Reclaiming the Black Past

Reclaiming the Black Past

The Use and Misuse of African American History in the Twenty-first Century

Pero Gaglo Dagbovie

02/2019

To Brother Keith,

In struggle for the cause of Black History!

Pero

VERSO

London • New York

First published by Verso 2018
© Pero Gaglo Dagbovie 2018

1 3 5 7 9 10 8 6 4 2

Verso
UK: 6 Meard Street, London W1F 0EG
US: 20 Jay Street, Suite 1010, Brooklyn, NY 11201
versobooks.com

Verso is the imprint of New Left Books

ISBN-13: 978-1-78663-203-6
ISBN-13: 978-1-78663-201-2 (UK EBK)
ISBN-13: 978-1-78663-202-9 (US EBK)

British Library Cataloguing in Publication Data
A catalogue record for this book is available from the British Library

Library of Congress Cataloging-in-Publication Data
A catalog record for this book is available from the Library of Congress

Typeset in Minion Pro by Hewer Text UK Ltd, Edinburgh
Printed by Maple Press, US

Contents

Introduction

The Enduring Mystique of Black History

"What do you do?" asks someone I am meeting for the first time.

Like clockwork, I respond, "I am a university professor."

"What do you teach?" is the next question posed to me in this familiar dialogue.

"History," I say, trying to keep things as simple as possible.

"Really? I love history," this eager conversationalist keeps the chitchat going, "What type of history do you teach?"

"American history," I reply, in anticipation of what the next question will most likely be.

"What area of American history?"

"Black history," I answer.

"Oh."

I often find myself having this type of friendly small talk when first encountering people my age and older in a variety of settings. Professional historians are undoubtedly familiar with this type of exchange. Over the years, I have noticed that after meeting people, particularly white people, for the first time and telling them what I do for a living, they tend to share with me their ardent interest in popular subjects in United States history such as the Civil War, World War II, the American presidency, or some notable historical icon or monumental event. It is not uncommon for my new acquaintances to share with me a book (usually authored by a journalist with whom I am not familiar) that they have recently read or a documentary that they saw on the History Channel, A & E, American History TV, Military History, and, from time to time, PBS. They rarely, if ever, share with me tidbits of information that they have learned about my area of expertise. Contemporary black culture permeates through American life, but black history does not explicitly shape most Americans' worldviews. The past experiences of black Americans, especially during the troublesome eras of slavery and Jim Crow segregation, do not make for friendly, lighthearted topics of conversation.

A different dynamic often occurs when engaging with elderly African Americans. I am almost always told a story about their experiences "back in the day" or an entertaining anecdote. Sometimes they fervently school me about how "history repeats itself" and how black America's past and present are inextricable. I particularly enjoy these conversations because they allow me to practice oral history and probe into an insider's perspective.

If the "facts" of those playing amateur historians are what I perceive to be inaccurate or imprecise, I hardly ever bother to correct them. Instead, I customarily participate in these brief exchanges by attentively listening to my acquaintance's rundowns of past events and personalities, nodding my head in appreciation of their curiosity about bygone days. After all, many people find history in its academic expression to be mundane, tedious, and off-putting. For those of my generation, this is epitomized by a popularly hilarious scene from the 1986 film *Ferris Bueller's Day Off* when actor Ben Stein lectures to bored-to-death high school students about the Great Depression. When I have the opportunity to alter such perceptions about history, I make modest efforts to do so.

For a host of reasons, the numbers of young Americans earning bachelor's degrees in history in the digital-centric twenty-first century is steadily declining. As cognitive psychologist and history education expert Sam Wineburg and others have argued, people's lack of enthusiasm toward the study of history is in part related to how they were taught history in secondary school. Most weren't and still aren't taught the value of "thinking historically" or the benefits of unraveling a "usable past."[1] US high school history, often subsumed under the broad and illusive category of social studies, is regularly reduced to the memorization of so-called "facts" and important names and dates. Time and time again, high school students are expected to demonstrate their historical knowledge by taking multiple choice, fill-in, and short-answer tests based upon so-called objective information from dry and conventional textbooks in which African Americans are at best discussed during slavery and Reconstruction and in the sidebars. With the exception of high school students in Philadelphia who, since 2005, have been required to take an introductory course in African American history before graduating, countless millennials and centennials or postmillennials were most likely first introduced to notions of African American history during their schools' annual perfunctory and token Black History Month activities.

Nonetheless, history—as memory, compelling and often unimaginable "facts" and details, the tales of influential people, artifacts that are housed in museums, and a record of consequential past events—does indeed fascinate many Americans across ethnic and generational lines. History is appealing in part because we all have our own personal histories that have profoundly influenced who we are and will become. Millions of Americans have used services offered by Ancestry.com LLC, and other genealogy companies and television shows like PBS's *Finding Your Roots with Henry Louis Gates, Jr.* and *Genealogy Roadshow*; NBC-TV's and The Learning Channel's *Who Do You Think You Are?* are popular. From family customs to national holidays to ethnic observances, historical traditions and rituals shape Americans' everyday lives.

---

1   See Sam Wineburg, *Historical Thinking and Other Unnatural Events: Charting the Future of Teaching the Past,* Philadelphia: Temple University Press, 2001.

Whether we are conscious of it or not, we all think historically on a routine basis. More than eighty years ago, historian Carl L. Becker argued just this, stressing that "every normal person" knows "some history"—"the memory of things said and done"—and practices rudimentary forms of historical research "at every waking moment" in order to resolve quotidian impediments and navigate their daily work life and existence. Without "historical knowledge," this former president of the American Historical Association maintained, peoples' "to-day would be aimless" and "to-morrow without significance." Ultimately, for Becker, "it is impossible to divorce history from life"; history "is so intimately associated with what we are doing and with what we hope to do." Becker also suggested that everyday Americans received heaps of historical information from their own personal experiences and from countless sources and outlets prior to "imaginatively" refashioning and interpreting these details and "facts" to create some sense of order and truth.[2] If Becker's "Mr. Everyman," as he contended, had trouble pinpointing the "mass of unrelated and related information and misinformation," then it would surely be impossible for Americans living in the information-overloaded twenty-first century to fully discern or explain how they know what they think they know about the past.

But one thing is a reasonably safe bet. In the late twentieth century and the twenty-first century, many Americans' perceptions of US history, including African American history, have not necessarily been shaped by professional historians but instead have been strikingly impacted by popular culture, journalists, political pundits and politicians, Hollywood films, and, of course, information from the easily accessible Internet.

Close to 20,000 doctorates in history have been doled by major research universities throughout the nation since the dawning of the twenty-first century. In 2014, as many as 1,043 PhDs in history were awarded in the United States, an all-time record at the time.[3] Notwithstanding the efforts of public historians, historians who have joined the ranks of public intellectuals, and the authors of historical narratives that have made the *New York Times* Best Sellers list, very few professional historians have released books or created institutions that have profoundly, directly, and speedily molded the public's opinions about US history.

Simply put, in this digital age, when social media, the Internet, and other forms of "new media" predominate, Americans, especially younger "digital natives," do not necessarily need to directly rely on the interpretations offered by professional historians when seeking to make sense of something from the past.

---

2   Carl Becker, "Everyman His Own Historian," *American Historical Review* 37, January 1932, 223, 227, 228.

3   Robert B. Townsend, "Report: Number of History PhD's Is at a Record, While the Number of Students Majoring in History Is Falling," historynewsnetwork.org, April 17, 2016 .

According to a recent report from the US Bureau of Labor Statistics, the "average" American spends very little time reading each week.[4] In the current digital era, as historian and archivist Abby Smith Rumsey has convincingly argued in *When We Are No More: How Digital Memory Is Shaping Our Future*, we now have "more knowledge than we know what to do with," "information travels at the speed of electrons," and an infinite numbers of "facts" that we can accumulate "sometimes get in the way of thoughtful concentration and problem solving." As Rumsey stresses, it is therefore important that we develop a digital literacy with an effective digital filtering system that will allow us to be able to, among other things, "read with appropriate skepticism" and discern which sources are reliable and trustworthy.[5] Similarly, in their recently published book on leadership in the United States following 9/11, Martin Dempsey and Ori Brafman highlight the challenges of living in what they call "the era of *the digital echo*," a time during which "facts" are no longer debated. On the other hand, they suggest that "competing narratives" prevail and that it is difficult to determine "what's real and accuate." In this era, "information passes from individual to individual more quickly, but in the process often becomes distorted."[6] Developing digital historical literacy for African American history during the "era of the *digital echo*" can be an especially challenging undertaking, particularly for those with little or no contact with African American people or culture.[7]

Although many blacks' views of African American history in general are informed by many of the same forces that shape whites' perspectives of their history, generally speaking African Americans have inevitably cultivated intimate relationships with black history. During each major phase or period of the black historical experience, young African Americans have drawn great inspiration from the black past that is characterized by perseverance, resistance, and survival in the midst of mind-boggling oppression. Black history is a vital part of contemporary black culture. African Americans' sense of history is shaped most by black institutions and traditions, such as the church, historically black colleges and universities, local and national organizations, and perhaps most significantly, the family. Since the era of emancipation, family reunions have played an important role in African American life and culture. History, specifically oral history, is the bedrock of these rituals. Epitomizing "living history" and functioning as direct links between the past and the present, elder

---

4 US Department of Labor, Bureau of Labor Statistics, "Time Spent in Leisure Activities in 2014, by Gender, Age, and Educational Attainment," TED: The Economics Daily, bls.gov; Jordan Weissmann, "The Decline of the American Book Lover," *The Atlantic*, January 21, 2014 ; Bijan Stephan, "You Won't Believe How Little Americans Read," time.com, June 22, 2014.

5 Abby Smith Rumsey, *When We Are No More: How Digital Memory Is Shaping Our Future*, New York: Bloomsbury, 2016, 4, 7, 12, 140, 145.

6 Martin Dempsey and Ori Brafman, *Radical Inclusion: What the Post-9/11 World Should Have Taught Us About Leadership*, Missionday, 2017, page xii.

7 One of the first reliable black history web-based sites, BlackPast.org, was founded in 2004 by historian Quintard Taylor.

generations share their past experiences and personal histories with younger generations. Younger African Americans are routinely reminded by their elders of the struggles that they, their parents, and their ancestors endured.

Some of today's millennial and postmillennial black activists have explicitly situated themselves within a history of black struggle. Founded in the summer of 2013, the Black Lives Matter (BLM) movement has actively sampled from past black freedom struggles. Though its founders have stressed how they are distinctly different from mainstream civil rights era black leaders, one of BLM's goals is to "(re)build the Black liberation movement." In doing so, those affiliated with BLM have marched, engaged in nonviolent direct action, and even organized a "Freedom Ride" to Ferguson, Missouri, in the summer of 2014. They have been inspired by who they view as being radical civil rights era leaders. For instance, the "Who We Are" section of their website pays tribute to civil rights strategist Diane Nash. Perhaps most important, in fostering a decentralized structure, BLM is modeled after the Student Nonviolent Coordinating Committee (SNCC). In 2015, in the midst of a resurgence in black student activism, students at the University of Missouri-Columbia founded an organization called Concerned Student 1950, named in honor of the year that the first African American student was admitted to the university. Such examples of new millennial black historical revivalism are not uncommon.

Historiography—simply put, historical scholarship or the writings of historians on historical subject matter—significantly influences how historians interpret the past. While historians must analyze a range of primary sources when deciphering and making sense of former times and the thoughts and actions of personalities from days of old, they are also expected to engage with the interpretations of their colleagues—other historians. At the end of the day, professional historians strive to generate original and innovative renditions of what transpired in the past. The same of course goes for experts in African American history, a subspecialty and distinct field of US history that has expanded at an exponential rate since it gained attention in the mainstream US historical profession during sometime between the late 1960s and mid-1970s. Influenced by Generation Xer and millennial black historians (what I broadly call "hip-hop generation historians"), the study of black history has significantly changed during the twenty-first century.

Yet notwithstanding recent innovations in the study of the black past, African Americanist historians, with few exceptions, are not usually socialized to make their scholarship deliberately relevant to the present and, therefore, do not strive to write for lay audiences. Many, moreover, tend to criticize their postmillennial students' and the general public's lack of historical knowledge, yet little has been written on the messages that the American public receives about black history from outside the province of the community of African Americanist historians.

Not only have historians undervalued contemporary black history, but very few have explored the contemporary implications of the actual African

American experience and how African American history has been brought into play, juggled, decoded, and represented in US politics and popular culture in the first decade and a half of the twenty-first century. Addressing this contributes to contemporary black history while also shedding light on how black history has been interpreted outside of the "ivory tower."

What we are told about African American history through Hollywood films, the mainstream media, Internet sites, entertainers, politicians, Black History Month commemorations, and museums can reveal a lot about how the general public thinks about black America and may conceptualize the black experience. For instance, one reason that many whites oppose race-based affirmative action and reparations has something to do with their inability to relate to black people's collective memory and historical consciousness, which is the byproduct of a lack of knowledge of black history, particularly prior to the passage of the Voting Rights Act. We must be critical of how black history is portrayed in US popular culture and politics. Framed largely by those who are depicting and interpreting it, the implications and meanings of black history are numerous.

Reclaiming the Black Past: The Use and Misuse of African American History in the Twenty-first Century seeks to explore how African American history has been regarded, depicted, and treated by a variety of spokespersons and public figures outside of the ranks of professionally trained historians—from politicians to comedians to filmmakers to hip-hop artists—and institutions (such as museums, mainstream Hollywood culture, and the US government) in the late twentieth century and the twenty-first century, the so-called pinnacle of "post-racial" American society. This book underscores the ubiquitous nature of African American history in American thought and culture. Each of the following chapters focuses on unpacking and deciphering how black history has been represented, interpreted, and remembered by people and institutions that arguably have at least as much (if not more) influence on the general public's impressions of black history than the vast majority of historians of the black past do.

How has black history been memorialized and, more specifically, packaged for publics and constituencies by an assortment of spokespersons in non-academic spaces? How might diverse historical message-bearers have shaped their depictions of the black past for their intended audiences? Though this book traverses many time periods, the "Age of Obama" is a common thread. How have developments in the twenty-first century and the years of Barack Obama's presidency impacted the ways in which black history has been unraveled in US politics and popular culture? How have these twenty-first century portrayals of black history persuaded their sometimes-uninformed consumers' views of African American culture?

I begin in chapter one by unpacking President Obama's complex philosophy of black history as revealed in many of his speeches and symbolic gestures. Obama's depictions of black history have foremost been influenced by his background and identity as well as inevitably by the particular context and the racial makeup of his audiences. Certain elements of his black history worldview have remained relatively constant, but Obama's representations of African American history were consistently carefully calculated.

Today, Black History Month is an established American custom. Yet, since widely acclaimed actor Morgan Freeman called Black History Month "ridiculous" in a 2005 interview with Mike Wallace on the popular CBS newsmagazine television program *60 Minutes*, debates about the purpose and relevance of Black History Month have increased. In chapter two, I explore the debates about the status of National African American History Month celebrations within a vast historical context. It becomes clear that the contemporary disagreements about the significance of Black History Month are not new.

During the new millennium, there has been an explosion of mainstream, commercially successful films that dramatize dimensions of black history. While most of these films have redemptive and educational qualities, all of them are problematic in their own ways. Chapter three unpacks how a collection of films released since *The Help* (2011) have interpreted and in many cases oversimplified and misinterpreted
s and historical icons from the annals of black history.

Often employing the medium of films and digital shorts, black comedians and satirists have offered their renditions of black history. Many have skillfully incorporated clever, yet often inaccurate, discussions of slavery, racism, and past racial injustices in their stand-up performances, albums, and sketches. In chapter four, I analyze how a group of black comics, satirists, humorists, and (for lack of a better term) jokesters have used their craft and positions as public spokespersons to put forward commentaries, sometimes sparking controversy, on the black past.

In 2005, the US Senate approved Resolution 39, in which it apologized for its predecessors' failure to enforce anti-lynching legislation. Four years later, the Senate unanimously passed a resolution apologizing for slavery. Beginning in the late twentieth century and into the twenty-first century, US politicians have apologized for a range of past atrocities committed against African American people while others have sought posthumous pardons for African American historical icons and the victims of legalized racial repression. Chapter five examines the implications and deeper meanings of US politicians' and the US government's revisiting of the past.

Opened in September 2016, the National Museum of African American History and Culture in the nation's capital became the world's largest African American history museum. In theory, the primary function of museums is to amass, display, protect, and exhibit historical materials and artifacts to the public for educational and entertainment purposes. In the "Afterword," I offer a brief appraisal of how the recently opened and critically acclaimed National Museum of African American History and Culture functions in this manner and portrays African American history, while considering how this representation might shape the general public's perceptions of the African American experience.

Reclaiming the Black Past is my contribution to understanding how African American history has been conceived, discussed, memorialized, and tinkered with by various groups and in different social spaces in US popular culture and politics.

1

"None of Our Hands Are Entirely Clean"

Obama and the Challenge of African American History

In what ways did Barack Obama conceptualize African American history during his presidential terms? How did he mull over black history in front of his different audiences and represent specific episodes in black history at key moments and in major speeches, such as his "A More Perfect Union" oration in Philadelphia on March 18, 2008? What types of code-switching did Obama engage in when discussing black history or policies, such as affirmative action, that have concrete historical antecedents? In what particular manners does his standing and approach as a black trailblazer / black "first" and leader compare with similar black luminaries from the past? How did Obama portray and make sense of hip-hop within the context of African American history and culture?

Such inquiries guide what I consider in this chapter. As a historian of black intellectual thought, I prioritize analyzing Obama as an intellectual and strive to unpack his carefully calculated thoughts about and characterizations of black history.

A HISTORIC OCCASION RECONSIDERED

Though it is not usually included in political commentators' lists of the most memorable US presidential elections, the election of Barack Obama as President of the United States on November 4, 2008 was a historic event. In varying degrees, of course, all US presidents have shaped the course of US political history. Accordingly, historians often use presidential administrations as opportune points of departure for broadly surveying and identifying particular eras in the American past. Presidents do indeed make history.

Obama, however, is a history-maker and catalyst of a peculiar type. He joined the pantheon of *black firsts* and arguably became a *black first* that eclipsed all others. He will forever be known and remembered as being the *first black president*, even though comedian Chris Rock and novelist Toni Morrison bestowed that title upon former President Bill Clinton nearly two decades ago.[1] Though the notion of Clinton's honorary commander-in-chief blackness continues to receive some attention (as late as 2015, for instance, journalist and author

---

1 Toni Morrison, "The Talk of the Town: Comment," *New Yorker*, October 5, 1998, 31–32. Rock called Clinton "the first black president" in a profile by David Kamp in *Vanity Fair* in August 1998.

Ta-Nehisi Coates sought to untangle and translate Morrison's thoughts for *The Atlantic* readers), Obama now holds the undisputed title.

The American mainstream media was obsessed with Obama's remarkable triumph and justifiably so. Until now, however, a great deal of print and online journalism as well as some trigger-happy scholars have haphazardly helped jettison Obama into the genealogy of black leadership and African American history and lore by portraying his presidency as an unprecedented milestone in the black freedom struggle, as evidence of America's monumental progress in race relations since the passage of the Voting Rights Act of 1965. Immediately following the 2008 election, droves of columnists, political pundits, and "everyday Americans" interpreted and presented Obama's presidency as a landmark event that somehow atoned for and even expunged several centuries of overt racial oppression.

The *New York Times* headline "Obama: Racial Barrier Falls in Decisive Victory" was followed by an article written by then chief political correspondent Adam Nagourney, who dramatically declared: "Barack Hussein Obama was elected the 44th president of the United Sates on Tuesday, sweeping away the last racial barrier in American politics with ease as the country chose him as its first black chief executive." Nagourney added that the election of 2008—"a striking symbolic moment in the evolution of the nation's fraught racial history"—also "ended what by any definition was one of the most remarkable contests in American political history." Even McCain in his concession speech could not ignore the historical significance of Obama's election. "This is a historic election, and I recognize the significance it has for African-Americans and for the special pride that must be theirs tonight." He continued, "We both realize that we have come a long way from the injustices that once stained our nation's reputation."[2]

The day after the election, renowned public intellectual Henry Louis Gates Jr. reiterated McCain's and others' prevailing sentiments with greater specificity but equal astonishment. For Gates, Obama's accomplishment was "the symbolic culmination of the black freedom struggle, the grand achievement of a great, collective dream," a sensational occasion that was only comparable to Lincoln's Emancipation Proclamation, Joe Louis' June 22, 1938 revenge defeat of Max Schmeling, and Martin Luther King Jr.'s legendary 1963 "I Have a Dream" oration.[3]

For the vast majority of black America, Obama's groundbreaking victory was their triumph as well. They took to heart his victory declaration—"I will never forget who this victory truly belongs to. It belongs to you. It belongs to you." They personalized and derived collective pride from his becoming a *black first* in a similar manner to how, one hundred years earlier, African Americans across the nation celebrated Jack Johnson when he became the first black

---

2 Adam Nagourney, "Obama Elected President as Racial Barrier Falls," *New York Times*, November 4, 2008, A1.

3 "Henry Louis Gates Jr. on Obama's Success," blog.oup.com, November 5, 2008.

heavyweight champion of the world by trouncing Tommy Burns in Sydney, Australia, and two years later when the brazen pugilist humiliated "The Great White Hope" James J. Jeffries in the "Fight of the Century."

Through Obama, black Americans from all walks of life enjoyed the vicarious thrill of feeling affirmed. Obama's coup unquestionably belonged to them and their forebears. The millions of African Americans who voted for him—especially between the ages of eighteen to forty-four years—recognized that they were shaping the trajectory of American political culture and making history; in other words, doing something consequential that had never been done before.

The symbolic importance of Obama's victory and presidency to generations of African Americans cannot be overstated. Yet along with the triumph came a declaration that the era of Obama's presidency represents a "post-racial" phase of American history. To those who scrutinize the contemporary realities of black life, this label is fallacious.

During Obama's presidency, there was a resurgence in anti-black thought and behavior in American culture. On one level, this is nothing new. Dating back to the Civil War and the short-lived era of Reconstruction, whenever African Americans have made major headway, groups of white Americans have pushed back, often violently. Riots ensued after Johnson beat Jeffries and after James Meredith began his quest to be the first African American to graduate from the University of Mississippi. Similarly, violent anti-black rhetoric shadowed Obama's victory, and violence against African Americans has mushroomed at the hands of police and domestic terrorists during and since his presidency. Just as it would have been optimistic to have thought that the Thirteenth Amendment would eradicate the exploitation of black labor or that *Brown v. Board of Education of Topeka* (1954) would swiftly put an end to Jim Crow segregation, it is naïve to assume that the status of African Americans would suddenly and magically improve under the administration of a black president.

Several years into Obama's presidency, historian Sundiata Keita Cha-Jua tendentiously dubbed the period from 1979 until 2010 the "New Nadir," contending that African Americans were living in "a state akin to the situation more than a century ago." Despite a black president and a noticeable increase in the "black petty bourgeois and bourgeois classes," Cha-Jua underscored that there had also been a rise in black incarceration, "spikes in racial violence," the "marginalization of black workers," and flagrant black disenfranchisement. "On most social indicators, since the decline of the Civil Rights and Black Power movements," he continued, "African American progress has stagnated and in significant areas, regressed."[4]

---

4 Sundiata Keita Cha-Jua, "The New Nadir: The Contemporary Black Racial Formation," *The Black Scholar* 40, Spring 2010, 38, 52.

Looking back on Obama's two presidential terms, public intellectual Michael Eric Dyson echoed Cha-Jua, unfavorably comparing him to presidents who are not considered progressive toward black people by any stretch of the imagination. Dyson, who provided a pensive and evenhanded assessment of the deeper meanings of "the black presidency," wrote:

> Under Obama, blacks have experienced their highest unemployment rates since Bill Clinton was in office. Obama doesn't even compare favorably to his immediate predecessor . . . The ranks of the black poor have also swollen under Obama . . . In Obama's administration, the disparity in wealth between blacks and whites nearly doubled . . . Obama's failure to grapple forthrightly with race underscores a historical irony: while the first black president has sought to avoid the subject, nearly all of his predecessors have had to deal with "the Negro question" . . . It is unfortunate that our nation's first black president has been for the most of his two terms uncomfortable with dealing with race; it is even more unfortunate that he could not, for the most part, openly embrace, in the course of his duties, the vital issues of the group whose struggle blazed his path to the White House.[5]

HISTORIANS AND THE "OBAMA PHENOMENON"

What journalist and op-ed columnist Bob Herbert dubbed the "Obama phenomenon" in early 2008 has spawned an earthquake of scholarship. "The historians can put aside their reference material," Herbert declared, "This is new. America has never seen anything like the Barack Obama phenomenon."[6] Since he won the presidency, countless journalists, biographers, scholars, social commentators, and polemicists have published books on various dimensions of Barack Obama's life, thought, and presidency. This steady flow of published writings has been inextricably bound to Obama's evolving leadership strategies and events and controversies that have characterized and shaped his governance. It seems that no stone has been left unturned; all perspectives have been publicized in some venue or another. It is not an overstatement to conjecture that Obama's presidency has been a lifeline for scores of academic careers.

More than any other single topic, the subject of Obama and race has been in vogue—and is still all the rage—among scholars and political pundits alike. After all, as Dyson has observed, "Race is the defining feature of our forty-fourth president's two terms in office."[7] Simply put, the "Obama phenomenon" cannot be adequately deciphered without understanding, if not centering, the meaning and history of race and the African American struggle in the United States. For the last eight years, many African American intellectuals, in particular, have

---

5   Michael Eric Dyson, *The Black Presidency: Barack Obama and the Politics of Race,* New York: Houghton Mifflin Harcourt, 2016, 165–68.

6   Bob Herbert, "The Obama Phenomenon," *New York Times,* January 5, 2008, A15.

7   Dyson, *The Black Presidency,* x.

understood this and some have produced excellent essays and books. Moreover, leading African American Studies journals, such as *The Black Scholar* and *The Journal of Black Studies*, have published "special issues" on the meaning of Obama's presidency and race.

In 2016 alone, the last year of Obama's second term in office, books on Obama and race continued to multiply. Such books include Dyson's wide-reaching and penetrating *The Black Presidency: Barack Obama and the Politics of Race*, political scientist and Africana Studies scholar Melanye T. Price's *The Race Whisperer: Barack Obama and the Political Uses of Race*, and Afrocentric pioneer Molefi Kete Asante's provocatively entitled *Lynching Barack Obama: How Whites Tried to String Up the President*. Even comedian D. L. Hughley has joined the fray by writing *Black Man, White House: An Oral History of the Obama Years*. The January/February 2017 issue of *The Atlantic* features Ta-Nehisi Coates's lengthy and somber appraisal of Obama's years in office, "My President Was Black: A History of the First African American in the White House—And What Comes Next" and in October 2017, Coates' contemplative *We Were Eight Yearts in Power: An American Tragedy* was released.

Thanks to numerous wordsmiths and scholars, we've learned a great deal about the ways in which race profoundly shaped Obama's presidency and influenced his calculated stance toward African Americans. Much can also be learned, I argue, by looking at how Obama has interpreted, portrayed, sampled from, and even manipulated African American history. Obama's relationship to African American history is kaleidoscopic. Yet Obama scholars have virtually ignored this subject, showing very little interest in his interpretation and approach to black history.

This may have something to do with the fact that professional historians, as a whole, have remained relatively quiet about the "Obama phenomenon." While recent editions of popular African American history textbooks like *The African-American Odyssey* and *From Slavery to Freedom: A History of African Americans* discuss Obama's presidency within the general context of black life during the twenty-first century (both books also unsurprisingly feature emblematic images of Obama on covers of recent editions), only a few professional historians—Thomas J. Sugrue, William Jelani Cobb, and Peniel E. Joseph—published book-length studies focusing on Obama while he was still in office. Ever so hip to the historical moment that they were witnessing, these historians, whose books were all published in 2010, partook in the public intellectual enterprise and the much-needed writing of contemporary history.

In his controversial 2017 *Rising Star: The Making of Barack Obama*, historian David J. Garrow approaches Obama in a much different manner than Sugrue, Cobb, or Joseph. Garrow's study is an exhaustive biography that drags on for close to 1,500 pages and details Obama's political and personal life, putting a spotlight on his sex life and relationship with one former love interest in particular. Unlike Sugrue, Cobb, and Joseph who wrote about Obama in the moment, Garrow worked on his biography for close to a decade and even shared drafts of it with Obama.

Sugrue dubbed Obama "the nation's most influential historian of race and civil rights." Wearing the hat of biographer, Sugrue charts how Obama's keen appreciation and interpretation of race, African American history, and the black freedom struggle transformed from his childhood through the beginning of his first term as president. He ultimately argues that Obama, the politician, had to adjust his treatment of black history by the time that he announced his candidacy for the US Senate. "Obama read widely in civil rights history; he taught antidiscrimination law; and he steeped himself in the historical and scholarly literature on race, poverty, and inequality," Sugrue observed. "This was a history he knew better than all but a handful of Americans. But none of that history was particularly useful for an ambitious politician. Situating himself in a current of civil rights history that emphasized its radical currents would be political suicide."[8] Instead, Sugrue suggests, Obama memorialized benign versions of the black past in order to endear himself to white voters.

A passionate Black Power era aficionado, Joseph examines the election of Obama as the byproduct of decades of vigorous black political mobilization and activism. Ergo, "Obama's climb to the top of American politics does not so much illustrate the end but rather the evolution" of a black politics that underwent significant transformations during the post–World War II era, especially during the highly contested and pigeonholed Black Power era. In Joseph's estimation, the "Obama phenomenon" would not have existed without the Black Power era. Simply put, "Barack Obama is a direct beneficiary of this rich legacy," a legacy that he perhaps consciously samples from but never really fully welcomed with open arms. Often drawing comparisons between Obama's nuanced approach to dealing with America's shameful racial history and democratic ideals and the strategies of civil rights activists as well as grassroots, militant champions of Black Power, Joseph repeatedly emphasizes that Obama "enjoyed the benefits of both the civil rights and Black Power movements while maintaining a safe distance from both."[9]

Sugrue maintains that Obama was intimately informed by the black freedom struggle of the 1960s and 1970s and possessed an informed conceptualization of Black Power and black history more generally at least a decade prior to announcing his decision to run for president. By contrast, Joseph deduces that for Obama, the Black Power crusade "represents a kind of racial anachronism" and that Obama, like the general American (white) public, possessed a flawed understanding of this pivotal movement. This is especially intriguing because the discussions of race in American society that emerged during what

---

8 Thomas J. Sugrue, *Not Even Past: Barack Obama and the Burden of Race*, New Jersey: Princeton University Press, 2010, 53–54.

9 Peniel E. Joseph, *Dark Days, Bright Nights: From Black Power to Barack Obama*, New York: Basic Books, 2010, 4, 164, 195.

has come to be known as "The Age of Obama" were reminiscent of those sparked during the Black Power era. Obama often, Joseph argues, avoided calling for "race-based solutions to historical discrimination" and "displays a lack of awareness of history that is at times stunning."[10] Joseph plays up the differences between Obama and Black Power era activists by taking notice of how many of these former militants were skeptical of and even opposed to Obama during his first presidential campaign. Still and all, Joseph does concede that Obama did in certain instances attempt to come face to face with the painful history of the oppression of African Americans during slavery and Jim Crow segregation.

Realizing that the immediate aftermath of election 2008 was too early to wholly historicize and evaluate Obama's foray into the White House, historian and op-ed columnist Jelani Cobb foreshadowed Dyson's *The Black Presidency.* Cobb's study offers a balanced appraisal of the evolution and early stages of the "Obama phenomenon." Like Dyson, who reminisces about his scatterings of interactions with President Obama, Cobb injects his own experiences into his narratives, vignettes that speak directly to the hip-hop generation. A salient phrase from Obama's 2009 inaugural speech serves as a useful point of departure for Cobb's portrayal of Obama: "There is not a black America or a white America . . . there is the United States of America."[11]

Of particular noteworthiness, Cobb explores and unpacks how Obama's diplomatic and multidimensional oratory skills simultaneously galvanized blacks and whites, his "tortured relationship" with Jesse Jackson and other members of the "civil rights old-boy network," how Obama's candidacy represented a "death knell for civil rights–era leadership" while energizing the often maligned hip-hop generation, the Obamafication of US popular culture, the debates surrounding Obama's biracial identity and blackness, the important role of Michelle Obama in her husband's quest to become president, and how Obama can be compared to other "First Blacks" as well as to Presidents Abraham Lincoln and Franklin Delano Roosevelt.

Like Sugrue, Joseph, and political scientist Frederick C. Harris, Cobb turns a spotlight on the fact that Jesse Jackson laid the foundation for Obama. "Examine Jackson's campaign, and you will begin to see the DNA of an Obama candidacy."[12] While Obama did routinely honor the "Moses generation," Cobb ultimately argues that Obama often denied his connection to the black past (as epitomized by his separation from Reverend Jeremiah Wright). Cobb reasoned:

> While his predecessors had struggled to prove themselves worthy of insider status, Obama became vastly successful by doing just the opposite: masterfully positioning

---

10 Ibid., 7, 161, 199.
11 William Jelani Cobb, *Barack Obama and the Paradox of Progress: The Substance of Hope*, New York: Walker & Company, 2010, 23.
12 Ibid., 50.

himself as an outsider. In reflecting the old ways, he necessarily blew off a portion of that history and that struggle. It was collateral damage of change.[13]

In the coming years, scholars and social commentators will certainly probe more deeply into the meaning, significance, and impact of the Obama years. The real explosion of Obama-centered African American historiography (that is, scholarship on Obama authored by professional historians who specialize in African American history) will most likely have to wait until around the 2030s, unless future African Americanist historians engage more deliberately in contemporary history (namely African American history since the late twentieth century and the dawning of the new millennium) and more explicitly draw connections between the past and the present.

ONE SIZE DOES NOT FIT ALL

As America's first black president, Obama inevitably encountered a unique set of challenges when addressing the country's checkered history of race relations. During his presidential campaigning and his administrations, Obama tactically discussed, depicted, and sampled from African American history in a variety of manners most profoundly shaped by the venue and historical context in which he spoke, the composition of his audiences, and the major talking points. Like black spokespersons from previous eras, he knew what was up. It is therefore unsurprising that some of Obama's most compelling insights about African American history sprang up in informal settings. After visiting the Cape Coast Castle (a slave fortress) in Ghana, for instance, he remarked: "I think that the experience of slavery is like the experience of the Holocaust. I think it's one of those things you don't forget about."[14] Likening slavery or the transatlantic slave trade to the Holocaust is controversial to say the least, and Obama would never say this in front of a podium in the Oval Office.

In deciphering Obama's references to, and descriptions of, black history, it is also important to pay attention not only to what he said, but when, during his eight years as president, he said it. For example, he tended to be more outspoken during his second term. Obama's vision of African American history has been relatively consistent in its malleability. Further, in his mind, black history has always been American history.

"Now, we gather to celebrate Black History Month, and from our earliest days, black history has been American history," Obama opened his remarks at a White House Black History Month reception in 2016. He insisted that black history should not be detached from "our collective American history" (another term for normative US history that prioritizes white America) or "just boiled

---

13   Ibid., 94.
14   Wayne Drash, "Obama on Slavery: 'Capacity for Cruelty Still Exists,'" cnn.com, July, 17, 2009.

down to a compilation of greatest hits" or a "commemoration of past events."[15] He also believes that black history can teach people about the value of balancing themes of victimization and perseverance. In his remarks at the groundbreaking ceremony for the National Museum of African History and Culture in Washington, DC, Obama announced: "I want my daughters to see the shackles that bound slaves on their voyage across the ocean and the shards of glass that flew from the 16th Street Baptist church." At the same time, he added, he wanted "them to appreciate this museum not just as a record of tragedy, but as a celebration of life."[16]

Clearly Obama and those in his camp were not wet behind the ears. They were cognizant of the racial maneuverings and power struggles that permeate American politics. An African American male seeking to become President of the United States could not focus on, draw excessive attention to, or critically unpack black America's past or present conditions when speaking directly to white audiences. Obama almost never discussed African Americans' historical or contemporary realities in his widely televised State of the Union Addresses and when he did, he was tactful and evasive. "We may have different takes on the events of Ferguson and New York. But surely we can understand a father who fears his son can't walk home without being harassed," Obama declared in his 2015 State of the Union Address, "And surely we can understand the wife who won't rest until the police officer she married walks through the front door at the end of his shift."[17]

The ways in which Obama talked about black history broadened over time. This is epitomized by the evolution of his National African American History Month proclamations considered in the next chapter, his routine speeches to the NAACP, and an assortment of unceremonious exchanges. Over time, he became increasingly forthright. When asked in 2008 if his daughters should benefit from affirmative action measures, Obama shrewdly responded that they should not be afforded "preferential" treatment. In the same year, he also did not endorse reparations. Yet, in an interview with the *New Yorker* in his last year as president, he opined that "racial preferences" should be applied in colleges and universities. Deciphering and untangling Obama's views of black history is a challenging endeavor.

This task is not made any easier by the fact that Obama delivered thousands of speeches and remarks on the eve of, and during, his presidency. Frederick C. Harris has reasonably cautioned and criticized those who have attempted to pry

---

15   Barack Obama, "Remarks by the President at Black History Month Reception," Washington, DC, February 18, 2016. Obama's various "Remarks" that I cite throughout this chapter can be found at www.whitehouse.gov under the "Speeches & Remarks" header under "From the Press Office."

16   Barack Obama, "Remarks by the President at the Groundbreaking Ceremony of the National Museum of African American History and Culture," Washington, DC, February 22, 2012.

17   Barack Obama, "State of the Union Address," US Capitol, Washington, DC, January 20, 2015.

too deeply into Obama's mind, "the armchair psychologizing of Obama that too often passes for serious political analysis" as he puts it. "Trying to dig into the inner thoughts of the president's view on race is at best left to presidential historians who, as time passes, will have the benefit of primary sources and the distance of time to reflect on Obama's views," Harris argues.[18]

Nevertheless, in order to unravel and appreciate Obama's varied renditions of black history, I argue that it is crucial to excavate his inner thoughts and strategies by closely reading his speeches and placing them within their proper contexts, paying special attention to his particular audience, actual and intended. In this sense, I engage in African American intellectual history, a subspecialty of black history that in some measure seeks to get into the minds and decipher the ideas of historical characters.

Though labeling Obama a "black leader" in the conventional sense is misleading, he can be considered among and compared with the pantheon of lionized African American icons. The similarities between Booker T. Washington (arguably the most powerful black leader during the Progressive Era) and Obama are remarkably appreciable.

OF MR. BOOKER T. WASHINGTON AND OBAMA

In one of the two most famous and enduring essays in *The Souls of Black Folk,* "Of Mr. Booker T. Washington and Others," Du Bois broke his silence and publically lashed out against Washington for asking African Americans to renounce political power, civil rights, and "higher" (liberal arts) education. He also grouped Washington with an earlier tradition of black leadership that championed a similar approach of "conciliation" and "submission."[19]

Following in the footsteps of the "father of the black intelligentsia," writers in the twentieth and twenty-first centuries have drawn parallels between Washington and successive generations of so-called "conservative" black leaders and (in the case of Adolph Reed Jr.) popular black public intellectuals of the 1990s. Such comparisons of black spokespersons from distinctly different historical epochs are now fairly commonplace. Cross-generational juxtapositions can be wrought by oversimplifications, sometimes leading students of history to give in to historic recurrence ("history repeats itself"). Still, such imaginative exercises speak to the ubiquitous nature of race in American culture, the enduring nature of America's consistent mistreatment of black people, and the lingering core and soul of particular strategies for combatting the oppression of black people.

Many scholars have compared Obama with Martin Luther King Jr. and other towering African American historical icons. For instance, Jelani Cobb has

---

18   Fredrick C. Harris, *The Price of the Ticket: Barack Obama and the Rise and Decline of Black Politics,* New York: Oxford University Press, 2012, xviii, xix.

19   W. E. B. Du Bois, *The Souls of Black Folk: Essays and Sketches,* Chicago: A. C. McClurg & Co., 1903, 41–59.

likened parts of Obama's 1995 autobiography to Du Bois's *The Souls of Black Folk* and has pointed out the "historical, personal, and political" connections between Obama and Jesse Jackson. Similarly, Peniel Joseph has identified "striking biographical and political parallels" between Malcolm X and Obama. More than a few emcees have grouped Obama with civil rights icons like Rosa Parks, Malcolm X, and King. In his classic track "My President," Jeezy keenly associated Booker T. Washington, his "homie," with Obama as members of the *black first* club. Perhaps Obama would not have been opposed to The Snowman's observations.

Obama's highest praise was reserved for John Lewis and King, but he did brand Washington "the leader of a growing civil rights movement," extolling his discipline, commitment to education as a compulsory passageway to social mobility, and work ethic. "Booker T. Washington ran a tight ship," he told the 2011 graduates of Booker T. Washington High School in Memphis, Tennessee. Playing historian, Obama created a humorous yet lucid and relatable anecdote about the iconic Washington:

> He'd ride the train to Tuskegee and scare some of the new students. This is before YouTube and TMZ, so the kids didn't recognize him. He'd walk up to them and say, "Oh, you're heading to Tuskegee. I heard the work there is hard. I heard they give the students too much to do. I hear the food is terrible. You probably won't last three months." But the students would reply they weren't afraid of hard work. They were going to complete their studies no matter what Booker T. Washington threw at them. And in that way, he prepared them—because life will throw some things at you.[20]

Though they obviously lived during distinctly different times, the lives of Washington and Obama mirror each other in some interesting manners that merit exploration.

To begin, both are biracial, and this complex and at times overly theorized identity lead their contemporaries and biographers to psychoanalyze them, especially in Obama's case. Both carefully constructed personal histories for public consumption in which they explained how they conceived their peculiar identities. In his widely selling neo-slave narrative *Up From Slavery* (1901) and his other autobiographies like *The Story of My Life and Work* (1900) and *My Larger Education* (1911), Washington rooted his identity in slavery and southern black culture while also, for his white readership, celebrating how white culture positively impacted him. In *Dreams from My Father* (1995), Obama grappled with how he discovered his blackness while being raised by his progressive white mother and her parents in Indonesia and Hawaii.

---

20 Barack Obama, "Remarks by the President at Booker T. Washington High School Commencement," Memphis, Tennessee, May 16, 2011.

Both Washington and Obama were not nurtured by their biological fathers. Washington's father was reportedly a white man who most likely took advantage of his enslaved mother. Obama's parents divorced when he was a toddler and his Kenyan father, who died when Obama was twenty-one years old, did not play an active role in his son's life. Psychologists could claim that, as young men, they longed and searched for father figures. Both found surrogates in elder white men when they were young—Hampton Institute's founder and Civil War veteran S. C. Armstrong in Washington's case; with Obama, his maternal grandfather and World War II veteran Stanley Armour Dunham.

On average, Washington traveled six months out of every year. Even so, family was an important dimension of his life. He maintained connections with his immediate family, enjoyed spending time with his children, and embraced the companionship that he shared with his three wives—he outlived his first two wives, Fannie Norton Smith and Olivia Davidson. His third wife, who he married in 1893, Margaret James Murray, served as the "First Lady" of Tuskegee until Washington's death. She was also a leader in her own right, focusing her energies on matters concerning black women in organizations like the Tuskegee Women's Club and the National Association of Colored Women.

"It just so happens that I'm fortunate enough to be surrounded by women. They're the most important people in my life," Obama wrote candidly in an essay in MORE magazine in 2015. "They're the ones who've shaped me the most. In this job, they are my sanctuary." Obama testified how he makes it his duty to frequently eat dinner with the family and dubbed First Lady Michelle Obama "the rock" of the family who truly sustains him.[21] Like other first ladies, Mrs. Obama was her husband's political partner and, like Margaret Murray Washington, she initiated many programs for African American women and girls.

Washington and Obama were both thrust into realms of leadership quite rapidly, causing onlookers to wonder, "How did that happen?" Relatively unknown on the national scale until more than a decade after he founded Tuskegee Normal and Industrial Institute in 1881, Washington became black America's sanctioned-by-whites leader in 1895 following the death of former slave and elder statesman Frederick Douglass and the delivery of his famous "Atlanta Compromise" oration in Atlanta, Georgia. More of a *symbolic* leader of black America than Washington, Obama rapidly rose through the ranks before officially announcing his candidacy for president on February 10, 2007.

Historians have not had too much trouble identifying black messiah leader(s) in each generation or major historical phase in the African American experience who not only achieved reverence from the black masses, but also the

---

21   Barack Obama, "How the Presidency Made Me a Better Man," *MORE* magazine *18*: 6, July/August 2015.

attention and support of white Americans. Washington and Obama were the most powerful black leaders of their respective times. In 1947, historian John Hope Franklin christened the period from 1895 until 1915 (the year of Washington's death) "The Age of Booker T. Washington." Analogously, the eight years of Obama's presidency are routinely called "The Age of Obama." Those historical personalities who have eras named after them have celebrity status. Washington and Obama both achieved megastar status, something usually reserved for actors, actresses, musicians, and athletes. As historian Michael Bieze has convincingly argued, Washington was truly a celebrity with his own sophisticated branding and propaganda. After he was elected president, "Obamamania"—the state of being a particularly enthusiastic supporter of Obama—swept across the nation.[22]

That Washington and Obama had their fair share of detractors and critics within the collective black community and among segments of white America is striking. Washington was attacked by major black leaders of the Progressive Era like Du Bois and his colleagues in the short-lived Niagara Movement, *Guardian* editor William Monroe Trotter, anti-lynching crusader Ida B. Wells, and others. Du Bois and company cried out for Washington to publicly denounce multileveled attacks on blacks' human and civil rights. "The Intellectuals," as Washington referred to his faultfinders, echoed some of the concerns raised by Obama's most fervent critics. Similarly, Cornel West, Tavis Smiley, Julianne Malveaux, Ta-Nehisi Coates, Michael Eric Dyson, and at one time Jesse Jackson and other civil rights veterans, among others, summoned Obama to abandon his strategy of race neutrality.

Although Washington's and Obama's unique posts as black leaders were dependent upon white patronage, both were caricatured, vilified, and attacked by white supremacists. Washington was demonized as being a black nationalist by *The Clansman* author Thomas Dixon Jr., was regularly called a "darkey" and "coon" by racist white southerners, was threatened so much that he at one point hired a private patrol to protect him, and was even brutally beaten by a white man in New York City in 1911.

Obama and Jesse Jackson are the only presidential candidates to have received death threats before receiving a nomination from their party.[23] From 2007 until 2017, Obama was the target of assassination attempts and purported conspiracies. Moreover, one only need to type *Obama* into any Internet search engine to uncover countless hateful and racist depictions of him.

---

22   John Hope Franklin, *From Slavery to Freedom: A History of American Negroes*, New York: Alfred A. Knopf, 1947. Stacks of books have been published with "the Age of Obama" in their titles since Gwen Ifill's *The Breakthrough: Politics and Race in the Age of Obama*, New York: Doubleday, 2008. For discussions of Washington's celebrity status, see Michael Bieze, *Booker T. Washington and the Art of Self-Representation*, New York: Peter Lang, 2008.

23   Jeff Zeleny, "Secret Service Guards Obama, Taking Unusually Early Step," *New York Times*, May 4, 2007, A21.

The most overriding connection between Washington and Obama is conspicuous, yet largely overlooked: by virtue of being representatives of "the race," or black leaders whose power-broking capital and abilities were more often than not subject to white approval and backing, they were compelled to master the art of communicating with two primary audiences—black and white America—separately and in some cases simultaneously. As they recounted in their autobiographies, this unique skill was something that they developed in their early years.

When interfacing with predominantly white audiences in the spoken and written word, Washington presented himself as a humble, nonthreatening, and compliant mouthpiece for black America. He personified the quintessential "safe Negro" leader. In *Up From Slavery*, he rewrote black history by labeling slavery a school for those in bondage, he claimed that the Ku Klux Klan no longer existed in 1901, he pandered to wealthy white philanthropists, he extolled the progress of US race relations since Reconstruction, and he publicized his own Horatio Alger tale as living evidence that all blacks descended from slaves could go on to accomplish great things.

In the multilayered, five-minute speech that he delivered on September 18, 1895, at the Cotton States and International Exposition in Atlanta, Georgia, Washington offered temporary solutions to the so-called "Negro Problem" that did not disrupt the white South's racial hierarchy. He meekly instructed blacks to remain in the South, to accept their positions as agricultural laborers, to obey the South's convoluted system of racial etiquette in the public sphere, to clinch onto vocational and industrial education, and to place notions of political and social equality on the back burner. Washington reassured southern whites that they would be "surrounded by the most patient, law-abiding, and unresentful people that the world had seen" and accepted segregation, famously declaring: "In all things that are purely social we can be as separate as the fingers, yet, one as the hand in all things essential to mutual progress."[24]

Be that as it may, when holding court with students in the Tuskegee Chapel during his routine "Sunday Evening Talks" or sermonizing to black Southerners during his whistle-stop speeches or educational tours from 1908 until 1912 that historian David M. Jackson meticulously sifted through, Washington propagated fundamental tenets of black nationalism—self-help, self-determination, economic independence, and perseverance. Like all influential black leaders of his times, he also believed in racial uplift and the politics of respectability.

The founder of Tuskegee Institute was bilingual, a master code-switcher who was well-versed in hamming it up with whites who believed in black inferiority; connecting with politicians (from congressmen to US presidents); keeping it real with poor black southerners; debating with his adversaries; and captivating his supporters abroad.

---

24   Booker T. Washington, *Up From Slavery: An Autobiography*, Garden City, New York: Doubleday and Company, 1901, 221–22.

Linguists H. Samy Alim and Geneva Smitherman are spot on in arguing that Obama's "ability to style-shift is one of his most compelling and remarkable linguistic abilities." They note that he knew when to speak "familiarly Black."[25] To be sure, in order to become the bona fide "first black president," Obama was compelled to study, get a grip on, and eventually master the art of consolidating and style-shifting, while communicating with black and white Americans. A mature chameleon, he calibrated his language and swag daily.

More important (and like Washington before him), Obama—who deliberately and logically avoided discussing issues of race and the unfavorable status of black America as much as possible during his campaigning and presidency— had to speak simultaneously to black and white America (to say nothing of other groups) about sensitive past and present racial matters. In perhaps the most consequential speech of his political career, "A More Perfect Union" (2008), Obama masterfully appeased large segments of both black and white listeners. In a sense, this speech foreshadowed Obama's future stratagem for coming to grips with issues of race and dreadful episodes in black history to white listeners.

Still, in numerous speeches that he delivered to predominantly black audiences, such as the NAACP, African American congregations, students at historically black colleges and universities, and impromptu meetings with African Americans, Obama spoke "familiarly Black" and more frankly revisited the black past and its lingering influence on African Americans' contemporary status. In speaking "familiarly Black," as Washington did when kicking it with black farmers, Obama also echoed the "pick yourself up by your own bootstraps" ethos and respectability politics of Washington and his contemporaries.

When deciphering Obama's rendering of African American history, as is the case with Washington and other crossover black leaders, one thing is crystal clear: it is essential to recognize to whom he was speaking and the specific circumstances and context.

REMIXING BLACK HISTORY: HISTORICAL DEBTS, MEMORIES, AND REVIVALISM

While running for the US Senate in Illinois, Obama delivered a memorable keynote address at the 2004 Democratic National Convention (DNC) in Boston in which he endorsed the then US senator from Massachusetts, John Kerry, in his quest to become the next commander-in-chief of the United States. While serving in the Illinois Senate from 1997 until 2004, Obama delivered numerous speeches, yet with this well-rehearsed seventeen-minute talk he captured notable attention, truly captivating and electrifying his audience. It marked a turning point in his political career. Three years later, on February 10, 2007, he

---

25   H. Samy Alim and Geneva Smitherman, *Articulate While Black: Barack Obama, Language, and Race in the U.S.*, New York: Oxford University Press, 2012, 5.

officially announced his candidacy for President of the United States. From this point on, he further honed his prowess as an orator by delivering thousands of different speeches.

In terms of substance, subject matter, and rhetorical style, Obama adjusted and modified his speeches based upon the racial and generational makeup of his targeted audiences. Certain features stand out when reading, listening to, or watching talks that he gave to predominantly white and black audiences and multiracial crowds. Obama offered these distinct audiences discrete and in some cases mismatched and conflicting depictions and interpretations of African American history.

In his 2004 DNC keynote address, for instance, he famously declared: "There's not a black America and white America . . ." He also intimated to his largely white audience that he was the epitome of the ever so elusive "American Dream" and owed a debt to his nation. "I stand here knowing that my story is part of the larger American story, that I owe a debt to all those who came before me, and that in no other country on earth is my story even possible."[26] Compare this to other speeches that Obama bequeathed unto his African American audiences and one immediately notices a different *modus operandi.* "And for most of this country's past, we in the African American community have been at the receiving end of man's inhumanity," Obama preached to the congregation—his "brothers and sisters" as he affectionately called his eager spectators—at Ebenezer Baptist Church in Atlanta, Georgia, ten months before he was elected President of the United States.[27] Similarly, in many heart-to-hearts with overlapping generations of African Americans, Obama emphasized that his success was due to the sacrifices of famous and uncelebrated black civil rights activists, that he indeed stood on the "shoulders of giants."

Of the many speeches that Obama delivered to predominantly black audiences, his first keynote address at a "Bloody Sunday" commemoration on March 4, 2007, at Brown Chapel AME Church in Selma, Alabama, was one of his most history-centric. It was in this sermonlike address that Obama established his often-cited discussion of the Moses and Joshua generations. The fact that Obama transmitted such an account in a black church is not surprising. He knew the importance of the black church, "our beating heart," as a conduit of black liberation theology and a vital movement center. His former mentor, pastor emeritus of Trinity United Church of Christ in Chicago, Reverend Jeremiah Wright, taught him this. In late June 2015 while reflecting upon the murder of Reverend Clementa Pinckney of Emmanuel AME Church in Charleston, South Carolina, Obama gave prominence to the black church. "The church is and always has been at the center of African-American life—a place to call our own in a too often hostile world, a sanctuary from so many hardships." All too often, however,

---

26   Barack Obama, "Keynote Address, Democratic National Convention," Boston, Massachusetts, July 27, 2004.

27   Barack Obama, "Ebenezer Baptist Church Address," Atlanta, Georgia, January 20, 2008.

black churches were terrorized as well. For him, the "Charleston Church Massacre" on June 17, 2015, "was an act that drew upon a long history of bombs and arson and shots fired at churches, not random, but as a means of control, a way to terrorize and oppress."[28]

Obama launched into his "Bloody Sunday" address by praising Congressman John Lewis, C. T. Vivian, and other members of the civil rights, or Moses, generation who paved the way for him. "It is because they marched that I stand before you today," Obama reiterated. After validating his Afro-diasporic blackness by drawing stark parallels between the British colonial system that oppressed his Kenyan grandfather and Jim Crow segregation in the United States ("Sound familiar?"), Obama underscored that the Joshua generation—those who came of age after the "classic" phase of the civil rights movement—owed a "debt," conceivably unrepayable, to their selfless predecessors.

Obama evoked a knowledge of the black past as a prerequisite for the Joshua generation's responsibility to "fulfill that legacy." He pronounced:

> I think that we're always going to be looking back, but there are at least a few suggestions that I would have in terms of how we might fulfill that enormous legacy. The first is to recognize our history. John Lewis talked about why we're here today. But I worry sometimes—we've got black history month, we come down and march every year, once a year. We occasionally celebrate the events of the civil rights movement, we celebrate Dr. King's birthday, but it strikes me that understanding our history and knowing what it means, is an everyday activity.[29]

He then enumerated the lingering problems facing the collective black community, from educational inequities to poverty to low-quality health conditions. Central to Obama's homily was his belief that the Moses generation set unattainable standards for everything from social and political activism to perceptions of "sacrifice," "dignity," "hard work and discipline," and morality. In doing so, upon more than a few occasions, he chastised young black people, mainly members of the millennial hip-hop generation. "I can't say for certain that we have instilled that same sense of moral clarity and purpose in this generation," Obama lamented as he joined forces with the Moses generation and beseeched the Joshua generation to become politically active and to "do for ourselves."

There are discernable patterns and themes concerning the meaning, utility, and application of black history from Obama's 2007 "Bloody Sunday" oration that would continue to surface in his future talks to black listeners. When sounding off to his "brothers and sisters," Obama positioned civil rights activists (the Moses generation) as being the progenitors and standard bearers of the

---

28   Barack Obama, "Remarks by the President in the Eulogy for the Honorable Reverend Clementa Pinckney," College of Charleston, Charleston, South Carolina, June 26, 2015.

29   Barack Obama, "Remarks at the Selma Voting Rights Act March Commemoration in Selma, Alabama," March 4, 2007.

long black freedom struggle, he situated himself within the history of black leadership, he drew connections between the past and the present, he commented on habitual obstacles that African Americans overcame, and he argued that the contemporary black community owed a debt to the past. Still, Obama often sidestepped indicting white America for its mistreatment of African Americans before black audiences.

A few exceptions stand out. On May 5, 2007, and June 5, 2007, Obama spoke to black mayors in Baton Rouge, Louisiana, and black ministers in Hampton, Virginia, respectively. In both of these speeches, Obama denounced white America's mistreatment of black people. Reflecting upon the beating of Rodney King and the riots that ensued in Los Angeles, he candidly remarked: "Much of what we saw on our television screens 15 years ago was Los Angeles expressing a lingering, ongoing, pervasive legacy—a tragic legacy out of the tragic history this country has never fully come to terms with." Obama added that Hurricane Katrina and its aftermath was "a powerful metaphor for what's gone on for generations." Throughout these talks, Obama outlined the major problems facing black Americans and US society as a whole, called for collective action, and concluded by highlighting the value of historical memory—"We won't forget where we came from. We won't forget what happened nineteen months ago, fifteen years ago, two hundred years ago."[30]

A well-traveled commander-in-chief, Obama was not reluctant to share this notion of a "tragic legacy" with non-white audiences abroad. For instance, when speaking in South Africa at Nelson Mandela's memorial service and at the University of South Cape Town in 2013, he drew correlations between race relations in South Africa and America. During his visit to slave castles at Gorée Island, Senegal, Obama remarked, "For an African American, and an African American President to be able to visit this site I think gives me even greater motivation in terms of the defense of human rights around the world."[31] This echoed his sentiments after visiting the Cape Coast Castle in Ghana in the summer of 2009. Similarly, when addressing the Turkish Parliament in 2009 about the troubled relationship between Turkish and Armenian people, he admitted that the US "is still working through some of our darker periods in our history" and "still struggles with the legacies of slavery and segregation."[32] That Obama brought up America's mistreatment of black people within the context of the Armenian Genocide or Holocaust adds further complexity to his representation of black history.

---

30   Barack Obama, "Remarks to the National Conference of Black Mayors in Baton Rouge, Louisiana," May 5, 2007; "Remarks to the Hampton University Annual Ministers' Conference in Hampton, Virginia," June 5, 2007.

31   Barack Obama, "Remarks of the President After Tour of Maison Des Esclaves," Gorée Island, Senegal, June 27, 2013.

32   Barack Obama, "Remarks by President Obama to the Turkish Parliament," Turkish Grand National Assembly Complex, Ankara, Turkey, April 6, 2009.

"REMEMBER WHAT IT WAS LIKE": BLACK HAGIOGRAPHY

From time to time, Obama gave nods to abolitionists and early twentieth century black historical icons, but his favorite historical role models came of age as activists and leaders during the 1950s and 1960s, like Congressman John Lewis and, of course, Martin Luther King Jr. Other civil rights champions that he paid tangential tributes to include Shirley Chisholm, Diane Nash, Julian Bond, Thurgood Marshall, Fred Shuttlesworth, and C. T. Vivian.

Obama hailed Lewis as "somebody who captures the essence of decency and courage, somebody who I have admired all my life." He added, "and were it not for him, I'm not sure I'd be here today." He routinely reminded his black listeners, especially those from the millennial hip-hop generation, that they could learn a lot from the sacrifices of John Lewis who was but "a twenty-five-year-old activist when he faced down billy clubs on the bridge in Selma and helped arouse the conscience of our nation." Obama told members of the NAACP in Cincinnati that he modeled his life after those who had paved the way for him. He explicitly placed himself in the context of black leadership history. "I turned down more lucrative jobs," he announced while reflecting upon his community organizing in Chicago, "because I was inspired by the civil rights movement and wanted to do my part in the ongoing battle for opportunity in this country."[33]

Although he did not actually mention King by name in his historic acceptance speech at the Democratic National Convention in Denver on August 28, 2008 (in passing he identified King as "a young preacher from Georgia" to the chagrin of public intellectuals Cornel West and Julianne Malveaux), throughout his two terms as president, Obama routinely praised him. In fact, Obama alluded to King in every speech that he delivered dealing with African American history or civil rights and gave him a shout-out in his second inaugural address in 2013.

Six months before his 2008 acceptance speech, he delivered a moving sermon at Ebenezer Baptist Church in Atlanta, Georgia. Martin Luther King Sr. led this church from 1931 until 1975 and his son became co-pastor in 1960. King Jr.'s funeral was held in this sacred space, which is a National Historic site and annually hosts events in honor of King and Black History Month.

In his thirty-minute oration on these consecrated grounds, Obama noted the abiding and transcendental nature of King's message of empathy and cooperation—"Unity is the great need of the hour." Furthermore, he annually released Martin Luther King Jr. Federal Holiday proclamations and delivered a passionate tribute to King in October 2011 in honor of the Martin Luther King Jr. Memorial located near the National Mall. He told the large crowd that Americans needed to heed King's teachings "more than ever." He placed King on the

---

33   Barack Obama, "Remarks at the 99th Annual Convention of the NAACP in Cincinnati, Ohio," July 14, 2008.

highest pedestal and often directly and indirectly sampled from him, in manner-isms and rhetoric. As he noted in a 2013 speech commemorating the fiftieth anniversary for the March on Washington, "His [King's] words belong to the ages, possessing a power and prophecy unmatched in our time."[34]

Between 2009 and 2016, Obama delivered more than twenty commence-ment addresses at a variety of colleges and universities. He spoke at several historically black colleges and universities (HBCUs) and First Lady Michelle Obama spoke at more HBCUs than her husband. Obama did exhibit a commit-ment to these institutions beyond speaking at a few commencements. He regu-larly supported National HBCU Week and the White House Initiative on HBCUs that was established by an executive order from President Reagan in 1981. In February 2010, he signed Executive Order 13532, "Promoting Excellence, Innovation, and Sustainability at Historically Black Colleges and Universities." For Obama, National HBCU Week served to "remember our history" and to "look forward to the future."

In 2013, during his thirty-three-minute commencement address at Morehouse College, he reflected on the history of this venerable university and celebrated King, who enrolled in Morehouse at age fifteen, and longtime Morehouse president Benjamin Mays. He called upon the graduates to embody the reformist and sacrificial leadership spirit that Mays encouraged and embodied.

"So the history we share should give you hope," Obama declared after describing the oppressive times that Mays, "black men of the '40s and '50s," and the Moses generation overcame. Juxtaposing them with those who came of age during the era of Jim Crow segregation, Obama told the Morehouse class of 2013 that they were "uniquely poised for success unlike any generation of African Americans that came before it." He brought to the fore that their collec-tive experience of struggle "pales in comparison" to what previous generations coped with and insisted that they could draw great inspiration from their ances-tors. Morehouse men, he declared, should, like Du Bois's "Talented Tenth," be committed to serving as role models and servants of the black masses. He chal-lenged them to use Mays as a guiding light. "Live up to President's Mays's chal-lenge . . . I promise you, what was needed in Dr. Mays's time, that spirit of excel-lence, and hard work, and dedication, and no excuses is needed now more than ever."[35]

Whom Obama praised to his black listeners often depended upon his particular audience. For instance, when speaking to members of the Congressional Black Caucus (CBC) in 2009, Obama conjured up a relatively overlooked black politician, George Henry White, a Republican congressman from North Carolina from 1897 until 1901 and the last black congressman until

---

34   Barack Obama, "March on Washington Fiftieth Anniversary," August 28, 2013.
35   Barack Obama, "Remarks by the President at Morehouse College Commencement Ceremony," Century Campus, Morehouse College, Atlanta, Georgia, May 19, 2013.

1928. Obama used White's prophecy—an optimistic prognosis that in the future other black congressmen would "rise up"—as a source of faith and inspiration for the CBC. He concluded by rallying members of the CBC to consider White's and others' struggles. "Remember what it was like for George Henry White in the early days of the twentieth century, as he was bidding farewell to the House of Representatives, the last African American to serve there for a quarter century." White and other early black politicians, Obama pleaded, did so much "to make it possible for us to be here tonight, to make it possible for you to be here tonight, to make it possible for me to be here tonight."[36]

"A LONG LINE OF STRONG BLACK WOMEN"

Like other black male spokespersons, leaders, and politicians, Obama tended to prioritize the legacies of black male heroes and icons. Beyond nominal remarks about Harriet Tubman, Rosa Parks, Shirley Chisholm, Diane Nash, and "women of soul" Patti LaBelle and Aretha Franklin; his 2012 National African American History Month proclamation, a tribute to black women as "champions of social and political change"; his honoring of two black women historians with the National Medal of the Arts and Humanities Awards (Darlene Clark Hine and Evelyn Brooks Higginbotham); or his Senate floor speeches commemorating the deaths of Rosa Parks and Coretta Scott King, he rarely celebrated black women's contributions to the black freedom struggle or black women's history. Black women were not, however, totally absent from his historical revivalism.

On April 20, 2010, Obama offered remarks at the funeral of Dr. Dorothy Height, chronicling why she deserves "a place in our history books." He praised Height for her work in the National Council of Negro Women and beyond—for fighting for "the cause" without needing "fanfare." In his commencement address at Hampton University, Obama used Height's life and work as a source of inspiration. As he said when referring to John Lewis and others, he imparted that she is "one of the giants upon whose shoulders I stand." He shared with Hampton graduates Height's struggle to get a college degree in hopes of motivating them to be tenacious:

> But I want you to think about Ms. Dorothy Height, a black woman, in 1929, refusing to be denied her dream of a college education . . . Refusing to let any barriers of injustice or ignorance or inequality or unfairness stand in her way. That refusal to accept a lesser fate; that insistence on a better life, that, ultimately, is the secret not only of African American survival and success, it has been the secret of America's survival and success.[37]

---

36 Barack Obama, "Remarks by the President at the Congressional Black Caucus Foundations Annual Phoenix Award Dinner," Washington, DC, September 27, 2009.
37 Barack Obama, "Remarks by the President at Hampton University Commencement," Hampton, Virginia, May 9, 2010.

Height was not the only black female civil rights heroine who Obama honored. On February 27, 2013, Rosa Parks became the first black woman to have a life-size statue erected in the Capitol. In National Statuary Hall, Obama delivered the dedication. "Rosa Parks tells us there's always something we can do." He continued, her "singular act of disobedience launched a movement." With these words Obama contributed to the archaic top-down notion of the civil rights movement. Yet, like her leading biographer Jeanne Theoharis, he acknowledged that before and after refusing to give up her seat on the bus, Parks was and continued to be an activist.

One of Obama's speeches stands out for its treatment of black women: his 2015 oration at the CBC's 45th Annual Phoenix Awards Dinner. On this occasion, he zeroed in on black women, past and present, because he, speaking for the black male collective, wanted them "to know how much we appreciate them, how much we admire them, how much we love them." Echoing scores of black women historians from the 1970s, 1980s, and 1990s, Obama pointed out that black women were at the forefront of the civil rights movement, "a part of every great movement in American history even if they weren't always given a voice." He stressed that black women were working "behind the scenes ... making things happen everyday." We are all, he pressed home, "beneficiaries of a long line of strong black women."[38] Obama, whose biological mother is white, closed ranks with black motherhood.

In addition to heaping praise upon black women, Obama was also critical of his male predecessors who at the March on Washington nearly five decades earlier snubbed black women, only allowing Daisy Bates the "honor" of introducing male speakers. "The men gave women just 142 words," Obama continued:

> America's most important march against segregation had its own version of separa-
> tion. Black women were central in the fight for women's rights, from suffrage to the
> feminist movement and yet despite their leadership, too often they were also
> marginalized. But they didn't give up. They were too fierce for that. Black women
> have always understood the words of Pauli Murray—that "Hope is a song in a weary
> throat."[39]

In the remainder of his speech, Obama linked the past marginalization of black women to their present status by stressing the necessity of continuing to fight for the "full opportunity and equality" for black women and girls. He identified the pressing challenges facing black women (namely unemployment, health disparities, unequal pay, stereotypes, incarceration, violence, and sexual abuse), yet celebrated black women's accomplishments in business, education, and motherhood.

---

38   Barack Obama, "Remarks by the President at the Congressional Black Caucus 45th Annual Phoenix Awards Dinner," Washington, DC, September 20, 2015.

39   Ibid.

He wrapped up his speech in a familiar tone, giving thanks to those nameless black women who "risked everything" not only for their survival but also for the welfare of future generations: "Their names never made the history books. All those women who cleaned somebody else's house, or looked after somebody else's children, did somebody else's laundry, and then got home and did it again, and then went to church and cooked—and then they were marching."[40]

"THANK YOU TO THE NAACP"

One of Obama's primary black audiences was the NAACP. On July 16, 2009, Obama spoke at the organization's centennial in New York City. This thirty-seven-minute speech was clearly crafted for a majority black audience, albeit middle class. There were certainly hip-hop generationers in the audience—it should not be overlooked that the then organization's president and chief executive officer, Benjamin Todd Jealous (b. 1973), is a hip-hop generationer who took office in 2008.

Immediately, Obama referenced the "journey" that African Americans had made since that time "when Jim Crow was a way of life; when lynchings were all too common, and when race riots were shaking cities across a segregated land." Unlike in "A More Perfect Union," in which he credits all Americans for challenging the past racial status quo, in this speech he specifically credited black leaders and civil rights activists like W.E.B. Du Bois, Charles Hamilton Houston, Thurgood Marshall, the Little Rock Nine, Martin Luther King Jr., John Lewis, "all the civil rights giants," and even Emmett Till's uncle, Mose Wright, for making history and paving the way for his presidency. He also affirmed personal links between himself and black America's past.

Obama unpacked how historical discrimination impacts the present by highlighting the major historically rooted problems that disproportionately affect black America and offered rudimentary remedies. Invoking the long tradition of black self-help and seemingly sampling from Malcolm X, Obama posited that African Americans have internalized oppression. "We need a new mindset, a new set of attitudes—because one of the most durable and destructive legacies of discrimination is the way that we have internalized a sense of limitation; how so many in *our* community have come to expect so little of ourselves." He also pointed to himself as being a role model for the hip-hop generation. He declared that "our kids" need to

> set their sights higher. They might think they've got a pretty good jump shot or a pretty good flow, but our kids can't all aspire to be the next LeBron or Lil Wayne. I want them aspiring to be scientists and engineers, doctors and teachers, not just

---

40 Ibid.

ballers and rappers. I want them aspiring to be a Supreme Court Justice. I want them aspiring to be President of the United States.[41]

Sampling from James Weldon Johnson's classic poem/song "Lift Every Voice and Sing" (later known as the Black National Anthem), Obama rounded off his speech by invoking a connectedness to the black past as well as to enduring spirits of survival and perseverance that characterize the African American experience. Sharing his family's experience at the Cape Coast Castle in Ghana, he avowed:

> There, reflecting on the dungeon beneath the castle church, I was reminded of all the pain and all the hardships, all the injustices and all the indignities on the voyage from slavery to freedom . . . I was reminded that no matter how bitter the rod or how stony the road, we have persevered. We have not faltered, nor have we grown weary . . . One hundred years from now, on the 200th anniversary of the NAACP, let it be said that this generation did its part; that we too ran the race; that full of the faith that our dark past has taught us, full of the hope that the present has brought us, we faced, in our own lives and all across this nation, the rising sun of a new day begun.[42]

In July 2015, Obama delivered one of his most fervent speeches to a large energized NAACP audience at the Pennsylvania Convention Center, a critical appraisal of the US criminal justice system, "one aspect of American life that remains particularly skewed by race and by wealth." This assessment of this flawed institution was more critical than the one he delivered eight months earlier at the Rutgers University Center for Law and Justice. Celebrating its 106th anniversary, Obama praised the NAACP for battling against lynching, segregation, and disenfranchisement and repeated one of his catchphrases—"I would not be here, and so many would not be here, without the NAACP." He observed that young blacks' life chances were threatened by a biased criminal justice system that had historically oppressed black America. "Part of this is a legacy of hundreds of years of slavery and segregation, and structural inequities that compounded over generations," Obama pronounced. "There's a long history of inequity in the criminal justice system in America."[43]

What's more, he suggested that this was a conspiracy of some sort: "It did not happen by accident." This declaration was welcomed with resounding applause. Despite their relatively privileged status and adherence to the age-old politics of respectability, his black listeners knew exactly what their

41   Barack Obama, "Remarks of President Barack Obama—As Prepared for Delivery," NAACP Centennial, New York, New York, July 16, 2009.

42   Ibid.

43   Barack Obama, "Remarks by the President at the NAACP Conference," Pennsylvania Center, Philadelphia, Pennsylvania, July 14, 2015.

commander-in-chief was saying. They gave credence to the time-honored belief in many black communities that the subjugation of African Americans has been and still is part of the American way of life. Such sentiments have been expressed by scores of African American radicals and conspiracy theorists. Obama echoed those figures as well as civil rights lawyer Michelle Alexander, who in *The New Jim Crow: Mass Incarceration in the Age of Colorblindness* (2010), detailed how mass incarceration systematically ravaged black communities.

He did, however, oversimplify how black communities were profiled and policed in the past. "Historically," he claimed, "the African American community oftentimes was under-policed rather than over-policed. Folks were very interested in containing the African American community so it couldn't leave segregated areas, but within those areas there wasn't enough police presence." There were certainly fewer state and federal resources invested into segregated black communities. Even so, Obama implied that black communities "historically"—during the vast era of Jim Crow segregation—were not policed. On the contrary, since *Plessy v. Ferguson* (1896) and earlier, black communities have been hyperpoliced. During the infamous "race riots" during the "Red Summer" of 1919 and the early 1920s (Tulsa and Rosewood), whites—sanctioned by the police and state—invaded black communities. This was, without question, turbocharged policing. Nevertheless, for the purposes of his argument, Obama effectually made his point.

Before his death, Booker T. Washington wrote an indictment of lynching that was published posthumously in the *New Republic*. He challenged and documented lynchings prior to 1915, yet refrained from publically speaking out against this genocide because he knew all too well that his power-broking abilities were sanctioned by white America. Similarly, during his first presidential administration, Obama did not subject the anti-black nature of the criminal justice system to critique in the blatant way that he did in 2015 toward the end of his second term in office.

"A WHITEWASH OF OUR HISTORY"?

In late August 2008 on "The Tavis Smiley Show," public intellectuals and outspoken Obama critics Cornel West and Julianne Malveaux rebuked Obama for failing to talk about African American history in his momentous acceptance speech, "The American Promise," at the National Democratic Convention in Denver, Colorado, on August 28, 2008, a date that marked the forty-fifth anniversary of the March on Washington where Martin Luther King Jr. delivered his famous "I Have a Dream" oration. West charged that Obama was "trying to escape from history" in order to win over white voters. Malveaux's criticisms were especially unsparing. "I think the brother dropped the historical baton," she declared. "The fact is that he basically perpetrated a whitewash of our history." She had hoped that Obama would have spoken more directly about the activism of King. Obama's reference to King ("a young preacher from Georgia") was prudent and inappreciable. Given Americans' lack of historical consciousness, it is not a stretch to conclude that many listeners did not realize that Obama was alluding to King.

West and Malveaux's observations that Obama skirted any discussion of an African American historical experience that has been most profoundly shaped by slavery and an enduring struggle for basic civil and human rights were certainly valid and refreshing. They also prompted the question: how did Obama represent black history at key moments before predominantly white audiences?

Months before his acceptance speech at the National Democratic Convention, on March 18, 2008, Obama delivered his monumental "A More Perfect Union" speech in Philadelphia, one of the speeches that he himself invested a great deal of time writing.[44] The mainstream American political media dubbed this speech his "Speech on Race" or "Race Speech," implying that this was his one and only speech dedicated to "race," a code word in white American society for "black people." In her introduction to the largely pro-Obama anthology *The Speech: Race and Barack Obama's "A More Perfect Union"* (2008), T. Denean Sharpley-Whiting insightfully pinpointed the significance of this speech as well as Obama's possible motivations:

> "A More Perfect Union" is "The Speech" that many say Obama always knew he would have to give someday in his run for the presidency. Despite his quasi-rock star status and numerous media-driven attempts to cast him as "post-racial" . . . Barack Obama is a black man, and one who had in March 2008 gone further than any other black man who had sought the American presidency. He could not avoid addressing the perilous conundrums of race and racism in America, though he may have wished otherwise . . . And if nothing else, Obama also clearly understood that despite all attempts—academic, scientific, and otherwise—to render race a social construction with no biological relevance, Americans cling, desperately, irrationally even, to race making, or "racecraft."[45]

The importance of this speech for Obama's debut presidential campaign cannot be overstated. He had to strategically respond to the nature of his relationship with the demonized Reverend Jeremiah Wright. In doing so, he tapped into his ability to speak to many different audiences simultaneously. In one sense, the

---

44   Like all US presidents, Obama has speechwriters. According to Mary Frances Berry and Josh Gottheimer, he worked with his speechwriter, Jon Favreau, in crafting "A More Perfect Union." Unlike other speeches, he reworked this one. See Mary Frances Berry and Josh Gottheimer, *Power in Words: The Stories Behind Barack Obama's Speeches, From the State House to the White House*, Boston: Beacon Press, 2010, 175–81.

45   T. Denean Sharpley-Whiting, *The Speech: Race and Barack Obama's "A More Perfect Union,"* New York: Bloomsbury, 2009.

speech is similar to Booker T. Washington's famous 1895 address. Whereas Washington belittled his militant contemporaries ("the wisest among my race understand that the agitation of questions of social equality is the extremist folly"),[46] Obama rejected Reverend Jeremiah Wright's indictment of (white) America.

Geneva Smitherman and H. Samy Alim have argued that Obama's "A More Perfect Union" speech was central to the hip-hop generation's admiration of him. "In the midst of the racially charged Reverend controversy," they suggest, "it was Barack's delivery of the 'Race Speech' in Philadelphia that was perhaps the single most important event that captured the heart of Hip Hop."[47] Smitherman and Alim add that members of the hip-hop community respected how Obama faced his critics head on and "rather than backing down, stood up and said the very words that his detractors were hoping to hear" about Wright. Still, Obama carefully calculated his statements and in the tradition of Booker T. Washington, satisfied large constituents of both blacks and whites in America. At one point, Obama "condemned, in unequivocal terms" Wright's indictments of America's racist past and present. Embracing his catchy "hope" and "change" slogans, he rejected Wright's, and many African Americans', beliefs that America "is still irrevocably bound to a tragic past."[48]

This goes against what he said on several occasions to black audiences. At the same time, he praised Wright for what he did in his Chicago community and deduced that his former pastor, like all people, "contains within him the contradictions—the good and the bad—of the community that he has served diligently for so many years" and was molded by his coming of age during an era when racial segregation reigned. In not totally disowning Wright but condemning his sentiments and rhetoric, he strategically compared him to his beloved white grandmother who, Obama confessed, adhered to anti-black racial stereotypes from time to time.

On one level, one could argue that from the generic hip-hop perspective—despite the sentiments of elder statesmen emcees who praised the "Race Speech" like David Banner, Common, and Jay-Z—Obama did not "keep it real." Obama's portrayal of African American history in his speech is multilayered and complex. This is similar to how many emcees rap about black history in passing, verses that simply rhyme well and are not necessarily linked to the other messages within the song.

Early in this long speech (approximately forty minutes in length), Obama deemed slavery "this nation's original sin," a description that he used years earlier and repeatedly later. He then gave kudos to "*Americans* in successive

---

46   Booker T. Washington, *Up From Slavery: An Autobiography*, New York: Doubleday & Company, 1900, 223.

47   Alim and Smitherman, *Articulate While Black*, 160.

48   Barack H. Obama, "A More Perfect Union," in Berry and Gottheimer, ed., *Power in Words*, 184, 190.

generations who were willing to do their part" to "deliver slaves from bondage."[49]

Unlike when addressing black audiences, he did not, by choice, offer a roll call of enslaved African Americans who themselves contributed to the destruction of slavery. He did not mention any of the countless slave revolts of the Nat Turner type. He did not empower African Americans with agency and did not position the abolition of slavery as a part of the enduring black freedom struggle. Instead, echoing Washington in his famous 1895 Atlanta oration, he understandably talked about *all* Americans "working together" to "move beyond some of our old racial wounds."[50]

At the same time, without delving deeply into the "history of racial injustice in this country," he maintained that "so many of the disparities that exist in the African American community today can be directly traced to inequalities passed on from an earlier generation that suffered under the brutal legacy of slavery and Jim Crow." He praised African Americans in the past who "overcame the odds" while also calling upon them to embrace "the burden of our past without being victims of our past." He did not summon his white audience to face the tangible realities of white privilege, but instead to realize that "the legacy of discrimination . . . is real and must be addressed." Obama ended his speech with a plea to Americans to unite in the spirit of "many generations" of Americans "over the course of the two hundred and twenty-one years since a band of patriots" created the US Constitution, a document that legalized slavery and the slave trade, created a fugitive slave law, and introduced the three-fifths clause.[51]

In arguably the most important speech in his political career, Obama established an approach to publicly speaking about black history to white America that he would continue to use. Most important, he further honed his skills at code-switching.

"My fellow citizens: I stand here today," Obama opened his historic inaugural address on January 20, 2009, "humbled by the task before us, grateful for the trust you've bestowed, mindful of the sacrifices borne by our ancestors." If *my fellow citizens* were removed from these opening lines, it would not be unreasonable to assume that Obama was addressing a predominantly black audience. After all, he routinely celebrated the far-reaching sacrifices made by previous generations of African Americans, especially the Moses generation. As was the case with "A More Perfect Union," in his inaugural address, he was, of course, speaking to a predominantly white audience; therefore, in evoking *our*, *us*, and *we* he was referring to all Americans. "Our ancestors" and "our forebears" for Obama was a double entendre: catch-all terms for past generations of Americans and a patriotic reference to "our Founding Fathers." In fact, he spoke of the pro-slavery "Founding Fathers" in a manner similar to how he previously and later

---

49 Ibid., 182 (emphasis mine).
50 Ibid., 189.
51 Ibid., 187, 189, 190, 193.

hailed the Moses generation to black audiences. "Our Founding Fathers," he pronounced, were "faced with perils that we can scarcely imagine." Under such circumstances, he maintained, they persevered and created enduring ideals. "We are keepers of this legacy," Obama announced. In charting the "work of remaking America," he revisited the black past only in passing, mentioning those who "endured the lash of the whip" and "tasted the bitter swill of civil war and segregation."[52]

Without delving into America's troubled racial history, Obama assured Americans that one of the best ways for the nation to move forward was by returning to the values and "truth" of the past, "the quiet force of progress throughout history." In doing so, he ignored the widespread oppression of African Americans. He concluded his inaugural address by citing the "timeless words" of George Washington. How did the first black president reconcile the fact that in 1799 America's first president owned 123 slaves at Mount Vernon? His veneration of Washington was similar to his praise song to "the small band of patriots" in his annual remarks on the South Lawn in honor of the Fourth of July. If Obama had been speaking to one of his black audiences, he would have most likely quoted Martin Luther King Jr. or another icon from the civil rights era (maybe even Douglass's famous 1852 speech).

At the beginning of his second term, Obama spoke on the steps of the Lincoln Memorial to commemorate the fiftieth anniversary of the March on Washington. He highlighted the interracial nature of the march and credited the marchers with profoundly altering American society—"Because they marched," he repeated. He expressed that Americans owed a debt to these activists, an obligation similar to the one that he assigned to younger blacks toward the Moses generation. In identifying martyrs, he strategically eulogized black and white freedom fighters—Medgar Evers, James Chaney, Andrew Goodman, Michael Schwerner, and Martin Luther King Jr.—and, in a sense echoing white conservatives who have appropriated King's "dream," he de-raced King's sentiments. "What King was describing has been the dream of every American," he commented. And whenever he singled out African Americans, he added "all races" or the phrase "regardless of race." He drew connections between 1963 and 2013, acknowledging that the 1960s belonged to a much more challenging era than the new millennium but that parallels did exist between the two. For Obama, the most important legacy of the March on Washington was unity, cross-racial coalitions and exhibiting "empathy and fellow feeling." For him, "the lesson of our past" is that "when millions of Americans of every race" unite, monumental change can be brought about.[53]

---

52 Barack Obama, "Inaugural Address," Washington, DC, January 20, 2009.
53 Barack Obama, "Remarks by the President at the 'Let Freedom Ring' Ceremony Commemorating the 50th Anniversary of the March on Washington," Lincoln Memorial, Washington, DC, August 28, 2013.

A month prior to this monumental speech, however, Obama spoke out in a very personal and persuasive way about racial profiling and the criminalization of black men.

"You know, when Trayvon Martin was first shot I said that this could have been my son," Obama divulged in the James S. Brady Press Briefing Room about one week after George Zimmerman was found not guilty of second-degree murder and manslaughter. "Another way of saying that is," he added, "Trayvon Martin could have been me 35 years ago." These phrases from Obama's speech made headlines nationwide and marked a noticeable shift in Obama's stance toward racial profiling. What most newshawks ignored was important. Obama historicized Martin's murder: "I think it's important to recognize that the African American community is looking at this issue through a set of experiences and a history that doesn't go away." He expanded on this unchanging and persistent history:

> The African American community is also knowledgeable that there is a history of racial disparities in the application of our criminal laws . . . And that ends up having an impact in terms of how people interpret the case . . . [B]lack folks do interpret the reasons for that in a historical context. They understand that some of the violence that takes place in poor black neighborhoods around the country is born out of a very violent past in this country, and that the poverty and dysfunction that we see in those communities can be traced to a very difficult history.[54]

Several years later, Obama continued to speak out about the lingering impact of tragic aspects of black history. "We gather here today to commemorate a century and a half of freedom," Obama introduced his fourteen minutes' worth of remarks celebrating the 150th anniversary of the passage of the Thirteenth Amendment. To soften the blow and connect with his white listeners in the US Capitol, he added that this ceremony was "not simply for former slavers, but for all of us."[55] Casting Lincoln as a stalwart abolitionist and honorary black freedom fighter in the company of Harriet Tubman, Frederick Douglass, and Martin Luther King Jr., Obama memorialized Americans—"black and white," "men and women"—who helped bring down slavery.

Conceivably steering away from potential queries about reparations (a struggle that he shrugged off early during his first presidential campaign), Obama did not mention how cotton was "King"; in other words, the incalculable wealth that slave labor generated for the US government for more than two hundred years. He did, nevertheless, make it plain that the legacy of slavery endured even though the country had made great progress. "For another

---

54   Barack Obama, "Remarks by the President on Trayvon Martin," Washington, DC, July 19, 2013.

55   Barack Obama, "Remarks by the President at the Commemoration of the 150th Anniversary of the 13th Amendment," US Capitol, Washington, DC, December 9, 2015.

century, we saw segregation and Jim Crow make a mockery of these amendments," he proclaimed as he did when speaking to the NAACP, "And we saw justice turn a blind eye to mobs with nooses slung over trees. We saw bullets and bombs terrorize generations."[56] Obama had referenced lynching in earlier orations, but this is perhaps the only time that he linked past maltreatment of African Americans with domestic terrorism. As to be expected, he chased up this indictment with an optimistic request that "our generation be willing to do what those who came before us have done" in standing up for others' freedoms.

In evoking lynching in this manner, Obama had come a long way since October 2009 when he signed off on the Matthew Shepard and James Byrd, Jr., Hate Crimes Act. The brutal, ritualistic, and premeditated murder of Byrd by three white men was by definition a lynching, a "lynching-by-dragging" as it has been dubbed. It was reminiscent of instances when white mobs—"the assemblage of two or more persons"—murdered black men during the "nadir" period. In his remarks at the reception commemorating the Act, Obama neglected to point out in his description of Byrd's death how similar his murder was to the killings of black men that were commonplace a century earlier. As historian Philip Dray has reminded us: "Almost every black family has a story in its history of an ancestor who 'come up missing' . . . Is it possible for white America to really understand blacks' distrust of the legal system, fears of racial profiling and the police, without understanding how cheap a black life was for so long a time in our nation."[57]

GENERATIONAL CRISSCROSSING:
OBAMA, HIP-HOP, AND BLACK HISTORICAL MEMORY

I think that the most vibrant musical art form right now, over the last ten to fifteen years, has been hip-hop, and there have been some folks that have kind of dabbled in political statements, but a lot of it has been more cultural than political.

—Barack Obama, "Ask Obama Live: An MTV
Interview with the President," October 26, 2012

On June 7, 1979, President Jimmy Carter designated the month of June to be Black Music Month. In celebration of this event, he invited Chuck Berry to perform at the White House. Following Carter, American presidents continued to issue Black Music Month proclamations and hosted similar programs.

During the first year of his presidency on June 2, 2009, President Obama changed the name of this observance to African-American Music Appreciation Month. In his first proclamation for this commemoration, he held in high

---

56 Ibid.
57 Philip Dray, *At the Hands of Persons Unknown: The Lynching of Black America*, New York: Random House, 2002, xi.

esteem a wide variety of black music traditions, including spirituals, gospel, blues, jazz, soul, and rock and roll. Complicating outworn notions of blackness, he alluded to how blacks had contributed to opera, classical symphony, and choral music. Hip-hop is conspicuously absent from Obama's first African-American Music Appreciation Month proclamation.

This oversight is thought-provoking considering the widespread support that the man who once had the moniker "The Hip-Hop President" received from hip-hop generationers as a whole and from artists like Jay-Z, Nas, Jeezy, MC Jin, Kidz in the Hall, Common, Talib Kweli, Puff Daddy, and scads of other emcees. In his African-American Music Appreciation Month tributes that followed, he did give shout-outs to "the urban themes of hip-hop," the "young wordsmiths," and "the young poet putting his words to a beat."

While campaigning for his first term, Obama's references to hip-hop expanded far beyond the aforementioned token nods.[58] He routinely disparaged young blacks from turning to hip-hop for salvation. In July 2008, Obama referenced Lil Wayne at a predominantly black town hall meeting in Powder Springs, Georgia. He directed his comments toward members of the millennial hip-hop generation. "You are probably not that good a rapper. Maybe you are the next Lil Wayne, but probably not, in which case you need to stay in school," Obama declared.[59]

A year later, he reiterated this message during a speech in celebration of the NAACP's centennial, insisting that young blacks who are socialized by millennial hip-hop should not primarily aspire to be a professional basketball player or rapper like Lil Wayne.[60] Obama's various calculated references to Lil Wayne—a device that he employed to demonstrate to young blacks that he was "down"—led one journalist to write a brief blog that chronicled the relationship between Young Weezy and Obama entitled "Does Obama Love Lil Wayne or What?"[61] Perhaps Obama shared a common veneration of King with Wayne, who in his 2007 mix-tape track "Love Me or Hate Me" spit: "I are the illest nigga Martin Luther King died for."

Obama has haphazardly been called "The Hip-Hop President" by more than a few newshounds. He is by no means a hip-hop head, and it is a stretch to label him a member of the hip-hop generation. He did not begin working with African American communities and intimately interacting with black culture until the late 1970s and the 1980s. He has disclosed that much of his intimate connections to African American culture grew out of his marriage to an African

---

58   For refreshing discussions of Obama and hip-hop, see Travis L. Gosa and Erik Nielson, eds., *The Hip Hop & Obama Reader*, New York: Oxford University Press, 2015.

59   Ed O'Keefe, "Obama Slams Hoop Dreams for High School Diplomas," abcnews.go.com, July 8, 2008.

60   Obama, "Remarks of President Barack Obama," NAACP Centennial, New York, New York, July 16, 2009.

61   Danny Groner, "Does Obama Love Lil Wayne or What?" *Huffington Post*, September 28, 2010.

American woman. "I am married to a black American who carries within her the blood of slaves and slave owners—an inheritance we pass on to our two precious daughters," Obama narrated in his "Race Speech."[62] Obama himself has also confessed that he was not socialized during his younger formative years by "old school" hip-hop, but by black music from the 1970s. Though familiar with some of the popular hip-hop artists by way of his daughters and younger aides, he has said that he listens most to Stevie Wonder; Marvin Gaye; Earth, Wind, and Fire; and the Temptations.

To the great dismay and chagrin of Donald Trump and his many co-conspirators in the half-baked "birther movement," in 2011 Obama released an official copy of his birth certificate, once and for all proving that he is a natural-born citizen of the United States and, therefore, eligible to serve as the President of the nation.

Several months before his birth in Honolulu, Hawaii, on August 4, 1961, a group of civil rights activists known as the Freedom Riders left Washington, DC, on a courageous quest to challenge the nonenforcement of the desegregation of public buses in the South. Obama belongs to a generation of African Americans who were not old enough to have been active in the classic phase of the civil rights struggle or even the heyday of the Black Power era. Nearing age sixty, he is also too old to be considered part of the hip-hop generation as delineated by journalist Bakari Kitwana—who, in 2002, identified "the birth years 1965–1984 as the age group of the hip-hop generation."[63] Situating Obama within a conventional generation in American culture is perhaps easier than placing him within a distinct African American generation. He belongs to the earliest cohort of Generation X (Gen X) and can also be considered a late "baby boomer."

Obama has directly spoken about hip-hop on several occasions. In a brief interview with BET's Jeff Johnson in early 2008 that has received roughly one million views on YouTube and has been sampled by more than a few deejays, Obama conveyed his stance toward hip-hop after he was asked a straightforward question: "Do you like hip hop?"[64] He promptly answered, "Of course." When he was asked which artists he admired, he responded that he had been listening to Jay-Z's popular tenth solo album, *American Gangster* (2007); that he appreciated it because it "tells a story." He also remarked that he was fond of Kanye, who he would later call a "jackass" for his shenanigans at the 2009 MTV Video Music Awards show. Obama qualified his veneration of modish hip-hop by insisting that he was "still an old-school guy." "Honestly," he said, "I love the

62   Obama, "Remarks of President Barack Obama," NAACP Centennial, New York, New York, July 16, 2009; Obama, "A More Perfect Union," in Berry and Gottheimer, eds., *Power in Words*, 183.

63   Bakari Kitwana, *The Hip-Hop Generation: Young Blacks and the Crisis in African-American Culture,* New York: BasicCivitas, 2002, xiii.

64   "USA President Barack Obama Opinion on Hip-Hop & Rap 2008," youtube.com.

art of hip hop, I don't always love the message of hip hop." Without specificity, he then criticized Jay-Z and Kanye for sometimes denigrating women, using "the n-word," and being preoccupied with making money and materialism. This mainstream and often elicited critique of hip-hop is something that Obama would continue to summon up.

On July 28, 2008, Christopher Brian Bridges (aka Ludacris) released his mixtape, *The Preview*, produced by DJ Drama. On the track "Politics as Usual," Ludacris leveled insults toward Hilary Clinton, George Bush, Jesse Jackson, and John McCain. A spokesperson for the Obama campaign quickly issued a statement condemning this "dis" track. "As Barack Obama has said many, many times in the past, rap lyrics today too often perpetuate misogyny, materialism, and degrading images that he doesn't want his daughters or any children exposed to." The Obama campaign spokesperson politicked:

This song is not only outrageously offensive to Mrs. Clinton, Rev. Jackson, Mr. McCain and President Bush, it is offensive to all of us who are trying to raise our children with the values we hold dear. While Ludacris is a talented individual he should be ashamed of these lyrics.[65]

This was situational politics in its purest form; Obama welcomed Ludacris into the White House in 2009 and 2015.

In his interview with BET in 2008, Obama pointed out that hip-hop could be effectively used to help educate African American youth. He remarked that hip-hop had the potential to help the youth think more critically; he labeled hip-hop "smart" and "insightful" and conceded that emcees can deliver, in his words, "a complex message in a very short space." He also urged artists to move beyond hip-hop's essence of "keepin' it real" and chronicling the realities of everyday life in urban America. Instead, he appealed for emcees to awaken the possibilities of a brighter future and "change." They should, he concluded, embrace his mantra, "the audacity of hope."

Several years after his interview with BET, on October 14, 2010, *Rolling Stone* magazine featured an absorbing interview with Obama. In response to the questions, "What music have you been listening to lately? What have you discovered, what speaks to you these days?" Obama rejoined:

My iPod now has about 2,000 songs, and it is a source of great pleasure to me. I am probably still more heavily weighted toward the music of my childhood than I am the new stuff. There's still a lot of Stevie Wonder, a lot of Bob Dylan, a lot of Rolling Stones, a lot of R&B, a lot of Miles Davis and John Coltrane. Those are the old standards. A lot of classical music. I'm not a big opera buff in terms of going to opera, but there are days where Maria Callas is exactly what I need. Thanks to

---

65   "Barack Obama Embarrassed by Ludacris Rap," telegraph.co.uk, July 31, 2008.

Reggie [Love, the president's personal aide], my rap palate has greatly improved. Jay-Z used to be sort of what predominated, but now I've got a little Nas and a little Lil Wayne and some other stuff, but I would not claim to be an expert. Malia and Sasha are now getting old enough to where they start hipping me to things. Music is still a great source of joy and occasional solace in the midst of what can be some difficult days.[66]

Obama's reference to Jay-Z is not surprising. The hip-hop mogul whose net worth is estimated at approximately half a billion dollars had been supporting him since the early days of his first presidential campaign. Obama included Nas most likely because of his 2008 "Black President" track. Obama's reference to Lil Wayne is more perplexing, especially given the subject matter of the vast majority of his rhymes. I wonder which Young Weezy tracks Obama had in his iPod and if he would be willing to share this with the public.

Since the Fisk Jubilee Singers performed for President Ulysses S. Grant in 1872 or soprano Marie Selika Williams sang for President Rutherford B. Hayes in 1878, numerous African American entertainers have showed off their skills in the White House. Obama has set himself apart from his post-Carter predecessors by welcoming hip-hop in the Oval Office. More than a few emcees—Doug E. Fresh, Jay-Z, Queen Latifah, Common, Big Sean, Wale, and Kendrick Lamar—visited and/or spit rhymes in the White House during Obama's presidency.

In May 2011, Obama was criticized by various Republicans, conservative political pundits, and police authorities for inviting Common to perform at the White House for Michelle Obama's "White House Music Series." Common's critics were offended by his anti-Bush, anti-police brutality, and pro-Assata Shakur lyrics. A veteran New Jersey State Trooper deemed the black activist who Common celebrated in his 2000 tribute, "A Song for Assata," "a domestic terrorist" who "executed" a New Jersey State Trooper on May 2, 1973.

In "A Song for Assata" from his commercially successful first solo album *Like Water for Chocolate*, Common played the role of an amateur historian; he evoked the story-telling tradition of hip-hop's early years in detailing the struggle of Assata from about 1973 until her escape to Cuba in 1979. Informed by Shakur's autobiography and interviews that he conducted with her in Havana, Cuba, Common stressed the relationship between her activism and the present state of black America. "I read this sister's story, knew that she deserved a verse / I wonder what would happen if that would've been me? / All this shit so we could be free, so dig it, y'all," Common rhymed.[67] This approach of imagining what life was like for previous generations of African Americans is something that Obama espoused when lecturing to young blacks.

---

66 Jann S. Wenner, "Obama in Command: The *Rolling Stone* Interview," *Rolling Stone* magazine, October 14, 2010.

67 Common, "A Song for Assata" (feat. Cee Lo Green), *Like Water for Chocolate* (MCA/Universal Records, 2000).

Public intellectual Mark Anthony Neal has convincingly lambasted Common for his sexism and "hyper-masculine" worldview. Yet, the Chicago-born emcee did produce one of the most elaborate and widely played tributes to a black leader in the history of hip-hop.[68] Unlike his male predecessors who at best have perhaps given "props" to Harriet Tubman, Common also venerated a black female leader.

Obama and his administration must have been aware of Common's politi-cized rap. By inviting him to the White House, Obama was, in a sense, validat-ing Common's appreciation of Black Power era history and his commemoration of a prototypical black radical who was added to the FBI's "New Most Wanted Terrorist" list at the beginning of Obama's second term.

Dressed in "all black everything" (rocking ripped jeans, a tight long-sleeve shirt, and an unostentatious gold chain with a cross pendant) and sporting Allen Iversonesque cornrows, 2015 Grammy award-winning emcee and future Pulitzer Prize winner Kendrick Lamar visited Obama in the White House in January 2016. Prior to this visit that received widespread attention on social media, Obama told *People* magazine that his preferred song of 2015 was "How Much a Dollar Cost" from Lamar's highly acclaimed *To Pimp a Butterfly* album. He added that he favored the Compton emcee over Drake. The differences between these two commercially successful emcees are numerous and clear, especially when one considers the content of their rhymes and freestyling abili-ties. Though he spits about struggle ("Started From the Bottom"), Drake does not rhyme about black history. Lamar, on the other hand, has creatively rapped about black history since his imaginative track "HiiiPower" (2011).

Inviting Lamar to the White House did not evoke the same response as Common's visit to the Oval Office did. Though he can be considered a "conscious" rapper (however problematic this label is), Lamar is also a black entertainer who has enjoyed white mainstream success. In choosing Lamar over Drake, it is not unreasonable to deduce that Obama approves of the more introspective, complex, and soul-searching rhymes. With "How Much a Dollar Cost," Lamar pleads guilty to turning his back on the poor, to abandoning the "Golden Rule" and Jesus's dedication to giving to the unfortunate.

During his first term, very few emcees—namely Dead Prez, Killer Mike, Lupe Fiasco, and Lowkey—openly condemned Obama for his racial neutrality and, in their minds, imperialistic foreign policy. Most emcees and members of the hip-hop community and expansive generation embraced Obama in part because he validated them, in some instances side-by-side with revered civil rights elders who shaped history profoundly. Hip-hoppers view Obama's presi-dency as epoch-making. As was the case with his philosophy of black history, Obama's outlook on hip-hop vacillated throughout his political career. As

---

68   For Neal's discussion of Common and *Like Water for Chocolate*, see Mark Anthony Neal, "*Like Water for Chocolate*: Common's Recipe for Progressive Hip-Hop," popmatters.com, May 4, 2000.

hip-hop studies scholars Erik Nielson and Travis L. Gosa noted in a 2015 *Washington Post* editorial, after Obama was elected, his relationship with hip-hop artists and activists began to deteriorate and hip-hop heads "took notice."[69] Rather than remembering Obama as "The Hip-Hop President," it would be more accurate to describe him as being a cautious consumer of and prudent apologist for hip-hop music and culture.

Whether speaking to or interacting with the millennial hip-hop generation, black and white audiences from various age groups, the mainstream media, or his fellow politicians, Obama made conscious decisions about how to portray African American history. Obama, who left the White House in January 2017, no longer needs to practice the hyper social awareness that he did during his presidency. He can now speak more plainly about a range of issues, including African American history. I would not be surprised if the Obamas' forthcoming Netflix series produces films and documentaries on dimensions of black history. As touched upon in the next chapter on Black History Month, his handling of this annual observance reflects his calculated stance toward the black past.

---

69 Erik Nielson and Travis L. Gosa, "Obama and Hip-Hop: A Breakup Song," *Washington Post*, September 25, 2015, washingtonpost.com.

2

Honoring "The Gift of Black Folk"

The Contested Meaning of Black History Month

"Who made America?" queried W. E. B. Du Bois in the preface to *The Gift of Black Folk: The Negroes in the Making of America,* first published in 1924. "Now that its foundations are laid, deep but bare, there are those as always who would forget the humble builders, toiling wan mornings and blazing noons, and picture America as the last reasoned blossom of mighty ancestors." He continued:

> America is America even because it shows, as never before, the power of the common, ordinary, unlovely man ... We who know may not forget but must forever spread the splendid truth that out of the most lowly and persecuted of men, Man made America.[1]

With great pride, the prolific editor of *The Crisis* was referring to the black "Man" and everyday African Americans as the "humble builders" who, in essence, contributed in monumental ways to America's economic growth, democracy, and culture. Like scores of self-taught black historians who preceded him, Du Bois spotlighted and memorialized how generations of African Americans "made America." For him, this story, the chronicle of African Americans' contributions, needed to be publicized in the name of "truth." Several years after *The Gift of Black Folk* was published, historian Carter G. Woodson created Negro History Week. The "high priest of Negro history" echoed Du Bois's search for the "truth" in describing the underlying objective of this celebration. Others felt the need to tell this story too. "Let truth destroy the dividing prejudices of nationality and teach universal love without distinction of race, merit or rank," Woodson declared.[2]

Fifty years after Woodson founded Negro History Week, the then Association for the Study of Negro Life and History (ASNLH) was at the forefront of a movement to transform this weeklong celebration in February into a monthlong tribute. "In celebrating Black History Month," Gerald Ford remarked in the first presidential observance on February 10, 1976, "we can seize the opportunity to honor the too-often neglected accomplishments of black Americans in every area of endeavor throughout our history." A decade later,

---

1   W. E. B. Du Bois, *The Gift of Black Folk: The Negroes in the Making of America,* New York: Washington Square Press, 1970, 1.

2   Carter G. Woodson, "Negro History Week," *Journal of Negro History* 11, April 1926, 241.

the United States Congress passed Public Law 99-244 (1986), designating the month of February as being National Black (Afro-American) History Month. During Bill Clinton's presidency, the celebration was renamed National African American History Month.

Most often called *Black History Month* (National African American History Month is a mouthful and comes across as being unduly formal and even portentous), today this annual commemoration constitutes a firmly established custom and institution in American life, especially among African Americans. During the twenty-first century, however, debates about the meaning and intention of this observance have proliferated. Countless people—journalists, political pundits, public intellectuals, educators, activists, and scholars—have wrangled over Black History Month's role in American life, even contemplating whether it is still necessary and of value. As historian Daryl Scott, former president of the Association for the Study of African American Life and History, remarked in 2014, thrashing out Black History Month's contemporary relevance and standing within American culture "is a cottage industry."[3]

On the eve of Black History Month 2016, a reporter for MSNBC covering the most recent chitchat about its observance in social media outlets contended that "the debate around Black History Month really began in earnest 10 years ago" when Academy Award-winning actor Morgan Freeman publicly raised objections to the celebration.[4] Though Freeman's comments undoubtedly reignited "the Black History Month debate," the contemporary war of words about this popular custom are not recent, avant-garde, or cutting-edge: such concerns have been looming in the minds of and articulated by a medley of thinkers for more than seventy years. In actuality, much of what is now being conjured up about Black History Month was present in the discussions of Woodson and his colleagues in the early years when Negro History Week was practiced.

Using provocative and in some cases quite entertaining discussions of Black History Month as instructive and engaging points of departure, this chapter opens by exploring how this observance has recently been reconceptualized by a group of citizen journalists. To illustrate that contemporary and widely publicized diatribes against Black History Month are reminiscent of past grumblings, I historicize twenty-first century debates and controversies surrounding this established celebration. I also unpack President Obama's ritualistic commemorations of the black past, recent "Black Future(s) Month" activities, and the paucity of scholarship on Black History Month. In conclusion, I consider Black History Month's unresolved future.

---

3   Larry Copeland, "Is Black History Month Still Needed?" *USA Today*, February 25, 2014, A5.

4   Adam Howard, "The Black History Month Debate Is Back," msnbc.com, January 22, 2016.

FEBRUARY 2016: A BLACK HISTORY MONTH TO REMEMBER?

By the middle of February 2016, many in the social media world were declaring that the 40th National African American History Month was the "best," "greatest," and "blackest" manifestation of this commemoration that the world had ever seen. One of the first bloggers to trumpet this conviction was Damon Young, co-founder of the popular daily digital magazine *VSB* (verysmartbrothers.com). In its own right, the title of his February 16, 2016, blog is alluring: "Kendrick Confirms It: February 2016 is the Blackest Black History Month Ever." For Young, Beyoncé's controversial half-time performance at Super Bowl 50 (one of the most watched programs in the history of the US television industry), Kendrick Lamar's success and Brittany Howard's closing performance at the 58th annual Grammy Awards, and Obama's opportunity to nominate a Supreme Court Justice confirmed that "February 2016 is the blackest Black History Month ever."

Throughout February 2016 and into March, countless bloggers—from unknown, amateur, personal bloggers to insightful public intellectuals—cosigned on Young's observations, adding other events, black accomplishments, and symbolic triumphs to the mix. Some developed interesting and sometimes humorous lists justifying why February 2016 was a historic month for black America in blogs bearing titles like "5 Reasons This Has Been the Most Unapologetically Black Black History Month Ever," "9 Reasons February 2016 Is the Blackest Black History Month Ever," and even "29 Reasons This Was the Blackest Black History Month Ever." When placed within the broader scope of African American history and the enduring black freedom struggle, most of the "reasons" that graced bloggers' inventories were insignificant: Stephen Curry's brilliance on the basketball court or Cam Newton's swagger, the "Black-ish" episode on police brutality, Kanye West's announcement of his ingenious "The Life of Pablo" album, Morgan Freeman's voice being used by the WAZE navigation app, the introduction of a black "American Girl" doll from the civil rights era, the release of several PBS-style black history documentaries, and so on.

CNN Digital joined the fray on the last day of the month. In an essay "From Beyoncé to Chris Rock: Best Black History Month Ever?" one multimedia journalist summarized what other bloggers before her concluded: "Even if we did not reach the absolute pinnacle of Black History Month, it's been pretty memorable."[5]

Why was there so much media attention and hype related to black America during the 2016 Black History Month commemorations? If we were to revisit past commemorations, we could certainly identify equally important

---

5 Emmanuella Grinberg, "From Beyoncé to Chris Rock: Best Black History Month Ever?" cnn.com, February 29, 2016.

achievements and landmark moments. As strange as it might sound, one of the reasons that the 2016 #BlackHistoryMonth movement deemed the 40th anniversary of this annual observance the "best," "greatest," and "blackest" Black History Month ever was arguably the byproduct of Beyoncé's popularity in African American and US culture. Her and her crew's superficial nods to the Black Panther Party during the Super Bowl half-time celebration evidently upset some of the older white viewers who were probably expecting an apolitical performance from this crossover megastar. On the other hand, younger African Americans, especially personal bloggers and public intellectuals in training, praised Beyoncé's actions as forthrightly challenging the white power structure by unapologetically vindicating dimensions of black womanhood and, most explicitly, honoring the Black Panther Party, one of the most militant organizations in the modern black freedom struggle.

Of course, Beyoncé is not the only hip-hop generation icon to exalt Black Power–era activism. There exists an identifiable tradition of Black Panther Party revivalism in hip-hop culture dating back to the "golden age" of hip-hop and earlier. Public Enemy, KRS-One, Paris, Nas, Lil' Kim, Dead Prez, Jay-Z, and Kanye West (just to name a handful) have all revered the Panthers in their lyrics and self-styling. Beyoncé was building upon hip-hop artists' proclivity to salute the Panther's "revolutionary" disposition. Yet, her status in US popular culture garnered much more attention for her nod to the Panthers than any of the acknowledgments of her predecessors. As feminist scholar bell hooks suggests in her tendentious critique of Beyoncé's *Lemonade* album, "Beyoncé's audience is the world and that world of business and money-making has no color."[6]

Was February 2016 really such a historic Black History Month? Assuredly, previous generations of African Americans could have compelling reasons for claiming that the Black History Month commemorations and achievements of their times were equally if not more important.

For instance, in February 1977, businessman and civil rights activist Vernon E. Jordan Jr. announced to readers of the *New Pittsburgh Courier*: "There's a degree of excitement about this year's observation of Black History Month missing from previous ones."[7] For Jordan, Blacks were poised to make economic advancements, "regional unity" was on the rise, Martin Luther King Sr. had just delivered a memorable sermon at the Lincoln Memorial, and the television miniseries *Roots* premiered on ABC. A decade later in a write-up entitled "This Black History Month Is Different from Others," editors of the *Atlanta Daily World* blazoned: "As we enter into 1987 Black History Month we hope the readers of your *Daily World* will take a broader view of the situation in the universe than ever before." They continued, "This is a time in history that mankind hangs

6   bell hooks, "Moving Beyond Pain," bellhooksinstitute.com, May 9, 2016.

7   Vernon E. Jordan Jr., "This Is Black History Month," *New Pittsburgh Courier*, February 26, 1977, 1.

in the balance . . . This hour in history confronts mankind with the most decisive test in history."[8]

Similarly, throughout the 1990s and into the twenty-first century, it was not
uncommon for events during February to be advertised as the "best" or "one of
the best" Black History Month programs ever. The editor of *Diverse Issues in
Higher Education* heralded that Black History Month 2006 was "memorable"
because of the plans to build the National Museum of African American History
and Culture in Washington, DC.[9] In 2009, numerous journalists declared that
with the election of Obama, the commemoration had a new meaning and would
undergo a facelift. And in 2014, one reporter even hailed Macy's "Eras of Black
Style" Black History Month receptions—held in ten major cities through the
nation—"some of the best Black History Month events ever."[10]

Online discussions of issues pertaining to black history, including Black
History Month, are in many ways refreshing, at times engendering critical reflections and discourse among young African Americans born after the modern civil
rights and Black Power movements. Michael Eric Dyson's recent veneration of
"an emerging black intelligentsia" in *The New Republic* is judicious.[11] Many of
these social critics have creatively used the Internet to disseminate and popularize their ideas. In some respects, they have altered the black public intellectual
landscape. At the same time, droves of today's black bloggers suffer from present-
ism, failing to analyze contemporary phenomenon in historical contexts. This in
part seems to be the case with much of the commentary surrounding Black
History Month during 2016 and earlier in the twenty-first century.

QUESTIONING BLACK HISTORY MONTH IN THE TWENTY-FIRST CENTURY

Black History Month 2016 was discussed and debated for reasons beyond those
identified by personal bloggers. On January 20, 2016, African American actress
Stacey Dash appeared on "Fox and Friends" to discuss disgruntled African American
celebrities who had recently called for a boycott of the Oscars because of an absence
of black nominees—namely Jada Pinkett Smith, Spike Lee, Al Sharpton, and others
who supported the #OscarsSoWhite movement. Dash denounced BET and its
annual awards ceremony and the NAACP Image Awards, deeming the event self-
segregation. While elaborating upon why BET should not exist, she added, "Just like
there shouldn't be a Black History Month. We're Americans. Period. That's it." The
prying host of the show egged Dash on by asking: "Are you saying that there

---

8   "This Black History Month Is Different From Others," *Atlanta Daily World*, February 5,
1987, 4.

9   Hilary Hurd Anyaso, "A Memorable Black History Month," *Diverse Issues in Higher
Education*, February 23, 2006, 4.

10   Debbie Norrell, "Black History Month is in the Books," *New Pittsburgh Courier, City
Edition*, March 5, 2014, B1.

11   Michael Eric Dyson, "Think Out Loud: An Emerging Black Intelligentsia Has Embraced
Online Technology to Change American Ideas," *The New Republic*, September 9, 2015.

shouldn't be a Black History Month because there isn't a white history month?" and Dash replied, "Exactly. Exactly." Dash, who endorsed businessman and Republican Mitt Romney in the 2012 election and was, from 2014 until 2017, a "semi-regular" personality on the Fox News Channel's daytime talk show "Outnumbered," was a hotly discussed newsmaker following her remarks. Unsurprisingly, many African Americans took to social media to criticize the former *Clueless* actress. Even her cousin, hip-hop mogul Damon Dash, condemned his kin's comments, surmising that she was paid by Fox News to make such statements.

As brief and perhaps insignificant as they were, Stacey Dash's statements spilled over onto a larger public stage. At the 2016 Oscars hosted by comedian Chris Rock, she was part of a skit in which she was introduced as being the new director of the Academy's "minority outreach program," an initiative that does not exist, of course. Dash announced, "I cannot wait to help my people out. Happy Black History Month." This parody failed to make a splash with the Oscars' primarily white audience probably because most were not aware of, or if cognizant took no particular stance toward, her statement about Black History Month. After all, some black people were the ones most baffled by Dash's comments, not whites. While it is easy to dismiss Dash's remarks, her brief observations did catapult Black History Month into the realm of social media and popular discourse, especially within black cyber communities. Yet, as Dash herself pointed out on her home page on patheos.com, she was not the first African American thespian to question the existence and purpose of Black History Month in the twenty-first century.

In a by now famous 2005 interview with Mike Wallace on the well-known news magazine *60 Minutes*, Morgan Freeman called Black History Month "ridiculous." Similar to Dash, Freeman whipped up the popular argument that there was not a month specifically designated to acknowledge white Americans' historical contributions (a "White History Month"). In highlighting this, both failed to acknowledge that in US popular culture and educational institutions white American history and culture is predominantly used as the universal frame of reference, that white American historical icons are routinely venerated. As Afrocentrist Molefi Kete Asante has repeatedly stressed, notions of Eurocentric and white American universality have been largely accepted in US culture. Take, for instance, the images that appear on US currency. Though Booker T. Washington and George Washington Carver appeared on US commemorative coins during the 1940s and in 2009 Duke Ellington became the first African American to be featured by himself on a US coin, history was made when it was announced that Harriet Tubman will become the first African American woman to be featured on a US paper note. A writer for the *New York Times* called this "the most sweeping and historically symbolic makeover of American currency in a century."[12]

---

12   Jackie Calmes, "Harriet Tubman Ousts Andrew Jackson in Change for a $20," *New York Times,* April 20, 2016.

Black History Month, in essence, exists because it is part of a time-honored tradition. It persists by virtue of this and because of the continued lack of consistent attention given to blacks' influence on American history and culture, especially in educational systems. If blacks' contributions and concerns were taken up in a manner that was at least proportional to their impact on American life, then, theoretically, Black History Month would no longer be needed.

Moreover, those who bemoan the absence of a "white history month," fail to recognize the truism that in the United States "every month is white history month" and that ten other groups of people have formally been awarded months: Asian/Pacific American Heritage Month (May); National Hispanic Heritage Month (September 15 through October 15); Irish American Heritage Month (March); Women's History Month (March); Older Americans' Month (May); Jewish American Heritage Month (May); Gay and Lesbian Pride Month (June); Caribbean-American Heritage Month (June); Italian American Heritage Month (October); and National American Indian Heritage Month (November 1990).

Why aren't these months, and others, contested in the ways that Black History Month is? A similar trend can be noticed with the critiques on affirmative action. This now passé practice is often presented to the American public as a "black thing," as if other groups have not benefitted from these policies.

Like others before him, and unlike Dash, Freeman called for an end to Black History Month because he believed that it denigrated the contributions that African Americans had made to US history and culture. "You're going to relegate my history to a month? ... I don't want a Black History Month," Freeman declared. "Black history is American history."[13] Though Freeman's comments triggered a social media frenzy, his thoughts were not original, evoking the age-old and prevailing contributionist and patriotic tradition of black thought and historiography that dates back to the nineteenth century. Frederick Douglass's steadfast belief in black contributionism was at the center of his consistent opposition—except at the outset of the Civil War—to the emigration and colonization movements during the nineteenth century. In his lengthy address "Lessons of the Hour" (1894), he underscored: "The native land of the American negro is America. His bones, his muscles, his sinews, are all American. His ancestors for two hundred and seventy years have lived, and labored, and died on America soil."[14] Echoing Douglass, countless twentieth-century black historians and activists argued that American history is incomplete without the contributions of African Americans. For decades, African Americans have argued that one month is "not enough" to recognize black American history. Negro History Week founder Carter G. Woodson himself knew that one week was not sufficient for memorializing the black past.

---

13   Morgan Freeman interview with Mike Wallace, *60 Minutes*, CBS, December 18, 2005.

14   Frederick Douglass, *Address by Hon. Frederick Douglass, Delivered in the Metropolitan A. M. E. Church, Washington, D. C., Tuesday, January 9th, 1894, on The Lessons of the Hour*, Baltimore: Press of Thomas and Evans, 1894, 26.

The beliefs of Freeman, Dash, and others that Black History Month segregates black people has been taken up by conservative spokespersons who see little value in the observance and create calculated arguments to jettison it. Take, for instance, an article published in the conservative semi-monthly magazine the *National Review* in 2013 entitled "Against Black History Month" by staff writer and author of the popular *The Conservatarian Manifesto* (2016). He begins by glossing over why Woodson created Negro History Week and then fast forwards to the present, marveling at how much things have supposedly changed. For him, unlike during Woodson's times, black history in the age of Obama was no longer snubbed in American society. He asserts that Freeman made his case "perfectly" and argues that Black History Month contributes to the swelling separation of the black past from the American experience, counters the "melting-pot" ideal, further segregates black people, is essentially antiquated, and, in the end, does nothing to address the "racial problems in America."[15] His pie-in-the-sky solution is to magically have curriculums in K-12 schools incorporate the black experience. If only the remedy were this simple!

Freeman's comments made an impression beyond conservatives. In mid-February 2012, Shukree Tilghman's documentary *More Than a Month* premiered on Independent Lens. The then twenty-nine-year-old filmmaker told one interviewer that Freeman's sentiments "resonated" so much with him that he was "determined to set out to find the truth about Black History Month." According to Tilghman, one fundamental question guides his documentary: "*What does it mean* that we have a Black History Month?" Like others before him, he sought to challenge Americans to "question why black history is taught as if it is somehow separate from American history." He carried on, "I hope as a country, we can imagine an America where Black History Month isn't necessary."[16] The existence of Black History Month, in Tilghman's estimation, contributes to the othering of African Americans.

Approximately one hour in length, Tilghman's film begins in 2010 with him traveling throughout the East Coast interviewing a range of people—from his parents to history professors and educators to high school students. One of the most compelling scenes from the documentary occurs when Tilghman, in the tradition of comedy sketches from *The Chris Rock Show*, engages with the public in the streets, walking around wearing a sandwich board sign with "END BLACK HISTORY MONTH" on the front and "BLACK HISTORY IS AMERICAN HISTORY" on the back. Tilghman's overarching argument is similar to earlier ones—that African American history is American history and should not be separated from mainstream representations of American history. Despite his recycling of conventional beliefs still lingering in the collective conscience of much of black America, *More Than a Month* is the first major film

---

15   Charles C. W. Cooke, "Against Black History Month," *National Review*, February 4, 2013.
16   Brooke Shelby Biggs, "Shukree Tilghman Wants to End (the Way We Think About) Black History Month," *Independent Lens Blog*, February 15, 2012, pbs.org.

that focused on Black History Month and consequently received plenty of attention.

Not only was the documentary screened at various venues during 2012 Black History Month celebrations, but Tilghman was interviewed numerous times and leading newspapers reviewed the documentary. In February 2012, the *New York Times* published a critical review of Tilghman's opus. The reviewer dubbed the documentary "meandering and indecisive" with such a "waffly ending that you can no longer tell whether he favors or opposes Black History Month." For this critic, Tilghman is "never less than a genial guide to the thorny question he raises from the start."[17]

Obviously, PBS and Independent Lens viewed Tilghman's work differently. For the sponsors and producers, *More Than a Month* is a useful teaching tool. Pedagogical devices—a "Discussion Guide" and "Educator Guide: Viewing and Discussion Guide"—were offered as supplements. The "Discussion Guide" includes a statement from Tilghman, a concise summary of the film, resources, discussion questions, and "suggestions for action." While the discussion questions could provoke critical thought and the "suggestions for action" echo practical exercises that Woodson put forward during Negro History Week celebrations, the recommended resources are lacking and problematic. For instance, readers are encouraged to learn about Woodson's life and career by perusing the overview of "the father of black history" on Wikipedia! None of the available published scholarship on Woodson is cited by PBS and Independent Lens. Aimed at middle school and high school students, the "Educators Guide" provides a host of useful tips for viewing the film, pointing out specific time-codes where the documentary can be stopped and unpacked with compelling inquiries.

The significance of *More Than a Month* cannot be ignored: it helped rekindle debates about the deeper meaning of Black History Month. Yet it appears as if Tilghman began to dislike the attention that his controversial film afforded him; he grew weary of being at the center of the debate about Black History Month's relevancy. In February 2014, he declined an invitation to be interviewed by Larry Copeland. "Unfortunately, I've all but retired from talking about Black History Month. I got tired, man," Tilghman told this reporter; "being the face associated with ending Black History Month is a peculiar burden."[18]

RESERVATIONS ABOUT NEGRO HISTORY WEEK CELEBRATIONS

There is a concrete tradition of questioning the purpose of Black History Month that emerged decades before Tilghman, Freeman, Dash, and others offered their sentiments in the twenty-first century. In fact, this skepticism predates the

---

17   Neil Genzlinger, "In Search of a Reason to Segregate American History," *New York Times*, February 15, 2012, C8.

18   Copeland, "Is Black History Month Still Needed?" A5.

establishment of this now monthlong celebration. From 1926 until 1950, the halcyon days of Negro History Week, African American activists, schoolteachers, and movers and shakers in the ASNLH plainly deliberated over how to most effectively carry out Negro History Week activities. In the pages of *The Journal of Negro History*, *The Negro History Bulletin*, and leading black newspapers, Woodson routinely shared his opinions on the most appropriate commemorative practices. Beyond advocating that the weeklong event eventually be transformed into "Negro History Year" (code words for the complete incorporation of the study of black history in American educational institutions), it is not surprising that Woodson never doubted his brainchild's function or aims. However, some within the black community did not always share his optimism or see eye to eye with his strategy.

Ideally, Woodson wanted Negro History Week to become what in 1935 he first referred to as "Negro History Year, the study of the Negro throughout the school life of the child."[19] In this sense, Negro History Week was meant to serve as a stepping-stone to the sought-after unabridged introduction of black history into secondary and high school curricula by African-American activists. By the late 1940s, Woodson still emphasized that he wanted this weeklong celebration to become "what it should be—Negro History Year."[20] Woodson did not discuss the logistics involved in converting Negro History Week into "Negro History Month." Others did, leading to the first Black History Month proclamation in 1976. While they did not disagree with Woodson's overarching mission, some black history enthusiasts during the era of Jim Crow segregation wanted his weeklong celebration to be transformed into a monthlong testimonial.

As early as 1932, members of the Bethel AME Church in Leavenworth, Kansas celebrated "Negro History Month" with "splendid programs."[21] Most likely unbeknownst to Woodson and the ASNLH, this congregation held this celebration in March. At the dawning and concluding of the 1940s, announcements in the *Chicago Defender*, the *Chicago Daily Tribune*, and *Masses and Mainstream*, respectively, dubbed February "Negro History Month."[22] In 1950, members of the Monroe Laboratory School in Washington, DC, became among the first to call for the observance of "Negro History Month" instead of Negro History Week with the blessings of the ASNLH. "The ever increasing interest of teachers, pupils and parents in Negro History led to the celebration of Negro History Month, instead of the usual one week," an editorial in the *Negro History*

---

19   Carter G. Woodson, "Negro History Week The Tenth Year," *The Journal of Negro History* 20, April 1935, 127.

20   Carter G. Woodson, "The Annual Report of the Director," *The Journal of Negro History* 33, October 1948, 392.

21   "Kansas State: Osawatomie, Kansas," *Chicago Defender*, March 26, 1932, 11.

22   Mabel Kountze, "Know About Yourself: Story of Booker T. Washington," *The Chicago Defender*, February 10, 1940, 15; "Negro History Month to Be Marked at Club Meeting," *The Chicago Daily Tribune*, February 8, 1947, 11; "Back Matter," *Science and Society* 13, Winter 1948/1949.

Bulletin reported.[23] During the remainder of the 1950s, the notion of a "Negro History Month" was sporadically evoked.

In 1951, Negro History Week was observed from February 11–18 and on February 17, 1951, "Negro History Month" by name was mentioned in the *New York Amsterdam News*.[24] A year later, a writer for the *Chicago Defender* argued that a monthlong celebration would better serve the black community. "'Negro History Week' could easily and profitably become 'Negro History Month,' for Old Negroes as well as Young Negroes pay so little attention to, and know so little about the history of the American Negro," a passionate Rebecca Stiles Taylor proclaimed. "Many college Negroes have knowledge of less than one half dozen historical Negro characters of yesteryears."[25] Perhaps in what was a typo, in 1953 a writer for the *New York Times* entitled an editorial "Negro History Month Is Set" while discussing New York Mayor Vincent R. Impellitteri's support of the ASNLH and its Founders Day celebration.[26] Four years later, the president of Texas College, a historically black college founded in 1894 in Tyler, Texas, offered an "official proclamation" designating February as "NEGRO HISTORY MONTH."[27]

Others more directly sought to revise and explicitly challenge Woodson's weeklong celebration. One of the oldest African American newspapers founded in Harlem in 1909, the *New York Amsterdam News*, served as a spirited forum for publicizing and contemplating Negro History Week. In a 1926 editorial, "Negro History Week a Popular Idea," the paper welcomed this celebration, observing: "It seems that the public has been awaiting such an idea."[28] Throughout the ensuing decades, this popular newspaper annually endorsed this event with recurring editorials in the 1950s like "Why Negro History?," by covering local and national events and festivities, and by publishing essays by Woodson in which he enthusiastically explained Negro History Week's primary objectives.[29]

During the second quarter of the twentieth century, Negro History Week was called into question by *New York Amsterdam News* writers, namely long-time managing editor S. W. Garlington. In a 1943 editorial, Garlington remarked that the celebration "is scheduled at the wrong time" because of the existence of other competing weeklong celebrations. Without mincing his words, he had the

---

23   "Negro History at the Monroe Laboratory School, Washington, D.C.," *The Negro History Bulletin* 13, May 1950, 182.

24   "Urge Bill to Restore B'klyn Night Court," *New York Amsterdam News*, February 17, 1951, 9.

25   Rebecca Stiles Taylor, "Federated Clubs: Mary Church Terrell Recalls Origin Mass Club Movement," *The Chicago Defender*, February 16, 1952, 8.

26   "Negro History Month Is Set," *New York Times*, September 10, 1953, 25.

27   "New Area of Activity in Texas," *The Negro History Bulletin* 20, May 1957, 171.

28   "Negro History Week a Popular Idea," *New York Amsterdam News*, January 20, 1926, 16.

29   Carter G. Woodson, "Assistance Needed for Study of Negro History," *New York Amsterdam News*, February 3, 1932, 8; Carter G. Woodson, "Negro History Week Different From Different Points of View," *New York Amsterdam News*, December 7, 1932, 6.

nerve to call out Woodson ("PAGING DR. CARTER G. WOODSON!") to change the date of Negro History Week. "Future observances of NHW should not (consciously or unconsciously) compete for attention," Garlington proclaimed. "Now Dr. Woodson, don't bring me that line about losing face if you change the date."[30]

Several years later in the midst of World War II, one of Garlington's *New York Amsterdam News* co-workers posited that Negro History Week celebrations should be refashioned into a more deliberate educational reform movement "for a new world order." The plea continued:

> Negro History Week, 1945, should have a deeper meaning, a greater purpose, and a more universal significance if the war aims of the United Nations are to be anything more than temporary morale-building propaganda or hypocritical and deceptive exhortations ... Negro History Week should, therefore, mean a new and keener awareness of the need for sweeping educational reform from the kindergarten to the university.[31]

It appears that Garlington abandoned his 1943 plea to Woodson as subsequent discussions of Negro History Week in the *New York Amsterdam News* maintained that February was a logical time for the celebration. He did not, however, totally refrain from criticizing the merits of Negro History Week. For instance, on February 11, 1950, in a broadcast on WEVD (a radio station founded in 1927 by the Socialist Party of America and named in honor of Eugene Victor Debs), the longtime managing editor of the newspaper unequivocally pronounced: "It is time to get rid of Negro History Week celebrations." Preceding later Black History Month detractors, Garlington argued that the African American past needed to be recognized as constituting an essential component of American history. In an unsigned editorial perhaps written by Garlington himself, his ideas were cited and summarized. "We want American History presented as the total record of the past activities and experiences of all grounds and races. We do not want it presented from any special angle." The editorial added, "What the Negro does is part of America and must be fitted into the American historical pattern or it is not the nation's history." Unsurprisingly, the editorial fully endorsed Garlington's views, stressing that "so-called standard" US history textbooks were biased and needed to be revised, that studying and honoring black history by itself amounted to "side show or Jim Crow history," and that, ultimately, the "integration" of all American groups into American historical narratives would require sustained reform in the shape of "moral suasion as well as the coercive force of law and the enforcement of law." The editorial did, nonetheless, conclude on a positive note, praising Woodson

---

30   S. W. Garlington, "Pointed Points," *New York Amsterdam News*, October 23, 1943, 15.
31   A. M. Wendell Malliet, "Urges Reform in Education System Here: History, Brotherhood Week Highlights Need for New World Plans," *New York Amsterdam News*, February 10, 1945, A6.

and the ASNLH for their efforts to create a "larger, broader balanced history for all Americans."[32]

Garlington's outlook did not entirely shape this leading newspaper's outlook on Negro History Week. The February 18, 1950, edition that showcased his comments also featured several different takes on the usefulness and impact of the annual celebration. In an essay entitled "Record of the Negro Past Now Being Kept," Constance Curtis exalted Negro History Week, Woodson's vision and commitment, and the undertakings of the ASNLH and its local New York City branch.[33] However, Chollie Herndon reported that judging by the lack of participation from colleges in New York City, Negro History Week "is a flop." At the twentieth century's midpoint, the *New York Amsterdam News* conducted a survey to measure the city's educational institutions' Negro History Week activities and reported that "69 percent of the colleges said they had never heard of the week." Though the newspaper insinuated that the local ASNLH branch could have improved its publicity efforts, in the end, Herndon concluded that "the failure of Negro student organizations to function successfully accounted for the dearth of Negro History Week activity."[34]

As iconoclastic and controversial as Garlington's comments were (more than four decades later, even the renegade Harold Cruse said that he was "shocked" by the anti-Black History Month remarks in the *New York Amsterdam News*), it does not seem as if they were widely considered beyond the newspaper's readership. The fact that the weekly student newspaper of Columbia University, the *Columbia Daily Spectator*, reported on Garlington's observations is thought-provoking. Apparently, the white staff deduced that his argument was valid, but underscored that Negro History Week was still relevant.[35] This issue also included a "letter to the editor" from Clarence B. Jones, who graduated from Columbia in 1956 and would later become a speechwriter and adviser for Martin Luther King Jr. The chairman of the CU Young Progressives stressed the importance of the observance. "Negro History Week is necessary because the role of the Negro in American history is either ignored or distorted in our schools," Jones wrote.[36]

On the 25th anniversary of Negro History Week, the ASNLH did not overlook dismissals by Garlington and a "strange assortment" of other "detractors" of their prized festivities. Prolific journalist, instructor and teacher trainer at Hunter College of The City of New York, and specialist in African and Middle East affairs, Marguerite Cartwright, authored a lengthy essay in the *Negro*

---

32   "'Do We Want Negro History," *New York Amsterdam News*, February 18, 1950, 14.

33   Constance Curtis, "Record of the Negro Now Being Kept," *New York Amsterdam News*, February 18, 1950, 1.

34   Chollie Herndon, "LIU Prof Denounces Negro History Week," *New York Amsterdam News*, February 18, 1950, 1.

35   "Approach to History," *Columbia Daily Spectator*, February 17, 1950, 2.

36   "Letter to the Editor: Hails Negro History Week on Its Twenty-Fifth Anniversary," *Columbia Daily Spectator*, February 17, 1950.

History Bulletin in which she systematically quashed those who called for the end of Woodson's beloved creation. According to Cartwright, during February 1950 the "*pros* and *cons* of Negro History Week were heard everywhere, from the breakfast table to the barbershop, from the press, over the airways." This staunch defender of Negro History Week pointed out, "Everyone was qualified to take a stand and everyone did."[37] Cartwright's assessment was in many regards ahead of its times, foreshadowing future defenses.

Cartwright agreed with those who argued that the study and dramatization of black history deserved more than one week of attention and pointed out that the ASNLH used this observance to "enrich" the curricula. Acknowledging that her personal experience was antidotal, Cartwright reflected on how the Negro History Weeks of her youth made her "better informed" about the black past. She appropriately asked if abolishing Negro History Week would really solve the problem of black historical marginalization in US culture, especially in schools.

By "abolishing the little toe-hold of recognition this provides, will the desired goal," queried Cartwright, "be reached any sooner?" After explaining the self-evident opposition of "white supremacy sources," without identifying them or the *New York Amsterdam News* by name, Cartwright challenged Chollie Herndon and Garlington, whom she called an "ignorant detractor." While she appreciated the ideal of having a US history that treated the black experience seriously, she realized, based upon the past and present state of race relations in the United States, that this was not going to happen overnight, that "changing history books is a slow and arduous task," and that Negro History Week was needed "while we are waiting for this total record of all groups and races." In retrospect, her observations were spot on. Prefiguring the beliefs of cultural nationalist Black Studies advocates, she maintained that "Negro History must be established as an independent discipline to meet today's need." Cartwright discredited the data compiled by the *New York Amsterdam News* that supported the claim that there was a lack of interest in Negro History Week in New York City, by drawing from a study of US history textbooks' treatment of Americans from various cultural backgrounds conducted by the American Council on Education that basically concluded that "prevailing stereotypes" about African Americans prevailed. She concluded her defense of Negro History Week in a pragmatic Woodsonian manner:

> Negro history, set apart if need be, and the obviousness of the need cannot be gain-said, is sadly needed to implement the study of American history, to strengthen our democracy, to produce wider scholarship thru increased culture contact, in short, to improve human relations.[38]

---

37   Marguerite Cartwright, "Negro History Week—1950," *Negro History Bulletin* 13, April 1950, 153.

38   Ibid., 165, 167.

Throughout the remainder of the 1950s, a few editorials in the *New York Amsterdam News* debated the meaning of Negro History Week. For instance, in a 1952 piece "Why the Need?" the newspaper supported Negro History Week but underscored that the celebration needed to be expanded in order to be more impactful: "All of us should understand each other not just one week in the year, but the entire 52 weeks."[39]

The criticisms offered by Garlington and his *New York Amsterdam News* co-workers were reinvoked and rehashed from the 1960s through the 1990s in varying degrees, from the peak years of the conventional civil rights era through the culture wars of the presidential terms of George H. W. Bush and Bill Clinton. Perhaps because of the focus on the civil rights mass movement, discussions of Negro History Week appear to have declined from the mid-1950s through the dawning of the Black Power era. Nevertheless, in 1963, controversial journalist, novelist, and conservative George S. Schuyler did call upon the ASNLH to "adopt a more effective method of indoctrination." In particular, the author of the satiric novel *Black No More* (1931) believed that "pilgrimages to historic sites" in New York City "with all of the consequent radio, television and newspaper coverage" would more powerfully "teach millions of people about Negro history."[40] Though Schuyler's proposed exercises in local public history were relevant, such a strategy would not have been as wide-reaching as more grassroots endeavors.

"WE NEED MORE THAN THIS"

During the early years of the Black Power era, there was a rise in outspoken skepticism about Negro History Week. In a 1969 editorial, "Making Negro History Week Last," writers for the *Negro History Bulletin* challenged how Negro History Week had been observed. "The exercises, speeches, plays, music, dance and public occasions of Negro History Week are not the true objectives toward which we move. We need more than this." Woodson's protégés continued:

> We should not confine ourselves to enthusiastic meetings in Negro History Week and then return to the same teaching as before until another year . . . It must therefore be apparent that Negro History Week serves as a point of departure, a motivation for continuing development of an American History which is inclusive of black people and all ethnic groups.[41]

In January 1970, a diverse group of black activists in New York City under the guise of the Black Solidarity Committee (including local activists Carlos Russell and Reggie Butts; Congressman Adam Clayton Powell; professor Charles

39 "Why the Need?" *New York Amsterdam News*, February 16, 1952, 14.

40 George S. Schuyler, "Views and Reviews," *The Pittsburgh Courier*, March 2, 1963, 11.

41 "Editorial: Making Negro History Week Last," *Negro History Bulletin* 32, April 1969, 4, 5.

V. Hamilton, African American students; and organizations such as the Urban League, the Communist Party USA, the Black Minister Conference of Greater New York, and the Black Panther Party) called for "Black Liberation Week" to take place from February 16 until February 22 as a replacement for Negro History Week.[42] The New York State Council of Black Democrats endorsed the event. Assemblyman Charles Rangel delivered a proposal in the New York State Assembly in which he summoned "all black people of the State of New York to observe Black Liberation Week by appropriate recognition and ceremony." Rangel added that the event was timely "as there are forces at work to deny us equality and freedom."[43]

The timeframe for "Black Liberation Week" was selected in honor of the birthday of Huey P. Newton, the first Pan-African conference that W. E. B. Du Bois organized, and the assassination of Malcolm X. Challenging the hero-worshipping nature of Negro History Week observances, the week's activities were "aimed at informing Blacks of the threat of genocide which faces them."[44]

Like Kwanzaa, founded by Maulana Karenga in 1966, each day focused on a specific theme. "Negro Liberation Week" focused on genocide, political prisoners, iconic freedom fighters, martyred black children, mothers, and the assassination of Malcolm X. The tone of the celebration was set by the opening day's theme, "We Charge Genocide," conceivably a tribute to William Lloyd Patterson's historic 1951 petition to the United Nations charging the United States with committing genocide against African American people. This observance was acknowledged by the *New York Times* in January and February 1970 but did not have the impact that Negro History Week did. Yet, in 1971, the *Chicago Daily Defender* advertised "Black Liberation Week" events that were scheduled to take place at Chicago State University and offered a peculiar description of the program. "Black Liberation Week is a nationwide celebration which, until two years ago, was known as Negro History Week," a brief editorial in the *Defender* stated. It continued, "The focus of the program changed when the name changed and is now directed to the future of Black American culture in comparison with its past."[45] To say that this editorial is confusing is an understatement, especially because "Black Liberation Week" did not replace Negro History Week.

In February 1971, one month before his death, Executive Director of the National Urban League Whitney Moore Young Jr. reiterated one of S. W. Garlington's complaints about Woodson. Garlington accused Woodson of inaugurating Negro History Week in February in part to honor Abraham Lincoln, "the mythical Lincoln" in Young's mind, and Young agreed with the critique.

---

42   "Negro History Week Now; Black Liberation Week Next: Black Liberation Week Feb. 16–22," *New York Amsterdam News*, February 14, 1970, 1.

43   "Liberation Week OKd By Blacks," *New York Amsterdam News*, February 21, 1970, 26.

44   "Next Is Black Liberation Week," *New York Amsterdam News*, February 6, 1971, 1.

45   "Will Observe Black Liberation Week," *The Chicago Daily Defender*, February 1, 1971, 2.

Young became one of the first to dub Negro History Week celebrations "educational tokenism." Like others, he called for the study of black people in all subjects "all year round" and encouraged black parents and communities to "assume a leadership role" in the struggle for culturally relevant education. According to Young: "Our kids are our most valuable asset and the education they receive is our most important task."[46]

Some were less direct in their critiques of Negro History Week and, following in the footsteps of those who preceded them as early as the Great Depression, celebrated black history for a month as opposed to a week. For instance, during the early years of the Black Power era, the House of Knowledge bookstore in Chicago, founded in 1950 by Pan-African activist Fidepe H. Hammurabi (born H. H. Robb), hosted a range of activities as a part of its "Negro History Month celebration."[47] In 1968, the then president of the ASNLH, Charles H. Wesley, noted that the Negro History Week celebration in 1967 was "more widely" celebrated "than in the years prior to it" and that the ASNLH granted permission to "one central city group" to celebrate "'Negro History Month.'" In the early 1970s prior to President Gerald Ford's inaugural "Message on the Observance of Black History Month," several groups and states had been observing "Negro History Month" with or without the ASNLH's endorsement.[48] The following appeared under the heading "Negro History Month in Observance" in a 1971 issue of the *Negro History Bulletin*: "February is being observed in a variety of ways throughout the Kansas City area as Negro History Month. Negro History Week, traditionally celebrated during the second week in February, has been expanded into a month-long observance."[49]

In the years immediately after President Ford's statement, discussions about the new manifestation of Woodson's brainchild continued. For Black Studies scholar Ralph L. Crowder, this "redefinition of terminology" was a step in the right direction. He did, however, caution Black History Month advocates from simply highlighting "great" black leaders' contributions to US history and culture; he argued that a more relevant approach was recognizing that history played a significant and practical role in "the struggle for Black liberation," that Black History Month be "the reaffirmation of struggle, determination, and creativity." In the end, he longed for a return to the utilitarian Woodson approach: "Let us strive to recapture the original legacy of Black History Month." What this "original legacy" actually entailed in Crowder's mind is unclear. His interpretation of

---

46 Whitney M. Young Jr., "Negro History Week," *New York Amsterdam News*, February 13, 1971, 14.

47 "House of Knowledge Marks 'Negro History Month,'" *The Chicago Defender*, February 4, 1967, 8.

48 "History Month to Conclude Afro-American Program," *The Chicago Defender*, February 25, 1967, 4; Charles H. Wesley, "Annual Report," *The Journal of Negro History* 53, January 1968, 108.

49 "Negro History Month in Observance," *Negro History Bulletin* 34, April 1971, 90.

the Negro History Weeks of Woodson's time was rather idealistic.[50]

During the late 1970s, members of the Association for the Study of Afro-American Life and History (ASALH) were also concerned with how Black History Month observances could be improved. At the annual 1978 convention in Los Angeles, for instance, there was a panel titled "Improving National Afro-American (Black) History Observances," and one year later, the ASALH Executive Director's ten recommendations for the new decade included the continuation and expansion of Black History Month.[51]

THE CULTURE WARS OF THE 1980S AND 1990S

In the 1980s, criticisms of relegating the celebration of black history to the shortest month of the year continued. As one writer for *The Atlanta Constitution* reflected at the end of February 1981:

> This weekend, February will segue into March, and the protest known as Black History Month will be over. The speeches and special programs—many attended by interracial crowds—will be put aside for another year, and the names of African Americans who contributed to the development of this country will return to their traditional non-existent status.[52]

Several years later, a *Los Angeles Sentinel* columnist echoed these sentiments and invoked the "black history is US history" mantra: "Our history is more than a month. Our history is American history itself, actually world history."[53] In the early 1980s, founder and director of the DuSable Museum of African American History in Chicago, Margaret Burroughs, wanted to alter Black History Month in one of the most puzzling manners ever suggested. In order to make Black History Month "more attractive to white Americans" and to inspire young whites to oppose racism, Burroughs proposed to "design Black History Month programs to bring into focus the white heroes, as well as the black." In Burroughs's mind, young whites needed "to know that all white people did not accept slavery, did not accept Jim Crow and even went so far as to resist racism against heavy odds—even in the South."[54]

The issue of acknowledging "white heroes" that Burroughs raised was revisited in later years. In the late 1990s, members of Fellowship Baptist Mission in

---

50 Ralph L. Crowder, "Historical Significance of Black History Month," *The Western Journal of Black Studies* 1, December 1977, 302–304.

51 "New Focus Projected for ASALH for 1980," *Negro History Bulletin* 42, October 1979, 111.

52 Roger Witherspoon, "Black History Month—Another Protest Made Necessary by Racism," *The Atlanta Constitution*, February 26, 1981, 9B.

53 Nelson L. Atkins, "A Legal Look: Black History Is More Than a Month," *The Los Angeles Sentinel*, February 17, 1983, B9.

54 Vernon Jarrett, "Blacks' White Heroes: Black History Month," *The Chicago Tribune*, February 21, 1982, A5.

Silver Spring, Maryland "took an unusual approach to Black History Month" by "honoring what it called 'white heroes' in the African American struggle for freedom."[55]

On the eve of the 30th anniversary of *Brown v. Board of Education*, law professor and critical race theorist Derrick Bell was concerned that the celebration of the 1954 landmark Supreme Court decision could be a part of what he called "the Black History Month Syndrome,"

> a brief period in which black America can parade its best, dust off its heroes, try to encourage its youth, and pretend that the annual ritual alone can make a lasting imprint on racist practices and beliefs that are reinforced throughout the year.[56]

While Bell saw some value in Black History Month programs for black and white children alike, he was worried that the anniversary celebration for *Brown v. Board of Education* would be converted "into the equivalent of an annual holiday with no more implication for the equal educational opportunity it promised than the celebrations dutifully carried out each year for Black History Month."[57]

Perhaps the most belligerent and contentious broadside against Black History Month during the 1980s—and possibly ever, for that matter—was organized by the Castillo Cultural Center, christened by one scholar as New York's most "radical" and "controversial" art and theater guild. In February 1986, Castillo activist and writer William Pleasant created the "Anti Black History Show." While some of the group's movers and shakers disagreed with Pleasant's idea, he stood firm in his harsh and unambiguous criticism of Black History Month, in his mind "an offensive celebration" that only offered reflections on the black past "one month when we need the whole year." Introduced with the bold manifesto, "Black History Month is Dead, LONG LIVE BLACK LIBERATION DAY EVERY DAY!," the art exhibition included untitled pieces by different artists that were "all related to black history." The Castillo Artists' Committee described their project as a direct protest against George Bush's Black History Month proclamation and, more specifically, "the corporate appropriation of Black History Month as either a celebration of petit bourgeois Black assimilationism or reaffirmation of the most deadly of all illusions, American pluralism." The Castillo activists prodded black people to avoid viewing black history as "an amalgam of relics" or a "romanticization of bygone triumphs and defeats." Instead, they endorsed what longtime *Ebony* historian Lerone Bennett Jr. and later public intellectual Manning Marable

---

55 Bill Broadway, "Room for White Heroes in Black History Month," *Washington Post*, February 22, 1997, C7.

56 Derrick Bell, "*Brown v. Board of Education* and the Black History Month Syndrome," *Education Week*, February 22, 1984.

57 Ibid.

called "living black history." Like many before them, the Castillo radicals insisted that US history "is black history." Foreshadowing Black Lives Matter's "Black Futures Month" observance three decades later, they maintained that art served "as a necessary tool in the progressive political movement."[58] Though the Castillo exhibition did not extend beyond New York City, it is not a stretch to conjecture that others shared the activists' views.

At the end of the 1980s, *USA Today* columnist DeWayne Wickham echoed earlier journalists, repeating that contemporary Black History Month celebrations strayed far from Woodson's heuristic approach. "I say let's end the insulting nonsense of 'Black History Month' and take a revolutionary step," Wickham shouted from the rooftops.

> Starting next month, let's insist that the history of African-Americans be required learning in schools, whenever classes are in session. The time has come to give people in this country what Woodson really wanted—the uncensored version of American history, year around.[59]

At the dawning of the next decade remembered in part for the expansion of and debates surrounding multiculturalism, Morgan State University in Baltimore, Maryland, tangibly expanded Black History Month, something that African American activists had been pushing for since the formative years of Negro History Week. Believing that the "history and culture of African-Americans should be treated with reverence and respect every day of the year," Morgan State initiated during the 1989–1990 academic year "a year-long celebration of African-American history and culture to be marked by monthly convocations." Representatives from the university viewed their program as being a "trailblazing initiative" that Woodson "would be proud of."[60] As part of this measure, the university also began requiring that all Morgan State students take a course in "African Diaspora History" before graduating.

Coinciding with the volatile culture war debates concerning the teaching of US history in public schools, during the 1990s, major black newspapers continued to feature articles and columns on Black History Month, and popular national newspapers, especially the *Washington Post*, provided a more mainstream forum for discussing the observance. Commentators tended to echo many of the previously articulated concerns, yet also raised new issues and criticisms. Two broad factions prevailed: Black History Month boosters or apologists and, as Marguerite Cartwright designated them decades earlier,

58   Eva Brenner, "Theatre of the Unorganized: The Radical Independence of the Castillo Cultural Center," *The Drama Review* 36, Autumn 1992, 39–40.

59   DeWayne Wickham, "This One-Month Focus Insults Black History," *USA Today*, February 1, 1989, 8A.

60   "Documents," *The Journal of Negro History* 84, Winter 1999, 94.

"detractors." Even so, these camps were heterogeneous and communicated nuanced interpretations.

With titles such as "Black History Month: 14 Years Later, Do We Really Need It?," "Black History Must Go Beyond February," and "When Will We No Longer Need a Black History Month?," think pieces published during the decade continued to debate Black History Month's usefulness and relevancy. In a lengthy essay in the *Los Angeles Sentinel*, Katherine Bankole conjured up Woodson, labeled Black History Month "an African American cultural tradition," enjoined African Americans to "control the dissemination of comprehensive historical and cultural information," and, like many before her, dreamed of a "curriculum of inclusion."[61]

Not all African Americans shared Bankole's belief that Black History Month was "an African American cultural tradition." For an African American school principal whose sentiments were featured in *Newsweek*, nothing could have been further from the truth. Apparently oblivious to decades of debate, this administrator viewed the observance as embodying "a thriving monument to tokenism which, ironically, has been wholeheartedly embraced and endorsed by the black community." Part of his argument was formulaic—that Black History Month trivialized the black experience and that US and African American history "are not mutually exclusive." Yet, he did suggest that instead of honoring the conventional icons of the black past, young African Americans pay tribute to the elders in their families and communities.[62]

BLACK HISTORY MONTH AND WASHINGTON, DC'S LARGEST NEWSPAPER

As stated earlier, the *Washington Post* devoted a great deal of coverage to Black History Month, and earlier to Negro History Week, and its approach was arguably more nuanced than any other white mainstream newspaper.

In late January 1926, the widely circulated *Post* announced the debut Negro History Week activities that would take place between February 7 and February 14. The editorial fully supported Woodson's endeavor and even directly quoted from his Negro History Week pamphlet, bringing to the fore one of his most famous adages: "If a race has not history, if it has no worthwhile tradition, it becomes a negligible factor in the thought of the world, and it stands in danger of being exterminated."[63] Two decades later, an unidentified writer for the *Post* promoted the observance and the basics of the early black history movement, writing: "There is something anomalous about the designation of Negro History Week in the United States. For the history of

---

61   Katherine Bankole, "When Will We No Longer Need a Black History Month?" *The Los Angeles Sentinel*, February 25, 1993, B7.

62   Wayne M. Joseph, "Why I Dread Black History Month," *Newsweek*, February 14, 1994, 11.

63   "Negro History Week Observed Next Month: Association Chooses February 7 to 14 for General Celebration Here," *Washington Post*, January 24, 1926, M18.

American Negroes is the history of the American people." The columnist continued:

> It is useful, however, to accord special recognition to the part they have played in the growth of this Nation—if only as an irrefutable answer to those who would deny them their just share in the heritage and the opportunities which they have helped to create . . . Full opportunity must be open to Negroes not only because of their services to American society, but because of the values which they can bring to it.[64]

Three decades later, after Negro History Week had been transformed into Black History Month, the *Post* was optimistic that "special 'black history' periods— whether a day, a week, or a month" would become less needed in the future. They advocated an integrated version of US history: "For what is important to remember is that African-American history had no business being separated from American history in the first place."[65]

Between 1977 and the end of the twentieth century, the *Washington Post* (like leading black newspapers such as the *New York Amsterdam News*, the *Chicago Defender*, the *Michigan Chronicle*, the *Los Angles Sentinel*, and the *Pittsburgh Courier*) published approximately one hundred articles, editorials, and/or columns that focused on Black History Month, often in nonconventional ways.

During the 1990s, the *Post* published more than a few intriguing editorials on Black History Month. In its pages, several schoolteachers lamented how Black History Month increasingly failed to have an impact on their students.[66] Staff writer and later the first black woman host for NPR Michele Norris examined how the observance had evolved from an educational reform movement into "a major corporate vehicle to reach black consumers while promoting cultural awareness" that "cause some debates in the black community." In another *Post* op-ed in 1996, journalist and poet Jonetta Rose Barras bluntly spoke out against the phenomenon that Michele Norris explored. In response to her local CVS Pharmacy's stereotypical Black History Month marketing scheme (for example, special sales for Luster Silk Right on Curl Moisturizer, Soft Sheen, Afro Pride No-Lye Relaxer), Barras called upon blacks to "boycott Black History Month and demand full representation throughout the year."[67]

---

64   "Negro History," *Washington Post*, February 15, 1946, 6.

65   "Black History Month," *Washington Post*, February 19, 1977, A12.

66   Marc Elrich, "The Stereotype Within: Why My Students Don't Buy Black History Month," *Washington Post*, February 13, 1994, C1; Patrick Welsh, "A Failing Grade on Race: Tense and Divided, My Students Are Rethinking the Whole Idea of Black History Month," *Washington Post*, March 3, 1996, C1.

67   Michele Norris, "Putting Black History Month on the Market," *Washington Post*, February 21, 1993, B1; Jonetta Rose Barras, "Black History Month Gone Wrong," *Washington Post*, February 28, 1996, A19; Todd Beamon, "A Black History Month Obligation or Celebration?: African Americans Question Whether Observance Has Become Just Another Uninspired Routine," *Washington Post*, February 20, 1997, D3.

The trend that Norris, Barras, and others identified was not, as they intimated, unique to the 1990s. Major corporations began strategic Black History Month marketing schemes and advertising campaigns as early as the inaugural observance. For example, in 1976, the Association for the Study of Afro-American Life and History worked to advertise the celebration with "a number of department stores" throughout the country and in 1978, Coca-Cola began its exploitation of Black History Month by producing 18″ x 24″ commemorative prints of black icons that could be purchased with "6 (six) crown liners from bottles of Coca-Cola along with 75 cents (for postage and handling) for each black leadership print." Advertisements such as these created by many different companies appeared in the pages of *Ebony, Jet, Essence,* and leading black newspapers. The *Atlanta Daily World* even published a flattering essay on Coca-Cola's so-called contribution to Black History Month.[68]

The marketing of the celebration expanded during the 1980s. Among others, Revlon, Coca-Cola, Sta-Sof-Fro, and Johnson Products Company created a range of Black History Month contests, sweepstakes, and scholarships. McDonalds even printed and sold hundreds of thousands of "Black History Through Art: A Recorded Account of Life in America," a black history curriculum kit with a filmstrip, cassette lecture, and teacher and student guides. One wonders how popular such materials were.

During the twenty-first century, the commercialization of Black History Month persisted. Black History Month sales, specials, and promotions are now commonplace. In addition to the usual suspects, many other businesses, companies, and organizations joined the fray. T. J. Maxx stores began selling arts and crafts from Kenya, Ghana, Zimbabwe, South Africa, and Swaziland just in time for Black History Month; Hennessy sponsored a traveling "African American Heritage" art exhibit; Coca-Cola, Albertsons, and Sav-On honored black entrepreneurs with in-store promotions and specific products; Nissan targeted the black community with a "Black Experience" marketing campaign; the National Alliance for Tobacco Cessation told blacks that "Black History Month Is Your Time to Quit Smoking"; Nike created its expensive BHM Collection to "honor Nike's kings and queens of the sport"; and Heineken USA launched a marketing scheme that solicited black artists to submit their work to be "showcased on a national platform."

The last major discussion that the *Post* had about Black History Month in the 1990s focused on a controversy: the case of a white school board member in Charles County who, using familiar arguments of old, sought to overturn a resolution for Black History Month because in her estimation it separated people "based upon genetic and chromosomal traits." Members of the black

---

68 "Coca Cola to Commemorate Black History Month with 'Glimpses of the Greats,'" *The Atlanta Daily World,* February 9, 1978, 3.

community organized against this and the *Post* offered at least one Black History Month supporter a platform to debunk this attack on the observance.[69]

SCHOLARS AND HISTORIANS CHIME IN

During the 1990s, black scholars, mainly historians, candidly and forthrightly debated on Black History Month, offering a range of opinions. Renowned historian John Hope Franklin was unwavering in his condemnation of contemporary Black History Month observances. "I very seldom give talks during Black History Month," he noted in 1990. "I refuse to confine discussions of African-American history to one week or one month."[70] The author of the classic *From Slavery to Freedom* later said that he opted to deliver lectures on black history "during the other 11 months." This approach, he recalled in 1998, "has been my one-man crusade to hasten the realization of Woodson's dream." Like others during the 1990s, Franklin was also bothered by the "hucksters," corporations, and self-proclaimed lecturers who exploited Black History Month for their own profits. Echoing Woodson, Franklin was convinced that those who reaped "so much benefit from Black History Month" should at a minimum assist the ASALH.[71] Franklin's juniors, historians Sterling Stuckey and Joe Trotter, were not as critical. Though they saw some flaws in the contemporary practices, they agreed that the celebration helped raise the general American public's interpretation of the black past.

Gerald Early, Earl Ofari Hutchinson, and Gayle Pembleton disagreed with Stuckey and Trotter. While Early contended that Black History Month had become "a spectacle as empty as the spectacle of transubstantiation in a Catholic church"[72] and Pembleton concluded that the observance "verges on the ridiculous,"[73] Hutchinson agreed that Black History Month had not changed most Americans' perceptions of the black past, yet blamed African American historians, educators, and Afrocentric thinkers "during the big push in the 1960s for Black Studies courses" for isolating the study of black history and culture and, thereby, allowing mainstream educational institutions to ignore the black past and limit discussions of black history to February.[74] Hutchinson's

---

69   Louise L. James, "Black History Month: Why Do We Continue?" *The Los Angeles Sentinel*, February 26, 1998, A7.

70   Quoted in Frank James, "Black History Month: 14 Years Later, Do We Really Need It?" *The Chicago Tribune*, February 28, 1990, 1.

71   John Hope Franklin, Gerald Horne, Harold Cruse, Allen R. Ballard, Reavis L. Mitchell Jr., "Black History Month: Serious Truth Telling or a Triumph in Tokenism?" *The Journal of Blacks in Higher Education*, no. 18, Winter 1997–1998, 88.

72   Gerald Early, "The Color Purple as Everybody's Protest Art," *The Antioch Review* 50, Winter-Spring 1992, 405.

73   Gayle Pemberton, "'All Right, then, I'll Go to Hell': The Power and Pitfalls of Literature Across the Curriculum," *Transformations: The Journal of Inclusive Scholarship and Pedagogy* 10, Spring 1999, 4.

74   Earl Ofari Hutchinson, "Time to Eliminate Black History Month," *New Pittsburgh Courier*, March 4, 1994, 5; "Black History Month: Serious Truth Telling or a Triumph in Tokenism?" 89.

solution was the genuine and complete incorporation of African American history. Gerald Horne, on the other hand, believed that Black History Month was necessary but needed some "tinkering" by mainly becoming more "transnational" in orientation. Echoing Hutchinson but in much harsher terms similar to how he lambasted black intellectuals and artists in his 1967 opus *The Crisis of the Negro Intellectual*, Harold Cruse claimed that black historians had failed to expand in meaningful ways on the efforts of Woodson. "The bulk of the new breed of black historians has little to say that is really new, inventive, or revealing," he bemoaned.[75]

Toward the end of the decade, Michael Eric Dyson introduced several creative monikers for February—"The Cruelest Month," the "Big Month" ("for most black petit-bourgeois intellectuals"), "National Negro Rental Month," and the "Colored Folks Festival." More than anything else, Dyson explained to white readers of the *New Yorker* that Black History Month, conceivably "a white conspiracy to keep the festivities as short as possible," was not enough time to adequately treat black life and culture and how black intellectuals were unreasonably in demand as speakers during February.[76] Dyson touched upon a point that resonated with his former and future colleagues.

The lengthy title of an article in the *Wall Street Journal* embodied the plight of black speakers during the shortest month of the year: "It's a Busy Month for Black Artists and Historians—Then a Quiet Year—African-American Scholars Say Invitations Dry Up After Black History Month Ends."[77] Many black intellectuals and authors have complained that they are disproportionately asked to speak during February and that their publications are merely marketed for one month of every year, thus overburdening them with scheduling conflicts and hyper-competition.

HONORING THE BLACK PAST WITH THE FIRST BLACK PRESIDENT

In late January or early February each year, every US president since Gerald Ford—Jimmy Carter, Ronald Reagan, George H. W. Bush, Bill Clinton, George W. Bush, Barack Obama, and Donald Trump (whose first proclamation, that focused on the "role of education in the history of African Americans," was delivered on February 2, 2017)—has delivered his own brief tribute to African American history at a reception in the White House that usually concludes by calling upon "public officials, educators, librarians, and all of the people of the

---

75   John Hope Franklin, Gerald Horne, Harold Cruse, Allen R. Ballard, Reavis L. Mitchell Jr., "Black History Month: Serious Truth Telling or a Triumph in Tokenism?" *The Journal of Blacks in Higher Education*, no. 18, Winter 1997–1998, 90.

76   Michael Eric Dyson, "The Cruelest Month," *New Yorker*, February 17, 1997, 33.

77   Nancy Ann Jeffrey, "'It's a Busy Month for Black Artists and Historians—Then a Quiet Year—African-American Scholars Say Invitations Dry Up After Black History Month Ends," *Wall Street Journal*, Eastern Edition, New York, NY, February 24, 2000, B1.

United States" to be heedful of February with "appropriate ceremonies, activities, and programs that raise awareness of African American history." Many expected that Black History Month tributes by Obama, the first black president, would be distinctly different from those of his white predecessors. In late January 2013, he concluded his remarks with this: "National African American History Month is a time to tell those stories of freedom won and honor the individuals who wrote them."[78] For some, Obama's speech left much to be desired.

Political scientist Frederick C. Harris has dismissed Obama's attitude toward Black History Month as passive and conventional. It is true that the Obama administration's Black History Month websites were unexceptional and run-of-the-mill. However, it is worth probing more deeply into how Obama acknowledged and ushered in the celebration of Black History Month since 2009. After all, it is not unreasonable to presume that Obama's commemorations would at the very least have a more emotional and personal flavor.

US presidents have issued a cornucopia of presidential proclamations for more than two hundred years, dating back to George Washington's 1793 Proclamation of Neutrality. Generally speaking, presidential proclamations range in terms of subject matter, scope, influence, and significance. Simply put, there are huge differences between policy-based proclamations and ceremonial or symbolic ones. Without doubt, the most famous and debatable proclamation related to African American history is Abraham Lincoln's 1863 Emancipation Proclamation—which did not, as many to this day still think, abolish slavery. (The abolition of slavery in the United States was accomplished by the Thirteenth Amendment to the US Constitution.) Passed by Congress on January 31, 1865, and ratified by the states on December 6, 1865, the monumental modification stated: "Neither slavery nor involuntary servitude, except as a punishment for crime whereof the party shall have been duly convicted, shall exist within the United States, or any place subject to their jurisdiction."

Between 2009 and 2016, Obama issued more than one thousand presidential proclamations, the vast majority of which are ceremonial in nature. Some of these statements deal with African American history and culture and include the proclamations for Martin Luther King Jr. Federal Holiday, National African American History Month, African American Music Appreciation Month, and even National Historically Black Colleges and Universities Week.

In his eight Black History Month tributes, Obama consistently mentioned, in passing, the contributions of famous and non-threatening black historical icons, acknowledged the obstacles that black people have endured and overcome, and alluded to how, in the present, black people still face certain lingering barriers to full equality. As a black man representing the nation, he adopted an integrationist approach to African American history by intimately linking the

---

78   Barack Obama, "Proclamation 8930—National African American History Month, 2013," January 31, 2013. Obama's proclamations that I cite in this chapter can be found at www.whitehouse.gov under the "Speeches & Remarks" header under "From the President's Office."

African American experience with the history of the nation. The opening line of his first Black History Month proclamation embodies this philosophy: "The history of African Americans is unique and rich, and one that has helped define what it means to be an American."[79]

When compared with his predecessors' first National African American History Month proclamations, Obama's was noticeably longer. Delivered on February 2, 2009, in his debut proclamation in honor of the black past, he did not shy away from harkening back to the days of slavery, noting that black people were once "recognized more as possessions than people." Unlike his famous 2008 "A More Perfect Union" oration, he highlighted African American agency in helping the United States reach its "full potential as a nation" and in fighting against "boulders of systematic racism and discrimination that pervaded *our* laws and *our* public consciousness for decades."[80]

The usage of *our* was, I would argue, deliberate. Though he mentions the slave trade, slavery, and racial oppression in general, Obama did not directly indict white America for its past mistreatment of African American people. Instead, he invoked "us" and "our" so as not to take sides. This strategy coincides with his universalist approach to addressing domestic racial policy issues. For their contributions to fulfilling "the promise of our Nation," he also strategically gave shout-outs to a very familiar cast of black historical icons from the antebellum era through the conventional civil rights movement. In summoning Frederick Douglass, Harriet Tubman, Booker T. Washington, George Washington Carver, Martin Luther King Jr., and Thurgood Marshall, Obama most likely reasoned that he would satisfy the black status quo while not offending whites.

Imagine if instead he had credited Martin R. Delany, Nat Turner, W. E. B. Du Bois, Ida B. Wells, Malcolm X, and Pauli Murray for contributing to the nation's progress. As an interracial mediator of some sort, he praised African Americans who possessed and exhibited "the same"—as white people, generally speaking—"sense of duty and love of country that lead them to shed blood in every war we have ever fought."

In his 2010 Black History Month proclamation, Obama called upon Americans to pay tribute to African Americans who overcame great obstacles through economic self-empowerment. He acknowledged the oppression that African Americans faced through the passage of the Voting Rights Act (1965), and while he admitted that "structural inequities" still adversely affected black communities, he reached a middle ground of some sort. "Racial prejudice is no longer the steepest barrier to opportunity for African Americans, yet substantial obstacles remain in the remnants of past discrimination."[81] He concluded by calling upon African

---

79   Barack Obama, "Proclamation 8345—National African American History Month, 2009," February 2, 2009.

80   Ibid (emphasis mine).

81   Barack Obama, "Proclamation 8476—National African American Month, 2010," February 1, 2010.

Americans to strive to push on like previous generations did. In this sense, he contributed to the notion that the activists of the civil rights movement are the measuring stick for black activism, and he placed the burden of racial progress on the shoulders of African Americans instead of challenging American society to change. Without fanfare, Obama's 2011 proclamation celebrated black participation in the Civil War, Lincoln's Emancipation Proclamation, and, like his previous commemorations, stressed how blacks had fought against oppression.

"The story of African Americans is a story of resilience and perseverance," was the opening of Obama's 2012 Black History Month proclamation. "It traces a people who refused to accept the circumstances under which they arrived on the shores, and it chronicles the generations who fought for an America that truly reflects the ideals enshrined in *our* founding documents." Notwithstanding that fact the nation's founding documents bolstered slavery and the oppression of black people, this is arguably one of the stronger openings of Obama's Black History Month proclamations. The next year, his tone was optimistic. Evoking the ever so familiar spirit of the "American Dream"—no matter what, "you can make it if you try"—and using Lincoln ("a great emancipator" who supposedly "called for the end of slavery") and Martin Luther King Jr. as points of departure, Obama declared that "we live in a moment when the dream of equal opportunity is within reach for people of every color and creed."[82]

Obama emphasized that the struggle for African American equality and upward mobility was a "shared" legacy, as symbolized by Lincoln, a representative of implied progressive racial politics for white America, and King, a powerful symbol for black America as well as a palatable black representative for white Americans. In 2014, he echoed this "shared" history motif, emphasizing that "the story of hard-won progress" is not only a defining feature of African American history, but "lies at the heart of our Nation as a whole."[83] Though he gingerly alluded to lynching and slavery, he underscored that much has been "gained through centuries of trial and suffering" and that true progress can be best achieved by coming together and uniting around the cause of social change. In 2015, Obama continued to celebrate this theme of togetherness while honoring the sacrifices made by the civil rights generation, an age group that he routinely revered to the point of hagiography. As he did in his earliest proclamation, he confessed that progress still lies ahead, but he did not center race relations or black uplift. He adopted his routine strategy of race neutrality and pinpointed historically rooted problems—such as poverty, substandard educational opportunities, and violence—that disproportionately and adversely impact African American communities, but can also be read to apply to many different groups of Americans.

---

82 Barack Obama, "Proclamation 8930—National African American History Month, 2013," January 21, 2013.

83 Barack Obama, "Proclamation 9080—National African American History Month, 2014," January 31, 2014.

On January 29, 2016, Obama delivered his last National African American History Month proclamation. When he began his second presidential term, many of his critics in the African American community understandably thought that he should abandon, or at a minimum adjust, his calculated stance toward racial issues. Though rhetoric by itself might not directly shape public policy, in his 2016 proclamation, Obama did proclaim: "For too long, our most basic liberties have been denied to African Americans." As usual, however, he did not assign accountability or blame to members of the white community. He avoided specifying who denied African Americans their basic human and civil rights. Instead, he disclosed how the US government oppressed black people. Identifying slavery as being "our Nation's original sin" and "antithetical to our country's conception of human rights and dignity" (something that he did in several of his earliest speeches), he celebrated those African Americans who struggled to transform American society.[84]

More than in his previous Black History Month proclamations, in his last ceremonial tribute to black history, Obama did draw more explicit parallels between the past and the present.

"We would do a disservice to all who came before us if we remained blind to the way injustices shape the present," Obama affirmed.[85] He did not, however, list with any precision those specific historically rooted inequities that continue to adversely impact African Americans, especially the most vulnerable members of the collective black community. Instead, he connected young activists to the heroes and heroines of the conventional civil rights movement who made public the glaring "disparities" in US society through strategies of nonviolent direct action. He did not point out that many young African American activists today (fists clenched in the air, often adorned in "all black everything" or political or Afrocentric t-shirts and cognizant of the messages of Malcolm X and the Black Panther Party) actively sample from Black Power era activists.

He could have identified the youthful movement by name (the Black Lives Matter movement), but he most likely purposefully avoided doing so. During Obama's second term, perhaps the most pressing problem facing black communities across the nation, beyond the everlasting dilemma of poverty, was the criminalization of black people as expressed in police brutality. This was not given notice in his proclamation.

Like other presidents before him, Obama hosted Black History Month receptions, activities, and events at the White House during February. During these festivities (some of which can be viewed on YouTube, C-Span, or the White House Black History Month website), Obama offers extended comments on African American history that stretch beyond his concise and often superficial proclamations.

---

84 Barack Obama, "Proclamation 9392—National African American History Month, 2016," January 29, 2016.

85 Ibid.

For instance, Obama's final major White House Black History Month gathering (held on February 18, 2016) was memorable; it marked the 40th anniversary of this celebration. "I would not be here if it were not for the battles they fought," Obama remarked at a meeting with civil rights leaders, past and present. "They," for Obama, specifically referred to civil rights activists Congressman John Lewis and Minister C. T. Vivian and collectively included those African American activists primarily from the civil rights generation.

At the larger reception in the White House East Room, Obama handed down a more extended discussion of the meaning of black history to him. His opening remarks caught the attention of social media, especially those catering to the black community. "We know it's Black History Month when you hear somebody say, 'Hey, Michelle! Girl, you look so good,'" Obama signified. H. Samy Alim and Geneva Smitherman would most likely point out how "the first Black Language–speaking president" adjusted to his predominantly black audience by "style-shifting."[86] What followed were comments that were clearly crafted for his predominantly black audience.

"Now, we gather to celebrate Black History Month, and from our earliest days, black history has been American history," Obama began his presentation. Co-signing on the sentiments of generations of Black History Month faultfinders, he insisted that black history should not be detached from "our collective American history" (another term for normative US history that prioritizes white America) or "just boiled down to a compilation of greatest hits" or a "commemoration of past events." On the other hand, he invited his audience to recognize that black history was made by legendary and unsung foot soldiers alike who profoundly shaped the course of American history and culture. In this oration, Black History Month for Obama was "about taking an unvarnished look at the past so we can create a better future. It's a reminder of where we as a country have been so that we know where we need to go."[87]

Early in this speech, he also evoked "we," not in reference to Americans in general, but specifically as a way to connect with the African Americans in the room, from young black activists to members of the Congressional Black Caucus. Obama trumpeted:

We're the slaves who quarried the stone to build this White House; the soldiers who fought for our nation's independence, who fought to hold this union together, who fought for freedom of others around the world. We're the scientists and inventors who helped unleash American innovation. We stand on the shoulders not only of

---

86   H. Samy Alim and Geneva Smitherman, *Articulate While Black: Barack Obama, Language, and Race in the U.S.*, New York: Oxford University Press, 2012, 2, 5–25.

87   Barack Obama, "Remarks by the President at Black History Month Reception," Washington, DC, February 18, 2016.

the giants in this room, but also countless, nameless heroes who marched for equality and justice for all of us.[88]

Interestingly, Obama gave props to young people. He extolled members of the millennial hip-hop generation for not, in his estimation, viewing "black history as a relic." He praised them for "making history" and gave "a special shout-out" to young African Americans who were "mobilizing people of all backgrounds." Again, he did not directly put a name on this campaign (the Black Lives Matter movement), but, nonetheless, he validated their message.

"TO CHANGE THE COURSE OF HISTORY BY SHAPING OUR FUTURE"

In honoring African American millennials as "history makers" during Black History Month, it seems that Obama would be sympathetic to "Black Future(s) Month." During the last several years, the notion of "Black Future(s) Month" has been promulgated by different groups of younger African American activists. Linking Black History Month to the future is not a twenty-first century phenomenon. In the early 1990s, one African American historian argued that while Black History Month observances were useful in helping blacks remember and learn from the past, "it is also important to use that history to chart new ways into the future."[89]

The exact phrase "Black Future Month" was evoked as early as 2003 by reporter and freelance writer Evan Narcisse in *Savoy* magazine. "Howzabout we rechristen February Black Future Month and devote it to issues that have slipped off our socio-cultural radar?" He insisted, "It's time to can the recaps and plot our advancement."[90] In 2011, one blogger suggested that "Black Future Month" should exist in the form of highlighting people from the African diaspora who "will make history." Chinaka Hodge added that the celebration should make "associations between the Black Future and the Black Past."[91] Several years later, Afrofuturists in Toronto, Canada, created the website blackfuturemonth.com and began hosting "Black Future Month," an annual black art exhibition that features art by OCAD University students and "renowned" professional artists. "The overarching theme of the annual Black Future Month (BFM) exhibition is the far-off distant future envisioned by Black people. The quantum leap into the future," the founders noted, "is meant to provide a platform that enables Black people to break from the historic ties of oppression still prominent today."[92]

88 Ibid.

89 "Black History Month Misconstrued by Many African-Americans, Says Prof.," *New York Amsterdam News*, February 29, 1992, 8.

90 Evan Narcisse, "Why I Hate Black History Month," *Savoy* 3: 1, February 2003, 64.

91 Chinaka Hodge, "Black Future Month // 2-1-11 // DoD.A.T.," chinakahodge.com, February 1, 2011.

92 "Black Future Month: The Afrofuturism Art Exhibition," blackfuturemonth.com.

The concept of a "Black Future Month" was popularized by those active in the Black Lives Matter (BLM) movement. On February 1, 2015, BLM co-founder Opal Tometi voiced her support of Woodson and Black History Month but maintained that simply commemorating the past was insufficient in times when anti-black violence is common. Tometi asserted:

> This year we find ourselves in the context of incredible and undeniable Black resistance and resilience—and so there can be no Black History Month as usual. We must seize the opportunity to change the course of history by shaping our future.[93]

"Black Future Month" 2015 was celebrated by BLM in the form of provocative blog posts "tackling 28 different cultural and political issues affecting Black lives" that were featured on *Huffington Post Black Voices*.

In a brief statement on their website on February 1, 2016, BLM launched the second annual "Black Future Month," changing the observance's name to "Black Futures Month" in order to acknowledge the multiplicity of blacks' potential destinies and prospects. Journalist and BLM lead communications strategist Shanelle Matthews characterized the days of reflection and jubilee as "a deliberate reinterpretation of the resistance and resilience of Black people as illustrated through art." The Arts and Culture Director for BLM stipulated that "Black Futures Month" employs art as a porthole into black America's unmapped future. Tometi added, "Black Futures Month is the visual representation for our lived experience." On each day in February 2016, BLM refashioned the month-long celebration by releasing "an original piece of art and an accompanying written piece to reclaim Black History Month."[94]

In an age of addictive social media that has given rise to a visible "black digital intelligentsia," BLM tactically employed the hashtag #blackfuturesmonth to publicize their efforts. Similar to "Black Liberation Week" from the Black Power era, each day of "Black Futures Month" 2016 had a specific theme, such as Afro-Futurism, climate and reproductive justice, children, youth, and elders, voting, immigration, mass incarceration, love, disability, LGBTQ issues, domestic violence, farming, faith, the body, labor, leadership, economics, and the black college student experience.

Though BLM has not outlined the long-term goals of this observance in great detail and it has yet to gain a large-scale following, "Black Futures Month" will most likely continue to evolve and clearly seeks to encourage Gen Xers and millennials, in particular, to think about how they can change and envision the future. It may not ever replace Black History Month, but it has the capability of growing into a new African American cultural ritual that the

---

93   Opal Tometi, "Black Future Month: Examining The Current State Of Black Lives And Envisioning Where We Go From Here," Huffington Post, February 1, 2015.

94   Shanelle Matthews, "Black Lives Matter Reinterprets February, Observes Second Annual Black Futures Month," Black Lives Matter Facebook group, February 1, 2016.

younger generations of black social activists can profoundly shape and learn from.

A significant amount of scholarship has been published on African American commemorations, holidays, and annual celebrations, from emancipation celebrations to Kwanzaa to Martin Luther King Jr. Day Federal Holiday and beyond. Historian Keith A. Mayes has convincingly argued that there exists "something called a black holiday tradition."[95] The history of Negro History Week has been unpacked by generations of historians since Woodson died in 1950. Though scholars, public intellectuals, and journalists have critically reflected upon and disputed the meaning and purpose of Negro History Week's legacy (later known as Black History Month, Afro-American History Month, and African American History Month), very few scholars have exhaustively addressed the ramifications of this observance. A comprehensive history of African American History Month still remains to be written. This is somewhat perplexing given the wealth of available sources, a sampling of which I have analyzed in this chapter. The most in-depth studies on Black History Month were published recently—two scholarly articles that offer particularly thought-provoking and creative explorations.

Education scholars have, unsurprisingly, discussed the strengths and weaknesses of incorporating Black History Month into their curriculums. Few, however, have been theoretical or, for that matter, meticulous.

LaGarrett J. King and Keffrelyn Brown have recently and efficaciously addressed this paucity of scholarship on "Black History Month teaching." According to these educational theorists, in K-12 schools, Black History Month activities have strayed far from Woodson's vision and have been plagued by inept "circular approaches." Employing what they call a tripartite "Woodsonian conceptual framework" and "Black History pedagogy," they argue that, despite the prevailing shortcomings of Black History Month to significantly reform the "standard" ways of teaching US history, the observance can furnish K-12 teachers unique opportunities to effectively introduce "an inclusive curriculum" by teaching students about the black past. In their study, King and Brown analyzed the strategies of three innovative and passionate middle school teachers who deliberately used Black History Month as a time to "interrupt the official curriculum" and to develop "pedagogy that aligned" with that of Woodson. Though a few of their lesson plans were problematic, in the end, these researchers found that the three teachers "explored Black history during February in critical and nuanced ways" by challenging the persistent normative US historical narratives,

---

95   Keith A. Mayes, *Kwanzaa: Black Power and the Making of the African-American Holiday Tradition*, New York: Routledge, 2009.

making the black past relevant to their students' daily lives, and adopting an ambitious "global approach."[96]

It is clear from this important study that prepared teachers can create impactful "Black History Month teaching." King and Brown's suggestion that K-12 schools should organize learning communities to help facilitate Black History Month educational programs is excellent. Equally important, their interview questions, methods, and data analysis could serve as blueprints for future studies of this nature that are much needed to help counter the mundane, status quo Black History Month schemes in K-12 schools throughout the nation.

In 2016, historian Kenan Van De Mieroop offered one of the most extensive discussions about the implications of Black History Month. Using Nietzsche's beliefs about the function of history as an analytical framework, Van De Mieroop questions the purpose of Black History Month in the twenty-first century, the so-called postracial era of American history. In his mind, Black History Month is "widely embraced" in the United States yet does little to address the "persistent problems of racism in America." In making this argument, he is suggesting that Black History Month's proponents view the annual ritual as being a remedy for racism in the United States, that "historical education can provide an antidote to current racial problems."[97]

The application of Nietzsche's and other European thinkers' theories of history will be best understood by those unfamiliar with African American history who feel comfortable applying Eurocentric road maps for understanding the significance of memory and commemoration to African American culture. Though timely and provocative, Van De Mieroop's assessment of Black History Month has its limitations. To begin with, he generalizes the "Black History Month" debate by identifying only two groups—"opponents" who believe that it is no longer necessary, that African American history, as Garlington argued more than sixty years ago, should be integrated into standard US historical narratives; and "proponents" who still steadfastly support this annual tradition. According to this scholar, contemporary mainstream Black History Month has "played a major role in constructing the post-racial era, and hence has ironically established the very conditions for its own irrelevance."[98]

While I agree that a "critical Black History Month" would be much better than "integrated monumental history" and that making connections between the past and the present is paramount, the major problems with this analysis are (a) that it relies on non-African Americanists' notions of history and (b) that it pigeonholes Black History Month celebrations by focusing on mainstream, commercial commemorations, presidential proclamations, and the opinions of

96   LaGarrett J. King and Keffrelyn Brown, "Once a Year to Be Black: Fighting Against Typical Black History Month Pedagogies," *The Negro Educational Review* 65, 2014, 24, 25, 27, 31.

97   Kenan Van De Mieroop, "On the Advantage and Disadvantage of Black History Month for Life: The Creation of the Post-Racial Era," *History and Theory* 55, February 2016, 3, 4, 5.

98   Ibid., 7.

a small group of social commentators, spokespersons, and politicians. Moreover, Van De Mieroop assumes that the proponents of Black History Month believe that the celebration's main objective is the elimination of racism through "historical education." This belief is a common oversimplification. Absent from this appraisal is the meaning of Black History Month within the context of Mayes's "black holiday tradition," the history of the Association for the Study of African American Life and History, and, more specifically, the deeper history of what is now officially called National African American History Month.

Negro History Week and the monthlong celebration that followed was and has been very important for the ASNLH and the ASALH. As Carter G. Woodson noted several years before his death, "the Negro History Week celebration has done more than any other effort to popularize the work of the Association since its organization."[99]

The purpose of Negro History Week that laid the foundations for the monthlong commemoration was never simply to stamp out racism. Woodson and his co-workers were not that naïve and short-sighted. When he created Negro History Week nearly one century ago, Woodson believed that it had the potential to help change not only how white people viewed and perhaps treated black people, but also the capacity to transform how black people thought about themselves through a historical lens. "The celebration of Negro History Week is no occasion for glossing over the tribulations and trials which Negroes have suffered because of man's inhumanity to man," Woodson wrote six months before his death, "but the desired end is more easily reached by showing the achievements of the Negro in spite of these handicaps."[100]

In justifying Negro History Week in 1926, Woodson argued that most African Americans knew "practically nothing" about their history and were, therefore, "a childlike race." Because the normative US history of his times did not acknowledge African Americans (and when the vast majority of white historians did mention black people, they usually deemed them inferior), Woodson believed that racism was bolstered by the suppression of black history:

A Negro is passed on the street and is shoved off into the mud; he complains or strikes back and is lynched as a desperado who attacked a gentleman.

And what if he is handicapped, segregated, or lynched? According to our educa-tion and practice, if you kill one of the group, the world goes on just as well or better; for the Negro is nothing, has never been anything, and never will be anything but a menace to civilization.

We call this race prejudice, and it may be thus properly named; but it is not something inherent in human nature. It is merely the logical result of tradition, the inevitable outcome of thorough instruction to the effect that the Negro has never

---

99   Carter G. Woodson, "The Annual Report of the Director," *The Journal of Negro History* 33, October 1948, 393.
100   Carter G. Woodson, "Annual Report," *The Journal of Negro History* 34, October 1949, 387.

contributed anything to the progress of mankind . . . In such a millennium the achievements of the Negro properly set forth will crown him as a factor in early human progress and a maker of modern civilization.[101]

Woodson viewed Negro History Week as a means to teach African Americans about their history and, equally important, to help change the ways in which they were viewed by whites.

Negro History Week changed during Woodson's times, between his death and the inauguration of Black History Month and since it became a monthlong celebration in 1976. And certainly anti-black racism still persists in the United States and is influenced by how black people have been and are dehumanized and stereotyped. The denial of blacks' historical achievements, contributions, and resistance is part of this anti-black belief system.

In the twenty-first century, however, it is fanciful to conjecture, as Woodson did during his time, that black historical knowledge will stamp out or cure anti-black thought and actions, especially in the realm of a reality like black mass incarceration.

WHAT LIES AHEAD?

The fate of Black History Month is unknown. Will it fade away because its leading campaigners will no longer believe that it is necessary? Will traditionalist educational administrators remove it from their schools' annual activities? Will conservative politicians at local and national levels deem it no longer relevant and even detrimental to national unity? Will Black History Month be replaced by "Black Futures Month"? Will it become a pastime within segments of the black community?

The response to all of these hypothetical questions is probably *no*. I find it hard to fathom that Black History Month will cease to be celebrated in American society (especially in African American communities and institutions) any time in the foreseeable future. It is "an African American cultural tradition" that predates Kwanzaa, Martin Luther King Jr. Day, and modern expressions of Juneteenth. The Association for the Study of African American Life and History (ASALH) has faith in, invests great time and resources in, and in some regard banks on annual Black History Month celebrations. They will not allow their founder's "most characteristic creation" to pass into oblivion. As ASALH National President Evelyn Brooks Higginbotham asserted in 2016, the Association "*always* takes special pride at the opening of the month of February."[102]

In future Februarys, the traditional press and social media will continue to bombard its readers with Black History Month suggestions, events, announcements,

---

101   Carter G. Woodson, "Negro History Week," *The Journal of Negro History* 11, April 1926, 240.
102   asalh100.org (accessed on June 15, 2016), emphasis added.

films, sales and promotions, TV and cable specials, quotables, quizzes, and salutes. In future Januarys and Februarys, Black History Month will spark various debates that, chances are, will harken back to those articulated during earlier periods that have been discussed in this chapter. As the scores of social commentators and scholars whose ideas I have unpacked demonstrate, there are countless and perpetual suggestions about how to reform and maximize the effectiveness of Black History Month.

As LaGarrett J. King and Keffrelyn Brown unambiguously argued, and as movers and shakers in the ASALH will in all likelihood forever trust, Woodson's vision should continue to inform our interpretations of Black History Month's role and relevance. Similarly, based upon its unwavering popularity, there is a sense of timelessness to Woodson's *The Mis-Education of the Negro*, even though it was published more than eighty years ago. Nonetheless, today, for obvious reasons, it would be unimaginative, shortsighted, and impractical to simply recycle Woodson's strategies for popularizing and teaching black history. Unlike during Woodson's times or even the first several decades that Black History Month was officially sanctioned, in large part thanks to the Internet and the digital revolution, we now have trouble-free access to an unprecedented wealth of innovative scholarship, primary documents, informative documentaries, and proven pedagogical devices pertaining to African American history and culture.

A major challenge in this age revolves around how K-12 educators decide to handle Black History Month and approach the study of African American life during the entire school year. The popular instructional disposition criticized by King and Brown should be replaced by effective and innovative "Black History pedagogy." Critics should be encouraged to chastise the commercialization and mainstreaming of this annual observance. But in a capitalist, consumer-driven society, these tendencies will prevail. At a minimum, scholars—namely African Americanists and historians—should play a leading role in working with K-12 educators and emboldening black communities and the broader American public to be conscious of and appreciate that, *yes*, African American history deserves to be interwoven into the multilayered fabrics of US history on a regular basis, not simply conjured up during February. Black History Month supporters and netroots can learn something valuable from the "Black Futures Month" campaign. During annual Black History Month commemorations, the intimate connections between the past, present, and future ought to be reckoned and vigorously interrogated.

3

Dramatizing the Black Past

Twenty-first Century Hollywood Portrayals of Black History

"A nation reveals itself not only by the people it produces, but by those it remembers," observed President Obama on Memorial Day in 2016 at Arlington Cemetery in Arlington, Virginia.[1] Founded in the immediate post–Civil War era under the name Decoration Day, this annual observance became an official national holiday in 1971 and pays tribute to those who died while serving in the United States Armed Forces. Though largely unacknowledged by US presidents and politicians, the US military, and the American public in general, African Americans have an intriguing relationship to this holiday that for many Americans today symbolizes the kickoff of summer vacation. According to slavery and Civil War historian David W. Blight, "the earliest and most remarkable Memorial Day" was celebrated by newly freed African Americans in Charleston, South Carolina, in 1865, when they honored deceased Union soldiers with proper burials, cookouts, orations, and a procession.[2] In a widely cited blog, Reconstruction historian Jim Downs added that African Americans created Memorial Day not only to pay respect to fallen Union combatants, but also to memorialize "members of their families and their community who died in a war that was meant to free them."[3]

The programs, services, and rituals of the 2016 Memorial Day that Obama ushered in were similar to previous ceremonies. For black America (the majority of whom were probably unaware of Blight's and Downs's revelations), the 2016 Memorial Day may have been subtly different than preceding commemorations.

On May 30, 2016, *Roots*, a remake of the classic 1977 miniseries that was based upon Alex Haley's *New York Times* best-selling historical novel *Roots: The Saga of an American Family* (1976), premiered on the History Channel, A & E, and Lifetime. By most accounts, the eight-hour long miniseries was a great success, attracting a huge audience even though it competed with a much anticipated Game 7 of the NBA Western Conference Finals between the Golden State Warriors and the Oklahoma City Thunder. Historians and scholars actively blogged about the *Roots* reboot, for the most part applauding its dramatization of crucial periods and possibilities in the black experience. Seasoned film

---

1   Barack Obama, "Remarks by the President on Memorial Day," Arlington Cemetery, Arlington, Virginia, May 30, 2016.
2   David W. Blight, "Forgetting Why We Remember," *New York Times*, May 29, 2011, A19.
3   Jim Downs, "Who Invented Memorial Day," *Huffington Post*, July 25, 2012.

studies scholar Stephane Dunn was not alone in conluding in an essay in *The Atlantic* that "*Roots* stands on sacred ground as the most in-depth, widely thought-provoking, and accomplished dramatic work of its kind."[4]

The minimal criticism of the remake of *Roots* from those with the expertise to do so has much to do with its executive producer Mark Wolper (the son of prolific television and film producer David J. Wolper, producer of the original *Roots* miniseries in 1977), who consulted with numerous experts in African and African American history and culture. Wolper was undoubtedly determined to make *Roots* as historically accurate as possible, exemplified by the era-specific costumes, make-up, and props; the diverse characters' dialects and mannerisms; the elaborate set constructions and picturesque filming locations; and the replica slave ship that was built from scratch. Nevertheless, the twenty-first-century version of *Roots* is not entirely unique.

During the "Age of Obama," a collection of Hollywood films has revisited the black past, several of which—namely *Django Unchained*, *The North Star*, *Lincoln*, *12 Years a Slave*, and *The Birth of a Nation*—use some creative license in depicting and updating how we can interpret slavery. In addition to *Roots*, the first ten episodes of the WGN America series *Underground* ran from March until May 2016. Chronicling the Underground Railroad in Georgia during the late 1850s, this series experiments by using music from artists like Kanye West to tell a story about what executive producer Misha Green calls "the revolution." Perhaps director Steve McQueen's assertion that Obama's presidency influenced a black film-centered movement in American film culture has something to it.[5] Even so, the history of black historical dramas runs deep.

Since D. W. Griffith's scandalous 1915 film *The Birth of a Nation*, Hollywood movies written, produced, and directed by people with varying intentions have depicted aspects of the African American historical experience. Notwithstanding the specific goals of the filmmakers, such representations have often molded American moviegoers' impressions of black history, especially when the films are marketed as being based on "true" or "actual" events and claim to accurately recount the lives of nonfictional historical icons and characters. Since the dawning of the new millennium, there has been an explosion of mainstream, commercially successful films that dramatize emotive and even controversial black historical subject matter, such as racism, slavery, Jim Crow segregation, racial violence, and, in the case of F. Gary Gray's *Straight Outta Compton* (2015) and Benny Boom's *All Eyez On Me* (2017), police brutality.

While most of these films have redemptive and educational qualities, all of

---

4   Stephane Dunn, "Why the Roots Remake Is So Important," *The Atlantic*, May 29, 2016.

5   Henry Louis Gates Jr., "*12 Years a Slave*," *Transition*, no. 114, 2014, 187. In an interview with Gates, McQueen asserted: "The fact that he's president can never be underestimated when it comes to the influence he's had on culture, and particularly film." He continued, "I guarantee you—well, I really strongly believe—that these films wouldn't have been made if Obama wasn't president."

them are problematic in their own ways. To begin with, historical dramas on black history—and on all historical subjects for that matter—are always scrutinized for their factual accuracy. What's more, in the most recent edition of his enduring study on blacks in American films, author Donald Bogle points out that during the "Age of Obama" new opportunities "sprang up for African Americans in the movie industry." But he added: "some of the very old images" about African Americans "continued to thrive into the new millennium."[6]

Paying attention to debates surrounding Hollywood filmmakers' portrayals of black historical phenomenon and keeping Bogle's observation in mind, this chapter chronologically and thematically unpacks how a cluster of commercially successful and widely talked about films released between 2011 (when *The Help* was released) and 2016 have construed aspects of black history.[7] Central to my discussion is testing the limits of scholar Derrick P. Alridge's assertion in 2001 that a "loss of black agency can be easily seen in Hollywood portrayals of African-American history," exploring how the directors of these films have discussed their approaches and intentions, and determining what dimensions of these films can serve as illuminating points of departure for teaching African American history to millennial learners.[8] Because such films are becoming more popular and will forever be with us (as I completed this book, Kathryn Bigelow's historical drama *Detroit* was released), I am convinced that we must know how to most prudently use and interpret these films. I begin with a detailed appraisal of *The Help*, one of the most popular films on the civil rights era.

---

6   Donald Bogle, *Toms, Coons, Mulattoes, Mammies, and Bucks: An Interpretive History of Blacks in American Films*, New York: Bloomsbury Academic, 2016, xviii.

7   During the "Age of Obama," many films were released that focused on black historical subject matter. If I decided to widen my scope and criteria, I could have included many other films. Blacks' roles during World War II, for instance, have been revisited during the last decade. Spike Lee's *Miracle at St. Anna* (2008) explores the adventures of four African Americans soldiers in the 92nd Infantry Division stationed in Italy in 1944. Though the film did not fare well at the box offices, the flashback scene during which the black soldiers are refused service at a diner in Louisiana is unforgettable, creatively getting into the minds of Lee's characters. Lee also expertly hints at how blacks from different walks of life considered the "Double V" campaign. Anthony Hemingway's *Red Tails* (2012) is also set in 1944 and tells a familiar story of what the renowned Tuskegee Airmen accomplished. Produced by Lucasfilm Ltd., the most redeeming features of the film are its special effects during the air-to-air combat scenes. Other black history centered films released since 2008 that I opted not to analyze include *The Express* (2008), *The Secret Life of Bees* (2008), *Cadillac Records* (2008), *Night Catches Us* (2010), *The North Star* (2013), *The Watsons Go to Birmingham* (2013), *Hidden Figures* (2016), and *Detroit, Marhsall*, and *Mudhound*, all released in 2017. Released when Obama began his presidential campaign, Denzel Washington's *The Great Debaters* (2007) is an excellent film for teaching about black life in the South during the era of the Great Depression.

8   Derrick P. Alridge, "Redefining and Refining Scholarship for the Academy: Standing on the Shoulders of Our Elders and Giving Credence to African American Voice and Agency. In *Retaining African-American Faculty, Administrators, and Students at Predominately White Universities: A Tale of Multiple Competing Paradigms*, edited by Lee Jones, (Sterling, Virginia: Stylus Publishing, 2001), 200.

"FOR THE SAKE OF ENTERTAINMENT"?: THE HELP

Released in the summer of 2011, *The Help* was a box office hit. With a $25 million budget, it made more than $200 million worldwide and won many awards. Octavia Spencer won an Oscar for Best Supporting Actress for her role as rebellious, headstrong domestic and cook Minny Jackson. It is worth noting that seventy years earlier, Hattie McDaniel became the first black woman to win this award for playing a strikingly similar role as Mammy in *Gone With the Wind*. Based upon Kathryn Stockett's 2009 *New York Times* bestselling novel, *The Help* is set in Jackson, Mississippi, in 1963 and focuses on the life of Eugenia "Skeeter" Phelan, an aspiring writer and recent graduate of the University of Mississippi who returns home for the summer, and the experiences of two domestic workers and best friends, Aibileen Clark and Minny Jackson, who are employed by Skeeter's privileged, cliquish, racist childhood friends Elizabeth Leefolt and Hilly Walters Holbrook, respectively.

The independent, twenty-three-year-old Skeeter (with "no man" and "no babies") is soon hired by the *Jackson Journal* to author a "domestic mainte-nance column" advice column. Because she has no real life experience in this province, she seeks advice from the fifty-two-year-old Aibileen. During the course of their conversations, Skeeter befriends Aibileen and becomes increas-ingly disturbed by how she, and other domestic workers, are routinely mistreated and abused. Though director Tate Taylor does not provide a back-drop revealing that Skeeter was exceptionally sympathetic toward black people (I wonder, for instance, how she responded to James Meredith's integration of "Ole Miss"), Skeeter apologizes to Aibileen for Hilly's racist rants and brazen support of the White Citizens Councils and refuses to support Hilly's home sanitation initiative that sought to enforce segregated bathrooms within household where domestics labored.

Perhaps more than anything else, Skeeter's compassion for black women seems to be rooted in her relationship with her treasured childhood maid, Constantine Bates, who raised her as if she was her own child, yet was unfairly fired by her mother. As a result of her interactions with Aibileen and triggered by a powerful memory of Constantine's unwavering love and support, she decides that she wants to write a book from the "point of view of the help." She shares her idea with Elaine Stein, an editor for Harper & Row, who agrees that her proposed story is never talked about, could challenge Margaret Mitchell's enduring *Gone With the Wind*, and is timely given the rising tide of the civil rights movement.

In order to "show what it's really like in Jackson," Skeeter needed to inter-view the maids themselves. When she was first approached, Aibileen did not want to collaborate with her employer's friend; she feared that her participa-tion in such a scheme would be life-threatening, "more than Jim Crow." Skeeter is portrayed as a white woman who, despite her privileged background, has the miraculous ability to understand Aibileen's trepidation. "I know it's scary," she tells Aibileen when first attempting to convince her to share her testimonies. After attending an uplifting sermon about courage, sacrificing for others, loving one's enemies, and praying for one's prosecutors, Aibileen had a sudden change of heart and agreed to cooperate with Skeeter. After she is baselessly fired, Minny also agrees to participate, and after Medgar Evers is savagely murdered and Hilly has her maid Yule May Davis violently arrested for theft, at least a dozen other domestics follow in Aibileen's and Minny's footsteps.

The stories that Skeeter includes in her book come from the mouths of her subjects. Yet she becomes their altruistic mouthpiece and liberator: a quintessential Hollywood white ally and savior who rescues powerless African American women. Again, somehow, Skeeter has the ability to relate to her subjects. Her novel, *The Help*, was a great success, shocking those white women who read it.

Proud of her daughter, Skeeter's mother—who succumbed to racist peer pressure from the president of the local chapter of the Daughters of the American Revolution and fired her longtime maid, Constantine, for breaching segregationist norms—told her daughter with tear-filled eyes that she "brought courage back to the family." All of the other white women depicted in the narrative were horrified by what they read, especially Holly, the victim of "the terrible awful." Skeeter's character is portrayed as being truly heroic and self-sacrificing. Not only did her novel cause her to lose her friends since girlhood, but her affluent boyfriend Stuart Whitworth leaves her because she, in his words, "stirs up trouble." Members of the black community praised Skeeter, symbolized by the copy of her book that members of Aibileen's and Minnie's church signed for her. Skeeter repaid her informants by sharing her royalties with them.

Toward the end of the film, Skeeter is offered a job from Harper & Row in New York City and she tells Aibileen and Minnie that she is not going to accept the offer and will, instead, remain in Jackson. "I can't just leave you two behind when things are getting bad from the mess that I created," the benevolent protector explained. Aibileen reassured Skeeter that they would be fine without her, retorting: "Bad things happen, ain't nothin' you can do about it."[9] In the end, despite excellent performances from Viola Davis and Octavia Spencer, Emma Stone's character Skeeter predominates. *The Help* is in toto the story of a selfless white female racial reformer.

The film received mixed reviews regarding its depiction of the civil rights movement. Many mainstream media and entertainment bloggers praised *The Help*, but the film was by no means universally welcomed. In a review with a title

---

9   Tate Taylor, dir., *The Help*, with Jessica Chastain, Viola Davis, Bryce Dallas Howard, Allison James, Octavia Butler, and Emma Stone, Burbank, CA: Walter Disney Studios Motion Pictures, 2011, film.

suggesting that the film centered the voices of black women, "'The Maids' Now Have Their Say," a film critic for the *New York Times* knocked *The Help* for the overacting "sometimes excruciatingly so, characterized by loud laughs, bugging eyes and pumping limbs."[10]

The most insightful critique of *The Help* was offered by the Association of Black Women Historians (ABWH). Founded in 1979, many members of this organization are leading figures in the contemporary black history movement, and the organization continues to support and promote historical scholarship "by and about black women." Early in 2012 in their widely publicized "An Open Statement to the Fans of *The Help*," five of the organization's representatives voiced their concerns with the film.

> Despite efforts to market the book and the film as a progressive story of triumph over racial injustice, *The Help* distorts, ignores, and trivializes the experiences of black domestic workers. . . . We are specifically concerned about the representations of black life and the lack of attention given to sexual harassment and civil rights activism.[11]

The ABWH spokeswomen maintained that the film evoked the enduring Mammy stereotype, gave its black female characters a "child-like, over-exaggerated 'black' dialect," oversimplified black manhood and black male–female relationships, ignored the pervasive sexual harassment faced by black domestic workers, downplayed civil rights activism within the black community, and softened brutal expressions of white supremacy in Mississippi. "In the end, *The Help* is not a story about the millions of hardworking and dignified black women who labored in white homes to support their families and communities," the ABWH members concluded:

> Rather, it is the coming-of-age story of a white protagonist, who uses myths about the lives of black women to make sense of her own. The Association of Black Women Historians finds it unacceptable for either this book or this film to strip black women's lives of historical accuracy for the sake of entertainment.[12]

The concise and insightful critiques raised by ABWH's collective response to *The Help* is instructive for exploring how this film functions in ineffective and perhaps informative manners.

The fact that *The Help* is set in 1963 is very important. This was a pivotal year in the African American freedom struggle for many reasons. Viewers are informed that the film is set in 1963 at several moments in passing. In one

---

10   Manohla Dargis, "'The Maids' Now Have Their Say," *New York Times*, August 10, 2011, C1.

11   The Association of Black Women Historians, "An Open Statement to the Fans of The Help," truth.abwh.org, August 12, 2011.

12   Ibid.

instance, Skeeter's editor, Elaine Stein, encourages her to complete her novel soon because it would build upon the momentum of the March on Washington for Jobs and Freedom. In another scene, viewers are presented with a thirty-second clip of original footage of Medgar Evers speaking out against segregation. Shortly thereafter, the murder of the Mississippi NAACP field secretary is revealed as well as the assassination of President Kennedy. This is the extent to which the historical context of *The Help* is established. In reality, the roll call of monumental events that occurred during 1963 is never-ending. Though a few scenes do briefly portray the everyday living conditions of African Americans in Jackson, it is not clear from the film that in 1963, more than 60 percent of African Americans in Mississippi lived in dilapidated homes and suffered greatly. Suffice it to say that 1963 was one of the most turbulent years of the modern civil rights era and Taylor did not do a thorough job of highlighting the importance of 1963.

Beyond inadequately historicizing 1963 and black life in Jackson, Mississippi, and reinvigorating the great white savior Hollywood trope, there are other problematic dimensions to *The Help*. We do learn more about Aibileen's life throughout the course of the film. Yet we rarely see her interacting with her immediate family. It is obvious through Viola Davis's powerful acting that Aibileen misses her beloved son, who died at age twenty-four in a tragic accident. Ultimately, it appears that she loves and cares for Mae Leefolt, her "baby girl," more than her own family members. There are flashbacks with Constantine nurturing Skeeter, but none with Aibileen mothering her deceased son. We do see a picture of her son, Treelore, hanging on the wall of her modest home, she recounts to Skeeter how he died, and at the end of the film she narrates that he perhaps aspired to be a writer. But we are left to imagine the nature of their relationship. Was she compelled to neglect her son when she was younger and raising one of the seventeen total white children she cared for? She refuses to answer Skeeter's compelling question: "What does it feel like to raise a white child when your own child's at home being looked after by somebody else?"[13]

The only notion of the black family that viewers are introduced to is Minny's dysfunctional relationship with her husband Leroy, who emotionally and physically abuses her. On one occasion, she is left with a massive gash above her left eye that her featherbrained employer Celia Rae Foote tends to. Imagine this: it takes a white woman to tell Minny that she should fight back. In the same way that there were some benevolent plantation mistresses during the antebellum era, there were some employers who were kind to their maids. In any case, the played-up relationship between Minny and "Ms. Celia" is nonrepresentational. Celia and her wealthy husband, Johnny, defy de facto segregation by dining in their home with Minny. Johnny even pulls out the chair for Minny at the dinner

---

13 Taylor, dir., *The Help*.

table before they enjoy a feast that Celia prepared thanks to Minny's lessons. After all, Minny is the "best cook in Mississippi."

The Jackson black community is presented as being a monolith—an uneducated and poor population. With the exception of two scenes including the Martin Luther King Jr.-esque preacher Green, a congregation of well-dressed churchgoers, and original television clips of Medgar Evers, most of the black characters in the background work in menial jobs like the humble waiter Henry who befriends Skeeter. Viewers are led to believe that a black middle-class or militant group of civil rights activists did not exist in Jackson. In terms of African American characters in the film, Aibileen is the closest to being an activist. She struggles with the decision to participate in Skeeter's project, fearing retribution. In one scene, she mentions that her cousin's car was bombed; viewers are left to assume that he or she was active in the black freedom struggle. This would have been an ideal opportunity to showcase African American agency. In another scene, members of Aibileen's church celebrate her for having the courage to share her story with Skeeter and emboldening others to do the same. In preacher Green's words, she stepped up at "an important time for our community." The "sassy" Minny's actions embody the ultimate form of resistance.

The most unimaginable example of fighting back involves Minny mixing her feces into her famous chocolate pie that her employer's daughter, the malevolent and bigoted Hilly Holbrook, eats. Skeeter describes this in her novel and it becomes known as "the terrible awful." Now deceased comedian Dick Gregory, among others, found this to be insulting to black women.

Many reviewers chastised the director for the film's use of an exaggerated, stereotypical, and antiquated black southern dialect. The African American English (AAE) spoken by blacks in *The Help* is a far cry from the dialogues that Zora Neale Hurston brought into being in her classic novel *Their Eyes Were Watching God* (1937). Unlike the director of *Roots*, Taylor apparently did not consult with AAE experts. "You is kind, you is smart, you is intelligent" is a mantra that Aibileen repeated to the young Mae. Resurrecting stereotypes dating back to the antebellum era, Minny tells Celia, "I love me some fried chicken."[14] Examples such as this abound.

Despite its troublesome shortcomings and omissions, *The Help* does illuminate some dehumanizing aspects of Jim Crow segregation, sometimes with subtle background images that could easily be overlooked.

Viewers do in fact gain some understanding of the experiences of domestic workers. Life was hard, to say the least. "We living in hell. Trapped. Our kids trapped," Minny laments after Medgar Evers was brutally murdered.[15] The film opens with Aibileen describing the demanding types of work that she performs

---

14   Ibid.
15   Ibid.

six days a week for a meager $182 per month. She recounts that she always knew that she was going to become a maid. Her mother was a maid and her grandmother was a "house slave." Aibileen and other maids are routinely denigrated and humiliated by their employers who call black people the n-word in their presence. Aibileen, Minny, and Yule May Davis are all accused of stealing and fired, a common reality for domestic workers.

To be sure, Taylor failed to acknowledge the sexual violence that black women faced but did include a scene in which Yule is arrested and beaten by a brawny police officer with a billy club in public. Even so, viewers are lead to believe that racism and Jim Crow segregation exists at the individual level. Police officers and particularly Hilly become the embodiment of racism. *The Help* also highlights how many white girls were influenced and raised by their maids, their surrogate mothers. At one point, Mae calls Aibileen her "real mother" in earshot of her biological mother.

Segregation is a prevailing theme in the film, as revealed by segregated bathrooms and buses, "colored only" movie theaters and taxi cabs, an extended monologue from Aibileen giving a run-down of the extensive and preposterous so-called "separate but equal" laws, and the segregated hospital system that contributed to Aibileen's son's death. The fate of Aibileen's son conjures up the myths surrounding the death of famous physician, surgeon, and medical scholar Charles R. Drew.

Unlike most of Spike Lee's films, *The Help* only provides fleeting glimpses into the intimate spaces of black culture and community life. We see Aibileen and Minny privately poking fun at their white employers, Minny schooling her teenage daughter about the proper etiquette for being a maid, and a church sermon that is inspired by the civil rights struggle. While select scenes such as these and a handful of others could be of service to students of African American history, the film would be best used in classroom setting for exercises in critical historical thinking. Unfortunately, the vast majority of the millions of people in the United States and abroad who saw *The Help* did not know much about the civil rights era, black women's history, or African American history in general and, as a result, probably believed what they watched.

REIMAGINING SLAVERY: DJANGO UNCHAINED, 12 YEARS A SLAVE, AND THE BIRTH OF A NATION

Slavery has been depicted by directors of US films since the early twentieth century in movies like *For Massa's Sake*, *In Slavery Days*, *Uncle Tom's Cabin*, and, of course, *The Birth of a Nation*. Released in 1977 and coinciding with an earthquake of "culture-and-community" historians' reappraisals of the "peculiar institution," the original *Roots* miniseries, despite its shortcomings, represents the first major revisionist dramatization of slavery.

Veteran West Coast emcee and amateur actor Snoop Dogg was one of the most outspoken critics of the 2016 *Roots* remake. "I'm sick of this shit. How the fuck are they going to put *Roots* on, on Memorial Day?" Snoop broadcast in an Instagram video. For this self-made businessman who founded Snoopadelic Films in 2005, the television and film industries as well as the mainstream media perpetually zoom in on "the abuse we took hundreds and hundreds of years ago." Snoop called upon "real niggas" to boycott *Roots*. "I ain't watching that shit . . . Let's create our own shit based on today, how we live and how we inspire people today. Black is what's real. Fuck that old shit."[16] While Snoop's diatribe is problematic at various levels (as journalist and syndicated columnist Roland Martin so aptly and passionately pointed out), he did raise a concern that has some validity, however minor and poorly communicated.

Slavery, at this point in time representing one-third of the total black experience in the United States, has for logical reasons been the focus of many network and cable television specials, documentaries, and Hollywood films. In addition to the conventional civil rights era, slavery seems to be a preoccupation of filmmakers. However, Snoop failed to realize that *Roots* presents the institution of slavery and the dynamic culture of the enslaved in nuanced manners. It goes without saying that historians, films studies scholars, and cultural critics have offered much more sophisticated analyses of how African Americans have been portrayed on television and in Hollywood films than Snoop. Digestible by millennials, the remake of *Roots*, Stephane Dunn suggests, "brings new light to the misconception that popular culture has done a good job telling stories about slavery and black history in the decades since *Roots* first gripped the nation."[17]

Like the *Roots* remake, Quentin Tarantino's *Django Unchained* (2012) and Steve McQueen's 2013 Academy Award Best Picture winning *12 Years a Slave* rejuvenated this re-envisioning of slavery in their own distinct ways. Tarantino's and McQueen's sagas both feature protagonists who grapple with the meanings and realities of bondage and freedom, but they present strikingly different renditions of black life during slavery.

In terms of profits, *Django Unchained* is Tarantino's most successful film, grossing more than $400 million in the United States and abroad. It is also his most controversial film. Without seeing it (he vowed that he was not going to watch it), prolific film director and social critic Spike Lee declared that Tarantino's film disrespected his ancestors. Lee was especially upset that slavery, a "Holocaust" in his mind, was being depicted in the form of a "Sergio Leone Spaghetti Western" and that the n-word was uttered more than one hundred times mainly by white slaveholders, racists, and passersby. Tarantino has a cameo appearance as Frankie, an Australian employee of the LeQuint Dickey Mining Company who is transporting Django after he is sold to them; his

---

16   Daniel Kreps, "Snoop Dogg Slams 'Roots' Remake, Calls for Boycott," *Rolling Stone* magazine, May 30, 2016.

17   Dunn, "Why the Roots Remake Is So Important."

character believes in black inferiority, but he does not use the contentious racial epithet, instead referring to Django as "black" and "blackie." A defensive Tarantino found Lee's criticism to be "ridiculous."[18]

Django Unchained was greeted with great fanfare by many scholars. *Transitions: The Magazine of Africa and the African Diaspora* and *Black Camera, An International Journal* published special issues exalting Tarantino's film. Nevertheless, a group of black scholars were critical of Tarantino's portrayal of slavery in greater detail than Lee.

According to Lonnie G. Bunch III, the founding director of the Smithsonian's National Museum of African American History and Culture, slavery in *Django Unchained* was "little more than a backdrop," only a few scenes critically probed the realities of enslavement, and the experiences of enslaved black women were problematic.[19] Like Lee, *New Yorker* columnist Jelani Cobb was troubled with Tarantino's careless use of the n-word and, in addition, argued that the director's focus on the conflict between Django and the "Uncle Tom" house servant named Stephen, played by Samuel L. Jackson, downplayed the conflicts between the enslaved and the slaveholding class.[20] Historian Daina Ramey Berry was among the first slavery scholars to offer a detailed review of *Django Unchained*. She was hypercritical of Tarantino's film, calling it an "exercise in counterfactual history." Berry added: "its absurdities trivialize the real violence of the slave system and everyday lives of the enslaved." She found fault with Tarantino's framing of gender roles in the slave community, his failure to expose more of the "horrors of slavery," and his contemporary musical score choices. Though she is open to using films and other nontraditional sources to teach millennials about slavery, Berry encourages those who viewed *Django Unchained* as their introduction into slavery to seek out available primary sources: "hearing the words of actual slaves may help a twenty-first audience imagine the experiences of life in bondage."[21]

Tarantino's action-packed and bloody Spaghetti Western begins "somewhere in Texas" in 1858 and chronicles the adventures of the once enslaved Django and erudite German bounty hunter Dr. King Schultz. The former dentist tracked down the slave-trading Speck brothers, who were transporting Django and other slaves who they purchased at a slave auction. Schultz was specifically looking for Django because he was previously enslaved on a plantation where three men, the Brittle brothers, used to work as overseers. Schultz is pursuing these three brothers because there is a sizeable bounty on their heads and he

---

18   Adelle Platon, "Spike Lee Slams Django Unchained: 'I'm Not Gonna See It,'" vibe.com, December 21, 2012. For a discussion of Tarantino's use of the n-word, see Chris Vognar, "He Can't Say That, Can He?" *Transition*, no. 112, 2013, 22–31.

19   Lonnie G. Bunch III, "What *Django Unchained* Got Wrong," smithsonianmag.com, January 14, 2013.

20   Jelani Cobb, "Tarantino Unchained," *New Yorker*, January 2, 2013.

21   Daina Ramey Berry, "Unmixed Blessin'?: A Historian's Thought on *Django Unchained*," notevenpast.org, January 2013.

hoped that Django would be able to identify the men for him. Django, who had been brutalized by these men, who also raped his wife Broomhilda, indicated that he could identify them for Schultz. The Speck brothers are not willing to sell Django to Schultz and one pulls a gun on Schultz. The skilled bounty hunter kills one of the brothers, shoots the other's horse, thereby breaking the slave trader's leg and trapping him under the horse, pays him $150 for Django, and frees the four other slaves. From this point, Django and Schultz become partners of some sort and later close friends and confidants, and together travel from Texas to Tennessee to Mississippi.

Schultz owns Django, but decides to enter into a business agreement and partnership with him. "I'm at a bit of a quandary when it comes to you," Schultz tells Django after purchasing him, "On one hand, I despise slavery. On the other hand, I need your help, and if you're not in a position to refuse, all the better. So for the time being, I'm going to make this slave malarkey work to my benefit."[22] Schultz is clearly not an abolitionist, but does not believe in black inferiority like the white southern characters in the film and develops a friendship with Django, treating him like an equal. He is shocked by the whip marks on Django's back, and throughout the film develops a disdain for the mistreatment of enslaved African Americans. In exchange for his help, Schultz agrees to free Django and gives the former bondsperson the surname "Freeman." After Django helps Schultz track down and kill the Brittle Brothers and Django helps Schultz locate and kill more wanted men, Schultz agrees to help Django find his wife, Broomhilda von Shaft, who is owned by Calvin J. Candie, the owner of the Candie Land Plantation in Mississippi.

Posing as slavers interested in purchasing slaves, Django and Schultz go to Candie's plantation, Django is reunited with Broomhilda without Candie's knowledge, and Schultz strikes a deal with Calvin to purchase Broomhilda. A major shootout ensues after Schultz refuses to close the deal of Broomhilda's purchase with a ceremonial southern handshake, as requested by Calvin, and then kills the Candie Land owner at close range with a derringer that he hid in his sleeve. Schultz is then killed, Django kills many white men, and in the end, the newly freed slave is forced to surrender because Broomhilda is taken hostage. He is tortured and then sold to a mining company. Drawing upon what he learned from Schultz, he is able to trick his guards into returning with him back to Candie Land in order to capture criminals who were wanted by the law. After his naïve escorts free and arm him, Django kills them and returns by himself on horseback to Candie Land armed with guns, ammunition, and dynamite. He finds Broomhilda and posts up in Calvin's home. When Calvin's henchmen, sister, and slaves return from his funeral, Django kills the whites, frees the two female house slaves, and shoots the loyal slave, Samuel, in the knees.

---

22 Quentin Tarantino, dir., *Django Unchained*, with Jamie Foxx, Christoph Waltz, Leonardo DiCaprio, Kerry Washington, and Samuel L. Jackson, New York: The Weinstein Company, 2012, film.

The saga ends with Django blowing up Candie Land and then riding away into the night with his wife. Like *Kill Bill: Volume 1* (2003) and *Inglourious Basterds* (2009), *Django Unchained* is a revenge film. In this case, a former slave is victorious in the end. I doubt that those who went to see Tarantino's neo-slave narrative fantasy were seeking to learn about slavery. He has a fan base that enjoys his characters' dialogues, his soundtracks and cinematography, his use of satire, the first-rate actors and actresses whom he casts, and perhaps above all, his profuse and often satiric use of violence.

"*Django Unchained* is *not* supposed to be experienced or understood as a historically accurate representation of slavery," English and African American Studies scholar Glenda R. Carpio has argued.[23] Tarantino's film is "an exciting adventure" starring a former slave who becomes a "magnificent heroic figure." In his words, his film is "a black story." Unlike *12 Years a Slave*, *Django Unchained* is not based upon a "true" story. At the same time, it does focus on an actual institution that profoundly shaped the evolution of the United States, and Tarantino did describe himself as being a historian of some sort.

In a revealing interview with Henry Louis Gates Jr., he explained how he perceived his role as an interpreter of the past. "I've always wanted to recreate cinematically that world of the antebellum South, of America under slavery, and just what a different place it was—an unfathomable place." He adds: "If I couldn't deal with the actual social strata inside the institution of lifelong slavery itself, then I wasn't really dealing with the story . . . I'm telling a historical story, and when it comes to nuts and bolts of the slave trade, I had to be real and had to tell it the right way. But when it comes to more thematic things and operatic view, I could actually have fun with stylization—because it is taking parts from a spaghetti Western. And I am taking the story of a slave narrative and blowing it up to folkloric proportions and to operatic proportions that are worthy of high opera." In describing how he treated life on antebellum-era slave plantations, Tarantino noted that he wanted to "do this subject justice." It appears that Tarantino wants to have it both ways. On the one hand, he claims to be treating slavery with some sense of historical accuracy and reality. On the other hand, he defends himself from criticisms about his representations of the past by reminding his critics that *Django Unchained* is a spaghetti "Western adventure" with "more of an entertainment value," that he does not "stare at the facts [of slavery] as much."[24]

So, can *Django Unchained* serve as a window into slavery, particularly in terms of educating millennial learners? Most historians of the African American past, especially slavery scholars, would probably refrain from using Tarantino's film as a porthole into slavery. The blatant oppression that bondspersons experience in *Django Unchained* could prompt viewers to rethink the violent nature of

---

23 Glenda R. Carpio, "I Like the Way You Die, Boy," *Transition*, no. 112, 2013, 1.
24 Henry Louis Gates Jr., "'An Unfathomable Place,'" *Transition*, no. 112, 2013, 50, 57, 58.

slavery. Like other filmmakers before him, Tarantino incorporated many scenes depicting the potential brutality of slavery, including whippings, brandings (the "r" that is branded on Django and Broomhilda's cheeks for running away), rape, and other forms of brutality, such as the killing of a disobedient slave by a pack of dogs and "Mandingo fighting" (orchestrated fights to the death between slaveholders' slaves). Primary sources provide us with ample descriptions of the brutality of slavery. At the same time, twenty-first-century interpreters certainly put their own spins of how things actually transpired. This is exactly what Tarantino did with the make-believe "Mandingo fighting" that is central to his plot.

While viewers are exposed to the complexities that "black love" could have entailed during slavery with Django and Broomhilda, overall, Tarantino does not adequately represent the slave community. Most of the slaves that we see in the film are exclusively working on plantations. During one of their conversations, Schultz asks Django if most slaves take marriage seriously and Django responds as if he does not know. As a slave who was married, he would have known that this was a common practice for slaves. In terms of resistance, there is a scene in which Django and Broomhilda are attempting to run away, Django kills overseers and slaveholders, and, of course, at the end of the film Django kills those at Candie Land.

Tarantino uses the loyal house slave Stephen as Django's nemesis. With Stephen, Tarantino sought to depict what he described as "how things work between the house slaves and the field slaves." For him Stephen was "the Basil Rathbone of house niggers" and portrayed the "actual social strata inside the institution of lifelong slavery." Samuel Jackson bought into his director's characterization of this quintessential "Uncle Tom" persona. "Do I have a problem with playing the most despicable motherfucker in the history of the world?" Jackson responded to Tarantino, "No, I ain't got no problem with that." While there were certainly conflicts that may have existed between "house" and "field" slaves, Tarantino's account is highly exaggerated and makes it seem as if those like Stephen were the chief villains during slavery. Django is clearly the primary hero. Yet Schultz is also a demigod of some sort, the familiar "white-savior character" in films recounting episodes in African American history. When asked by Henry Louis Gates Jr. why he decided to make Schultz a "Christ figure," Tarantino claimed that the German bounty hunter was not a white savior in the conventional sense. He explained that Schultz allowed Django, his former apprentice, to develop into a professional bounty hunter in his own right. According to Tarantino, Schultz "is coming from almost a twenty-first-century perspective. He understands slavery, intellectually, but he's never seen the everyday horrors and degradation of it."[25]

"*12 Years* has been called the anti-Django. Do you think of it that way?" Henry Louis Gates Jr. asked Steve McQueen during an interview. "No,"

---

25   Ibid., 57, 55, 62, 65.

responded the Academy Award-winning director. "I'm a huge admirer of Quentin Tarantino; it's just different. One is action, adventure, comedy; one is drama. What's important is that people are talking about and looking at that subject."[26] McQueen's *12 Years a Slave* was a huge hit on all accounts. Though it grossed less than half of *Django Unchained*, this historical drama earned many prestigious awards, including three Academy Awards. The London born director made history by becoming a "black first"—the first black African descendant to win an Academy Award for Best Picture.[27]

McQueen's film is an adaptation of Solomon Northrup's by now famous 1853 slave narrative, *Twelve Years a Slave: Narrative of Solomon Northrup, a Citizen of New York, Kidnapped in Washington City in 1841, and Rescued in 1853*. During the pivotal 1850s, when slavery was intensely debated, Northrup's tale sold widely (more than 30,000 copies) and shared with its readers the trials and tribulations of a free black man, skilled laborer, and talented musician from Saratoga, New York. Northrup was drugged and kidnapped by two white men posing as circus performers who transported him to Washington, DC. From there, he was sold into slavery in New Orleans, Louisiana. For the next twelve years, Northrup is owned by two different slaveholders on cotton and sugar plantations. Northrup eventually befriends a carpenter and abolitionist who is working on the plantation where he is held captive. This soon-to-be confidant, Samuel Bass, sends word back to New York explaining Northrup's plight. With the help of a white politician and lawyer whose family owned Northrup's father, Northrup is eventually given his freedom back and he returns to New York.

Like those involved in the production of the *Roots* remake, McQueen collaborated closely with scholars, including Henry Louis Gates Jr. and experts on Northrup. As he has recounted in several interviews, McQueen had been interested in doing a film on slavery for some time and when he finally discovered, for himself, Northrup's memoir, he believed that "it was a script already."[28] He justified his film by arguing that slavery was a subject that filmmakers did not adequately treat. In depicting Northrup's experiences, he deviated somewhat from the 1853 classic. Part of McQueen's goal was to spark larger conversations about slavery in popular culture and, in many ways, he succeeded in doing so.

Unsurprisingly, a diverse group of scholars have creatively deconstructed McQueen's film. For instance, several essays featured in *Black Camera, An International Film Journal* sought to "go beyond judging" the "historical veracity" of *12 Years a Slave*.[29] While I agree that scholars of contemporary black

---

26   Gates, "*12 Years a Slave*," 193.

27   Steve McQueen, dir., *12 Years a Slave*, with Benedict Cumberbatch, Chiwetel Ejiofor, Michael Fassbender, Lupita Nyong'o and Sarah Paulson, Los Angeles, CA: Fox Searchlight Pictures, 2013, film.

28   Elvis Mitchell, "Steve McQueen," *Interview Magazine*, October 7, 2013.

29   James Edward Ford III, "Introduction," *Black Camera* 7, Fall 2015, 110–14.

cinema should not be obsessed with deciphering how accurate filmmakers' portrayals of the past are, historians' analyses of historical films are inevitably shaped by their profession and can help society better deromanticize and unravel Hollywood versions of the past.

Slavery historian Brenda Stevenson's meticulous critique of McQueen's dramatization of slavery in *The Journal of African American History*, the oldest and leading black history journal, epitomizes the historian who is committed to the notion of "historical veracity" in Hollywood portrayals of the past. For Stevenson, *12 Years a Slave* did not drastically revise how filmmakers and mini-series directors have envisioned slavery. At the same time, she contends that *12 Years a Slave* is "probably the first Hollywood production to incorporate some version" of all of the previously established "characters and scenarios of southern US slavery in one film." She adds: "It does so, moreover, while unflinchingly stamping the institution and its benefactors with a savage, violent brutality—physical, psychological, and sexual—that leaves no room for excuses."[30]

Situating *12 Years a Slave* within the context of slavery-centered cinema, Stevenson dubbed McQueen's film "a flawed and incomplete masterwork." She had high expectations and standards for McQueen. She seems to have wanted him to adopt a more scholarly approach to slavery and to more accurately deal with "the intricacies of the institution." For Stevenson, McQueen misled his viewers by erroneously portraying the slave community, resistance patterns among the enslaved, and the experiences of free people of color and specifically enslaved women. In her legitimately nitpicky critique based upon close readings of archival documents and Northup's account, she points out how McQueen failed to demonstrate how enslaved workers owned by Epps were "a relatively tight-knit community" and that the Epps home was not a plantation mansion.

But Stevenson's harshest criticism of *12 Years a Slave* concerns how it portrays enslaved women. With Eliza, Patsey, and Harriet Shaw, she contends, McQueen "readily adopts this favorite Hollywood trope of the black woman as sexually bound to powerful white men." Though she does not have a problem with including the prevalent sexual exploitation of black women, she argues that McQueen portrays black women one-dimensionally, ignoring how enslaved women resisted and persevered. Simply put, the women described by Northup in his narrative were not exclusively defined by how they were mistreated. If she were to have been consulted instead of Gates, Stevenson would have urged McQueen to have given significant screen time to how enslaved women worked, survived, found joy, and resisted. In the end, Stevenson implies that people should read Northrup's account before seeing the film.[31]

I agree with Robert Brent Toplin, the longtime editor of the American Historical Association's *Perspectives on History* news magazine, who was project

---

30   Brenda A. Stevenson, "*12 Years a Slave*: Narrative, History, and Film," *The Journal of African American History* 99, Winter-Spring 2014, 108.

31   Ibid., 108, 112–16.

director and principal director of PBS's 1984 *Solomon Northrup's Odyssey* and has published three book-length studies on how Hollywood films interpret US history. Like Stevenson, he is critical of McQueen's failure to detail the dynamic inner workings of the slave community. But, he suggests: "*12 Years a Slave* offers many teachable moments for historians. Attention to detail in the story can open opportunities for classroom discussion."[32]

McQueen did a marvelous job of recreating episodes from Northrup's life—actual and fictionalized—that can be used to explore broader themes of enslavement. Violence is central to McQueen's rendition of slavery. When asked by Henry Louis Gates Jr. if the scene when Epps rapes Patsey was "too much," like Tarantino, McQueen responded: "Either I was making a movie about slavery or I wasn't, and I decided I wanted to make a movie about slavery." He added:

> People talk about what happened, but when you visualize it, when you see it . . . I'm making a picture of what took place in those times, and if I didn't do it justice, I wouldn't be able to look at myself.[33]

There are countless other scenes that reveal the inhumane nature of slavery.

While being held captive in a slave pen in Washington, DC, in the shadows of the nation's capital after he had been drugged and abducted by his kidnappers, he is severely beaten with a paddle and cat-o'-nine tails by his captor Burch. The beating is brutal. Burch breaks the paddle on Northrup's back after striking him fifteen times. He then gives him a dozen lashes with the whip. The slave trader Burch beats Northrup until he is exhausted. Northrup's shirt is bloodied and while he is bathing in the courtyard outside of the dungeon, viewers see the vicious whip marks on this back. There are several rape scenes in the film and Patsey is brutally whipped in a manner similar to how slaves were whipped in films like *Amistad*. During Northrup's transport from Washington, DC, to Louisiana, a male slave Robert who attempts to protect a female slave from being sexually assaulted by a sailor is killed. As was the case during the infamous middle passage, his body is thrown overboard. This scene, however, raises questions. It is very unlikely that an ordinary sailor involved in the illegal domestic slave trade would have had the authority to kill a slave. After all, Robert—like the slave who is devoured by ravenous dogs in *Django Unchained*—could have been sold for great profit.

Because he physically assaulted the sadistic chief carpenter on the Ford plantation, a white man named John Tibeats, Northrup is tortured by Tibeats and two other white men. With his hands tied behind his back, he is left hanging by his neck so that his toes can barely touch the muddy ground beneath him preventing him from strangling to death. "That picture of Solomon standing

---

32   Robert Brent Toplin, "12 Years a Slave Examines the Old South's Heart of Darkness," *Perspectives on History*, historians.org, November 2013.
33   Gates, "*12 Years a Slave*," 191, 192.

there," McQueen recounted, represented "all the hundreds of thousands of people who were lynched."[34]

In another instance when Northrup is running errands for Epps, he stumbles upon a group of white men in a wooded area who are lynching two young black men who appear to be slaves. This scene is haunting, reminiscent of the lynching scenes in John Singleton's *Rosewood* (1997) and Denzel Washington's *The Great Debaters* (2007). Still, one wonders why these two men were being murdered. Slaves were certainly punished and tortured for a variety of reasons, and there were barbarous slaveholders during the antebellum era. But why would two enslaved, young, and healthy men—worth between approximately $1,000 and $2,000—be killed? Were these men convicted of leading a revolt? Could they have been free blacks who, in the eyes of the murderers, violated whites' notions of proper racial etiquette? Such questions remain unanswered.

In addition to the prevailing themes of violence and coercion, the characters in McQueen's film effectually dramatize the routine dehumanization of bondspersons. While being held captive in the holding pen in the nation's capital, Northrup and the other captives are fed poor quality food and forced to bathe completely naked in front of each other and their white captors. At the private slave auction at Freeman's home in New Orleans where William Ford purchases Northrup and Eliza, the potential buyers are told to "inspect them at your leisure." The enslaved men, women, and children are, in some cases, naked and forced to open their mouths and demonstrate the good physical shape that they are in. The most powerful moment in this scene is the separation of Eliza from her two children. This was a common practice, and through Eliza, who never fully recovers from this tragedy, we are able to better imagine the impact of such an atrocity. Eliza's daughter (who was fathered by her previous owner) is cherished by the slave dealer Freeman, who indicates that she is expensive because of her complexion. It is implied that she will be sold to the highest bidder as a concubine or "fancy maid." This was not uncommon in Louisiana.

In McQueen's film, viewers do get a glimpse of what the enslaved did to survive and resist. When he is being transported to New Orleans, Northrup meets several others who have met a similar fate. A conversation between Northrup, Clemens Ray, and Robert reveals some potential responses to enslavement. Northrup suggests: "The crew is fairly small. If it were well planned, I believe they could be strong armed." Robert, who is clearly a disobedient bondsperson (as revealed by him being restrained with shackles and an iron mask), agrees. Clemens Ray, on the other hand, argues that "three can't stand against a whole crew," that survival "is about keeping your head down."[35]

It seems that Northrup draws from both of these approaches. He learns to survive by concealing and revealing his intelligence, winning the favor of

---

34   Ibid.
35   McQueen, dir., *12 Years a Slave*.

William Ford and dealing carefully with Epps. His unique talents as a violinist helped him on both the Ford and Epps plantations. It is clear that Northrup's memories of his life as a free man and his dreams of reuniting with his family helped sustain him. He also drew inspiration from the slave community, Negro spirituals, and his relationship to Patsey, who he tried to protect from Epps to the best of his abilities. Perhaps the most explicit example of Northrup's resistance that seems like a page from Frederick Douglass's 1845 popular autobiography or Tarantino's script for *Django Unchained* is when he beats down John Tibeats with a whip that he used on him. Though he knew that there would be severe consequences for such actions, we can tell that this was very cathartic for him.

Unlike recent films that touch upon slavery such as Steven Spielberg's 2012 *Lincoln* or Gary Ross's 2016 *The Free State of Jones*, with *12 Years a Slave* McQueen also, sometimes subtly, depicts day-to-day life within the slave community that existed outside of the purview of their owners. We see slaves singing work songs and spirituals, showing concern for each other's well-being, and burying one of their own. In an early scene in the film, Northrup also has a sexual encounter with a female slave during which she pleasures herself with his hand. Northrup seems to be a passive participant. The interaction is quick and after she climaxes, she turns her back to Northrup and weeps. McQueen said that he included this moment that of course did not exist in Northrup's narrative in order to show some "tenderness" that the enslaved were able to experience.

Despite the fact that *12 Years a Slave* presents realistic and moving accounts of slavery and the slave community, it also in some measure supports the enduring Hollywood white savior trope.

Northrup's first master, William Ford, is at times presented as being a reluctant slaveholder and abolitionist; Samuel Bass and one of Northrup's white friends from Saratoga, New York, Mr. Parker, are portrayed as liberating Northrup. They come to his rescue and he is not credited with attaining his own freedom. This leads many viewers unfamiliar with US slavery to perhaps think that benevolent whites were most responsible for challenging slavery in a similar manner to how many Americans still presume that Lincoln freed the slaves with the Emancipation Proclamation. In addition, McQueen depicts life for free blacks in New York as being problem-free, when in fact the fate of Northrup reveals that free blacks could be re-enslaved. Yet, the flashbacks of his life as a free black man make it appear as if free blacks in the North were on equal footing with whites. The life that McQueen's free Solomon Northrup leads is a far cry from the landscape that historian Leonard P. Curry describes in *The Free Black in Urban America, 1800–1850: The Shadows of the Dream* (1981). Before he was kidnapped, he exchanged greetings with whites in the street, he was a respected musician, he lived in a nice home and community, and he received first-class treatment while shopping in white-owned establishments.

At the end of the film after he is rescued and reunited with his family, McQueen listed a few facts on the screen related to Northrup's case. Highlighting his exceptionalism, perhaps the most impactful was this: "Solomon Northrup was one of the few victims of kidnapping to regain freedom from slavery."[36]

Unaware that McQueen was working on *12 Years a Slave* while he was plugging away at his own film on slavery, in 2016, actor Nate Parker directed and starred in the imaginative and powerful film *The Birth of a Nation*. This historical drama that, in Parker's words, "reclaimed" the title of D. W. Griffith's racist 1915 film and "repurposed it as a tool to challenge racism and white supremacy in America," tells of Nat Turner and the notorious 1831 Southampton Rebellion. After its premiere at the prestigious 2016 Sundance Film Festival, Fox Searchlight Pictures (which also distributed *12 Years a Slave*) purchased the rights to Parker's debut film for a record-breaking $17.5 million.

More like *Django* than *12 Years a Slave* only in the sense that Tarantino and Parker do not shy away from graphic violence from the hands of enslaved protagonists, *The Birth of a Nation* represents Parker's interpretation of a controversial historical personality and slave revolt that, like most historical phenomenon, is still open to widely varying interpretations.[37] Parker has been candid with the public about what this film means to him. Several years before Tarantino's or McQueen's films were released, Parker began thinking about his biopic. As an undergraduate student at the University of Oklahoma, he first learned about Turner's revolt in an African American Studies course. "Nat Turner was my hero long before I became an artist. Knowledge of his exploits," Parker told an interviewer, perhaps getting caught up in the moment, "provided the courage needed to set aside my college degree to pursue my purpose in the arts."[38]

According to Parker, who did not consult closely with slavery scholars or experts on Turner, Styron's controversial 1967 Pulitzer Prize-winning novel *The Confessions of Nat Turner* and US history in general "has strategically painted him with the brush of villainy and controversy."[39] By challenging oversimplified renditions of Turner, and building upon McQueen's film (which he viewed as being pioneering), Parker wants his audience to recognize how slavery rendered "even the most well-intentioned complicit" as well as the prevailing "resistance and self-determination from the position of the enslaved." In his portrayal of Turner, Parker has said that he strove to reveal Turner's "humanity" and to create a "hero that fought against this system." Because the story of his revolt has

36   Ibid.

37   Nate Parker, dir., *The Birth of a Nation*, with Nate Parker, Armie Hammer, Colman Domingo, Aja Naomi King, Jackie Earle Haley, Penelope Ann Miller, and Gabrielle Union, Los Angeles, CA: Fox Searchlight Pictures, 2016, film.

38   Soheil Rezayazdi, "Five Questions with *The Birth of a Nation* Director Nate Parker," *Filmmaker Magazine,* January 25, 2016.

39   Ibid.

been so hotly debated, historians will perhaps not be as quick to attack him for misinterpreting this controversial African American icon.[40]

Early in the film, Parker reconstructs Turner's early years and, through some of young Nat's visions, draws connections between Turner and his African ancestors, depicts how Turner became a preacher, shows how Turner and an enslaved woman named Cherry experience love, and, like *Django Unchained* and *12 Years a Slave*, lays bare the violent horrors of slavery. It is impossible for anyone in the twenty-first century to get into Turner's mind, especially since he did not, unlike Solomon Northrup, leave behind his own account of his life. Nonetheless, Parker challenges his audience to ponder what may have going on in Turner's mind as he made the decision to lead a revolt and, in the process, sacrifice his life for a greater cause that resulted in the deaths of more than fifty whites and two hundred blacks, drastically impacting how slave conspiracies and black preachers were dealt with in the South. Parker's debut film did not have the impact that Tarantino's or McQueen's did, perhaps in part because of the re-invoked controversy surrounding his involvement in a 1999 rape case.

ENVISAGING THE CIVIL RIGHTS ERA

Similar to slavery, episodes and personalities from the ritualistically memorialized conventional civil rights movement (a period lasting from approximately *Brown v. Board of Education* until the Voting Rights Act) have been the subjects of popular American films for decades. Two of the last Hollywood films about episodes in African American history that were released during the "Age of Obama" take place during the antebellum era and the civil rights period. While Parker reckons with slavery, Jeff Nichols's *Loving* (2016) focuses on the 1958 marriage of a black woman, Mildred Jeter, and a white man, Richard Loving, who are arrested for violating Virginia's anti-miscegenation laws and whose case was at the center of the monumental US Supreme Court case *Loving v. Virginia* (1967).[41]

While *The Help* does not challenge status quo cinematic portraits of the black freedom struggle, *The Butler* and *Selma* have helped chip away at the one-dimensional portrayals of the civil rights movement that films like *Mississippi Burning* (1988) evoked. Civil rights era films have tended to spark heated debates in part because the legacy of this movement and many of its key movers and

---

40   Alex Billington, "Sundance Interview: *The Birth of a Nation* Director/Star Nate Parker," firstshowing.net, February 3, 2106.

41   I opted not to analyze *Loving* in this chapter because the civil rights movement is not prominently featured. The film centers the relationship between Mildred and Richard and their historic case. See Jeff Nichols, dir., *Loving*, with Joel Edgerton, Ruth Negga, Nick Kroll, Martin Csokas, and Michael Shannon, Universal City, CA: Focus Features, 2016, film. *Loving* supplements Nancy Buirski's highly informative 2011 documentary *The Loving Story*.

shakers are still with us today. "There has never been an honest movie about the civil rights movement," veteran civil rights activist Julian Bond wrote four months before he died when asked what he thought about Ava DuVernay's *Selma*. According to Bond, Americans "will have to wait a long, long time" for a trustworthy film on the civil rights era.[42]

Bond was right. Recently released Hollywood films on the civil rights movement are not wholly "honest." That said, the same could be alleged about historical scholarship on this climacteric in African American history and about all historical films and historical scholarship. Like films, historiography is based upon interpretation. With the risk of sounding cynical, the ultimate truth is as elusive as unmitigated objectivity.

Released in the United States three months before *12 Years a Slave*, Lee Daniels's *The Butler* is based upon the real life of Eugene Allen, an African American who worked as a waiter and butler in the White House from 1952 until 1986.[43] Though they grossed about the same and were both widely admired, *12 Years a Slave* won more prestigious, mainstream awards than Daniels's film. Neither were screened in the White House, but Obama was especially moved by *The Butler*. "I teared up just thinking about not just the butlers who have worked here in the White House, but an entire generation of people who were talented and skilled, but because of Jim Crow, because of discrimination, there was only so far they could go," Obama told Tom Joyner in an interview in the White House. "And yet, with dignity and tenacity, they got up and worked every single day, and put up with a whole lot of mess because they hoped for something better for their kids."[44]

Influenced by a brief 2008 article in the *Washington Post* about Allen's experiences working in the Executive Residence and voting for Obama in the historic election of 2008, *The Butler* chronicles the experiences of Cecil Gaines and his family for more than five decades. Central to the film are generational worldview conflicts and the historical contexts and turning points that molded the film's main characters. In an interview in August 2013, Daniels insisted that his film was not intended to be about the civil rights movement. "I felt to keep the movie alive," he maintained, "we needed to make sure that the family was the focal point of the film not the Civil Rights movement, not the history lesson that was going on in America."[45]

Leading authority on the Black Power era Peniel E. Joseph admired

---

42   Daniel Judt, "Feeling Versus Fact: Reconciling Ava DuVernay's Retelling of Selma," thepolitic.org, March 28, 2015. It appears that Bond had mixed feelings about *Selma*. In several interviews, he praised the film but disagreed with how DuVernay portrayed Lyndon B. Johnson's relationship with Martin Luther King Jr.

43   Lee Daniels, dir., *The Butler*, with Forest Whitaker, Oprah Winfrey, and David Ayelowo, New York: The Weinstein Company, 2013, film.

44   "Obama Says He Teared Up While Watching 'The Butler,'" cbsnews.com, August 28, 2013..

45   Edward Douglas, "Interview: Talking With the Butler's Lee Daniels," comingsoon.net, August 14, 2013.

Daniels's film but disagreed with his description of what it accomplishes. According to Joseph, *The Butler* "details a sort of counter-narrative of the civil rights era." While he accurately pointed out that the "movie's depiction of the Black Panthers falls largely flat," he maintains that its rendition of key episodes of the civil rights movement "are pitch perfect." He especially appreciated Daniels's representation of black activism, Jim Crow era violence, and "key moments" and icons of the civil rights era. *"The Butler* provides the most nuanced depiction of black life during the civil rights movement," Joseph concluded.[46]

Hailing Daniels's film the most innovative and sophisticated Hollywood account of the civil rights era is not necessarily a tendentious appraisal. In other words, prior to *The Butler*, major Hollywood films on the civil rights era were by and large flawed, often relegating black characters to the background while elevating white deliverers. Despite Daniels's explicit intention to not make the civil rights movement the "focal point," *The Butler* is as much about Cecil's life and his relationship with his wife Gloria (played by Oprah Winfrey) and two sons as it is about the civil rights movement. Daniels's film can be tellingly used as a point of departure for discussing black life during the civil rights era.

The Butler effectively uncloaks dimensions of black life during the civil rights movement. Many turning points and important topics of this era receive more than simply token nods, including the lynching of Emmett Till, Little Rock, the student led sit-ins and Freedom Rides, the debates between Malcolm X and Martin Luther King Jr., the Civil Rights and Voting Rights Acts, "Bloody Selma," the assassination of John F. Kennedy, black participation in the Vietnam War, and the assassination of King and the ensuing riots. (Interestingly, Daniels does not specifically acknowledge the assassination of Malcolm X.) *The Butler* also sheds light on the experiences of African Americans before and after this crucial period. Narrated by Cecil Gaines (played by Academy Award-winning actor Forest Whitaker), the film begins on a cotton plantation in Macon, Georgia, in the mid-1920s when Gaines, the son of sharecroppers, is about seven years old. Life for the Gaines family and the other workers eerily resembles slavery. Later in the film, an elderly Cecil visited the cotton plantation with Gloria and commented: "We hear about the concentration camps, but these camps went on for twenty years right here, in America."[47]

In a gut-wrenching scene, Cecil's mother, Hattie Pearl, is pulled from the cotton fields where she is laboring side-by-side with her family and is raped by the plantation owner, Thomas Westfall. Although we do not see the assault, we hear her screaming in the background. Earl Gaines, Cecil's father, is defenseless during the attack and warns Cecil not to do anything. "Don't lose your temper with that man," he tells his son, "This is his world." After Westfall emerges from

---

46   Peniel E. Joseph, "A Civil Rights Professor Reviews *Lee Daniels' The Butler*," indiewire.com, September 16, 2013 .
47   Lee Daniels, dir., *The Butler*.

the building where he raped Cecil's mother, an angry Cecil asks his father, "'Pa . . . What you goin' to do?" Earl then tells Westfall, "Don't you ever do that to my wife."[48] Almost immediately, Westfall shoots Earl point blank in the forehead. Not only does this early scene foreshadow more violence to come and highlight the traumatizing effects of the sexual exploitation faced by black women in the Jim Crow South, but it also reveals how meaningless black life was in the eyes of the white South. We can assume that like countless white southerners who lynched and murdered black men during the era of Jim Crow segregation, Westfall was not punished for his actions. Westfall's grandmother feels pity for Cecil and teaches him how to be a top-grade domestic servant, "a house nigger," in her words.

In his later teens in 1933, Cecil leaves the Westfall plantation on foot in search of a new life. Like McQueen's Solomon Northrup but under much different circumstances, while Cecil is walking through a southern town on a rainy night he stumbles upon two black men hanging from a light pole. The brief image resembles postcards that can be found in the shocking book *Without Sanctuary: Lynching Photography in America* (2000).[49]

"Any white man could kill any of us at any time and not be punished for it," an elderly Cecil narrates, "The law wasn't on our side. The law was against us." Cecil's life takes a turn for the better when he meets a black man in his fifties named Maynard, a butler who works in a hotel in North Carolina that Cecil broke into for food. Maynard feels pity for Cecil and takes him under his wing, teaching his young disciple the ins and outs of being an exemplary butler. Maynard then recommends Cecil for a job that he was offered at the Excelsior Hotel in Washington, DC. Cecil is initially nervous about the opportunity of working with "high falootin' white people." Invoking Paul Laurence Dunbar's famous 1896 poem "We Wear the Mask" and echoing what Cecil's father told him when his mother was being summoned by the sadistic Westfall, Maynard counsels him: "Cecil, we got two faces. Ours, and the one we got to show white folks. Now to get up in the world, we have to make them feel unthreatened."[50]

While working diligently at the ritzy Excelsior Hotel, Cecil impressed the supervisor of the White House butlers and in 1957 he is offered a job as a butler in the Oval Office. He accepts the position and holds it until he retires during the Reagan administration. Cecil serves all of the presidents from Eisenhower through Reagan, and Daniels centers his daily work life around the struggle for African Americans' civil and human rights. Daniels's portrayal of US presidents' attitudes toward civil rights and black people is refreshingly critical. While he celebrates Eisenhower and Kennedy through Cecil's staunch admiration of them, he breezes over Carter's presidency but exposes the racist sentiments of

---

48   Ibid.
49   James Allen and John Lewis, *Without Sanctuary: Lynching Photography in America*, Sante Fe, NM: Twin Palms, 2000.
50   Daniels, dir., *The Butler*.

Lyndon B. Johnson, Nixon, and Reagan. Johnson, especially, is portrayed as a southern-bred, at times comical and simple-minded, racist who signs off on civil rights legislation because of the external pressures he faced. It is a bit curious that Daniels's depiction of Johnson did not elicit the same criticism that Ava DuVernay's did in *Selma*.

In the remainder of *The Butler*, spanning from 1957 until the election of Obama in 2008, Cecil's son Louis becomes a leading character who embodies the black freedom struggle. He develops into a "Superman" of civil rights activism who seems to be at many major events in the movement. It becomes crystal clear that because they came of age at different stages within the black experience and had totally different upbringings, they find it onerous to understand each other.

The friction between Cecil and Louis poignantly typifies the disagreements between different generations of African Americans who in their own distinct ways were seeking to survive and contribute to black liberation. While Cecil cannot understand his son's evolving militancy, Louis cannot come to grips with his father being a butler, despite his mother's pledge that his father's sacrifices paved the way for his success and a moving mini-lecture he received from Martin Luther King Jr. about the historical importance of black domestic servants to the black community. As a high school student, Louis begins developing a sense of black consciousness that is at odds with that of his father, who did not have the privilege of attending high school. In one instance, we see Louis attempting to shield a flyer from his father's purview that reads: MAMIE TILL, MOTHER OF EMMETT TILL, SPEAKS OUT. Upon noticing this, Cecil orders his disgruntled son not to attend the rally.

While at Fisk University, Louis is free from his domineering father's reign; he able to pursue a life as an activist. He meets civil rights activist James Lawson, a leading mentor to the Nashville Student Movement and the Student Nonviolent Coordinating Committee. Louis joins the Nashville Student Movement and participates in the sit-in movement. Daniels does a superb job of recreating the training that these activists underwent and the violent white resistance that they encountered while sitting at a "white only" Woolworth's lunch counter. As he does throughout the film when depicting the civil rights struggle, Daniels includes actual footage from the times. Cecil learns about his son's activism while watching him being arrested on national television. In 1961, Louis is one of the Freedom Riders who was on the bus that on May 14 was attacked by the Ku Klux Klan in Anniston, Alabama. Daniels juxtaposes the attack with a famous image of the actual Greyhound bus that was fire bombed.

Louis becomes a hardcore activist, telling his mother after he served three months in jail in Mississippi and she had warned him about the consequences of his activism, "Ma, then they just gonna have to kill me."[51] Apparently

---

51   Ibid.

recognized for his steadfast commitment to the civil rights movement, Louis joins Martin Luther King Jr.'s inner circle: he marches in Birmingham, where he and other protesters are sprayed with water hoses and attacked by police dogs and Bull Connor's men, he marches in Selma, and he is in the Lorraine Motel with King on the day that he is assassinated.

With Louis, Daniels captures the shift in many young blacks' thinking when the cry "Black Power" gained commercial popularity in 1966. Following King's death, Louis drifts away from the philosophy of nonviolent direct action and joins the Black Panther Party for a brief stint, abandoning them because he is at odds with Eldridge Cleaver's rhetoric of armed self-defense and an eye-for-an-eye mentality. Louis goes on to earn a MA degree in political science and in the 1980s becomes a congressman who is concerned with the plight of black and Latino people and who joins the anti-apartheid movement. In 1986, Cecil has a major change of heart, an epiphany. While sifting through boxes of Louis's keepsakes, it seems that he suddenly becomes cognizant of the sacrifices that his son made over the years for the black freedom struggle. Cecil decides to join Louis at a protest outside of the South African Embassy and both are arrested. This moment represents the meeting of the different generations.

The film ends with the 2008 election of Obama to the amazement of Cecil and Louis. Cecil's wife Gloria did not live to witness this historic moment, but Cecil relished in it for both of them. When African Americans born in the decades before *Brown v. Board of Education* like Congressman John Lewis and Reverend Jesse Jackson Sr. shed tears when Obama was elected president, many younger African Americans could not quite understand or appreciate their elders' joyfulness and wonderment. After seeing *The Butler*, Cecil's and his generation's exuberance is completely understandable.

Released in time for the festivities that accompanied the fiftieth anniversary of the Voting Rights Act, Ava DuVernay's *Selma* did not come close to shattering any records at the box offices, but it was widely praised.[52] On rottentomatoes.com, the film received 99 percent on the Tomatometer. President Obama screened the film in the White House in January 2015. In 2015, DuVernay also made history by becoming the first black woman to be nominated for best director in the history of the Golden Globes and to have a movie nominated for best film by the Academy Awards. Like countless other films based upon actual historical events and icons, *Selma* was also the subject of some frenzied controversy. She was accused of falsifying the historical record mainly based upon her portrayal of Lyndon B. Johnson.

Director of the Lyndon Baines Johnson Library and Museum Mark K. Updegrove kicked off the waves of criticism of *Selma* on December 22, 2014, when he argued that the film skewed the relationship between Johnson and

---

52   Ava DuVernay, dir., *Selma*, with David Oyelowo, Tom Wilkinson, Carmen Ejogo, Giovanni Ribisi, and Tim Roth, Hollywood, CA: Paramount Pictures, 2014, film.

Martin Luther King Jr. and characterized Johnson in a manner that "flies in the face of history."[53] Joseph A. Califano Jr., Johnson's top assistant for domestic affairs from 1965 until 1969, agreed with Updegrove, maintaining that DuVernay grossly misinterpreted Johnson's stance toward civil rights and his relationship with King. He was baffled as to why DuVernay supposedly did not consult the wealth of primary sources on Johnson and King. "The film falsely portrays President Lyndon B. Johnson as being at odds with Martin Luther King, Jr.," Califano avowed.

> Contrary to the portrait painted by *Selma*, Lyndon Johnson and Martin Luther King Jr. were partners in this effort. Johnson was enthusiastic about voting rights and the president urged King to find a place like Selma and lead a major presentation.[54]

Soon, other social commentators and scholars echoed Updegrove and Califano's concerns, including Diane McWhorter, David J. Garrow, Richard Cohen, Elizabeth Drew, and Maureen Dowd.

In the heat of the moment, DuVernay's immediate response to her haters most likely ruminated with other filmmakers who have directed historical dramas. "I'm not a historian. I'm a storyteller," this self-proclaimed "Spike Lee devotee" said. In tweets and interviews, she stood firmly by her right to portray Johnson in the manner that she did and thought it "unfortunate" that her film was reduced to "one talking point" by a small group LBJ loyalists. In early January 2015, she also offered her view of thinking historically: "I think that everyone sees history through their own lens . . . This is what I see, this is what we see. I'm not gonna argue history. I could, but I won't."[55] In a later interview in the *New York Times Magazine*, she summarized her thoughts about her critics. "Nobody was thinking about Lyndon Johnson," DuVernay said:

> We were showing King, living and breathing, having an ego, smoking. And so I didn't think twice about L.B.J., because as far as I'm concerned what I portrayed is what I feel about L.B.J. Yes, he was a hero, but he was a reluctant hero.[56]

DuVernay, in essence, maintained that, as a filmmaker, she has the right to interpret the past in the manner that she sees fit. Though Julian Bond was not convinced that *Selma*, or any film for that matter, adequately dramatized the

---

53   Mark K. Updegrove, "What *Selma* Gets Wrong: LBJ and MLK Were Close Partners in Reform," *POLITICO Magazine*, December 22, 2014.

54   Joseph A. Califano Jr., "The Movie Selma Has a Glaring Flaw," *Washington Post*, December 26, 2014.

55   Taylor Lewis, "Ava DuVernay Responds to 'Selma' Critics," essence.com, January 7, 2015.

56   A. O. Scott, "Ava DuVernay Didn't See the Reaction to 'Selma' Coming," *New York Times Magazine*, February 22, 2015, MM218.

civil rights movement, "living history" Congressman John Lewis and Andrew Young Jr., both of whom knew King well, for the most part backed DuVernay's rendition of what transpired in Selma.

Several hip-hop generation historians defended their contemporary. For Peniel Joseph, *Selma's* portrayal of the relationship between Johnson and King and civil rights "hews close to the historical record." He added that "the events depicted in Selma were driven largely by African American activists portrayed in the film" and suggested that DuVernay received so much criticism from Johnson supporters and the mainstream media because she did not buy into the ever so familiar Hollywood white man savior trope.[57] Historian Crystal Feimster agreed with Joseph. "For DuVernay, the central driving force of the narrative was about black people, and that's an important narrative to tell," she observed.[58] "The real problem many critics have with this film is that it's too black and too strong," Joseph surmised, "the beating heart of this film rests not with its portrait of LBJ, or even King, but with the larger truth that the civil rights movement's heroic period reflected our collective strengths and weaknesses as a nation, something Americans are loath to recognize let alone acknowledge."[59]

Scholar Brittney Cooper viewed *Selma* as being a "magnificent and powerful film" that was undeservedly attacked by Johnson apologists. For Cooper, *Selma* "displaces a white gaze" and provides its viewers, especially black youth, with an "affective" portrayal and interpretation of a pivotal moment in the civil rights movement. Cooper asked that people "trust" and allow a black woman like DuVernay to offer us a deeper history of the Selma to Montgomery marches, one that sheds light on the experiences of often marginalized black women. In Cooper's estimation, *Selma* "is the unique result of what black feminist scholars call the 'visionary pragmatism of black women filmmakers.'" She does not believe that filmmakers like DuVernay are bound to tell *the* "truth" or to adhere strictly to the "facts," both of which, she rightly points out, are determined by those in positions of power. She calls upon those who view the film to focus on what we can learn about the habitual struggles of African Americans during the civil rights movement.[60]

Not all African American scholars were as enthusiastic about *Selma* as public intellectuals Joseph or Cooper. For instance, political scientist and iconoclast Adolph Reed Jr., who came of age several decades before Joseph and Cooper, situates *Selma* within a genre of historical dramas that "treat the past like a props closet, a source of images that facilitate naturalizing presentist sensibilities by dressing them up in the garb of bygone days." Reed challenges DuVernay's argument that she did not want to promote the white-savior

57   Peniel Joseph, "Selma Backlash Misses the Point," npr.org, January 10, 2015.
58   Judt, "Feeling Versus Fact."
59   Joseph, "Selma Backlash Misses the Point."
60   Brittney Cooper, "Maureen Dowd's Clueless White Gaze: What's Really Behind the *Selma* Backlash," salon.com, January 21, 2015.

storyline by claiming that she replaced this with "another iteration of King idolatry" and venerations of "the black (haute) bourgeoisie." DuVernay's film, in his estimation, does not adequately contextualize how the campaigns in Selma contributed to blacks' struggle for voting rights or its relationship to "contemporary problems bearing on race and inequality."[61] *Selma* does not, for Reed, "lay out an historically richer and thicker account of the struggle for voting rights enforcement and the impact of the [Voting Rights Act] on the South," something that he overviews in the bulk of his lengthy commentary.[62]

Former editor and columnist for *USA Today* Barbara Reynolds disagreed with Cooper's feminist reading of *Selma*. Reynolds contended that DuVernay portrays Coretta Scott King as a "tormented victim" and "an accessory to her iconic husband's story." Reynolds, who knew Coretta Scott King for thirty years, would have appreciated a depiction of her friend as the "strong-willed woman" that she maintains she was. She took issue with the notable scene in which Coretta Scott King, with tears in her eyes, asks her husband in a telephone conversation, "Did you love the others?" Reynolds claims that "this is not something that Coretta would have said." According to this self-proclaimed expert on Mrs. King, she was hip to the FBI's well-orchestrated attacks on her husband that included the spreading of rumors that he was an adulterer. Reynolds also conjectures that Mrs. King never received a tape recording from the FBI containing "sexual sounds that were meant to incriminate Martin." Based upon her belief that "historic truths" exist, Reynolds believes that filmmakers should respect "the truth" and not "fictionalize our heroes."[63]

A hip-hop generation historian of the black past with some "old school" tendencies, I believe that the directors of historical dramas like *Selma*—especially those that posture as history or are based upon actual events—should ideally seek to present fact-based renditions of the past. At the same time, I understand Hollywood and do not have a problem with filmmakers, like some of the most preeminent historians, using their imaginations when reconstructing the past. History is indeed fluid. History is interpretation. Much like novels, films can be judiciously used as portholes into what might have been said and done.

Like *42*, *Race*, and *Detroit*, *Selma* covers a brief period of time. The film begins in 1964 when King accepted the Nobel Peace Prize in Oslo, Norway, on December 10 and ends on March 25, 1965, when he delivered his speech "How Long, Not Long" at the Alabama State Capitol. *Selma* does not come close to being a biopic. In fact, in order to appreciate King's role in the Selma campaign, viewers would have to know something about King's life, especially the years

61   Adoph Reed Jr., "The Real Problem with *Selma*," nonsite.org, January 26, 2105.
62   Adolph Reed Jr., "The Strange Career of the Voting Rights Act: Selma in Fact and Fiction," newlaborforum.cuny.edu, June 1, 2015 .
63   Barbara Reynolds, "The Biggest Problem with 'Selma' Has Nothing to Do with LBJ or the Oscars," *Washington Post*, January 19, 2015.

between the Montgomery Bus Boycott and the March on Washington. After all, these experiences, as well as his early years, molded him into the leader that he became by 1965. Before focusing on King and the Selma to Montgomery marches, DuVernay contextualizes the state of race relations in the South with a few moving examples.

Approximately five minutes into the film while King delivers his moving acceptance speech, in which he symbolically bestows the Nobel Peace Prize to the civil rights movement, we are bombarded with DuVernay's graphic recreation of the bombing of the 16th Street Baptist Church on September 15, 1963, that took the lives of four young girls. It is a haunting set of images; the youthful victims' lifeless bodies are floating around in slow motion among the rubble. Those unaware of this terrorist act would not have been able to identify it, unless they paid close attention to a later conversation with King and Johnson. Nonetheless, viewers were exposed to the prevalent anti-black violence that took the lives of many blacks in the South. In another early scene, we see civil rights activist Annie Lee Cooper attempting to vote in Selma. Having previously failed the tests in the eyes of the city's white officials, Cooper is prepared this time. Her written responses are on point, so the examiner asks her to recite the preamble to the US Constitution, which she does perfectly. She is then asked to name all of the county judges in Alabama, which she cannot do, so she is denied her constitutional right to vote.

Unfortunately, much of the discussions about *Selma* have revolved around certain critics' preoccupation with how DuVernay portrays the interactions between King and Johnson, so much so that it is easy to underappreciate the strengths of the film. Given the fact that she was unable to use King's speeches, DuVernay adroitly creates dialogues for her version of King, played by David Oyelowo who not only looks like King, but also embodied his spirit. DuVernay's King is not the prototypical, sanitized "I Have a Dream" or "turn the other cheek" incarnation. From the get-go, her King speaks out against the brutalization of black people. "There has been thousands of racially motivated murders in the South, including the four little girls," King tells Johnson, and "not one of these criminals who murders us when and why they want has ever been convicted." Later in a stirring speech in a Selma church, King proclaims: "We're not asking. We're demanding. Give us the vote!"[64]

There are plenty of historically authentic teachable moments in *Selma*. Among others, DuVernay's characters dramatize the violence that King, at a personal level, and blacks in Selma faced and endured. King is assaulted in a Selma hotel by a random white man who pretends to be an admirer and he receives numerous telephone death threats. The scene in which marchers are attacked, especially while attempting to cross the Edmund Pettus Bridge, lasts for about four minutes, showing in slow motion the indiscriminate nature of

---

64   Ava DuVernay, dir., *Selma*.

the beatings at the hands of the police. Women and the elderly were assaulted the same as grown men were. DuVernay recreates the shooting of determined activist Jimmie Lee Jackson on February 18, 1965, that resulted in his death roughly a week later. Viewers are exposed to FBI Director J. Edgar Hoover's well-known targeting of King and his Southern Christian Leadership Conference (SCLC) co-workers, the debates between SCLC and Student Nonviolent Coordinating Committee (SNCC) as well as the internal conflicts that troubled the latter, the tensions between King and Malcolm X, the decisive role television and print-media coverage played during the civil rights movement, and the debates between advocates of nonviolent direct action and armed self-defense.

In Brian Helgeland's *42* and Stephan Hopkins's *Race*, we do not get introduced to what Jackie Robinson and Jesse Owens, respectively, might have been thinking during their struggles. In *Selma*, DuVernay assiduously probes into King's mind and psyche. He exchanges intimate thoughts with Coretta Scott King that reveal his vulnerabilities, he jokes with his SCLC colleagues, he demonstrates to younger SNCC leaders James Forman and John Lewis that while he may not agree with them, he understands and respects their grassroots approaches and strategies, he stresses out while imprisoned, he questions the validity of his nonviolent movement in the aftermath of violent white retaliation, and he seeks spiritual support from friends like Mahalia Jackson. In sum, DuVernay directed a film in which we really get to know a version of King the man. While her interpretation of this icon can certainly be debated, she successfully transcends the conventional renderings of this icon, in turn creating a complex King that historians themselves have striven to reconstruct.

CELEBRATING BLACK ATHLETIC PROWESS

Early in my teaching career (before the full-scale Internet revolution), I routinely required students in my survey course on African American history since 1876 to submit an elaborate annotated bibliography project on practically any topic of their choice relevant to the course material. I encouraged students to think creatively and critically in selecting a topic. "Research something that you are passionate about or interested in," I routinely responded to students who asked me to help them identify topics. Many students developed intriguing and original projects. There were others, however, who submitted generic papers on the Negro Leagues and popular sports icons like Muhammad Ali, Michael Jordan, and especially on Jackie Robinson. In gravitating toward Robinson, they were probably drawn to the familiar. Most likely in their high school history and social studies courses, they learned that in 1947 Robinson became the first African American in the "modern era" to play major league baseball, that he, in essence, integrated the MLB or "broke the baseball color line."

Robinson is one of the most revered African American athletes. In 1950, he even starred in *The Jackie Robinson Story*, a largely successful seventy-seven-minute film that chronicles Robinson's illustrious baseball career. A year after the MLB inaugurated "Jackie Robinson Day" in honor of his monumental accomplishments, in 2005 20th Century Fox and Legend Films brought out a colorized edition of *The Jackie Robinson Story*. US popular culture continues to memorialize Robinson. In 2013, screenwriter and director Brian Helgeland, whose most successful films include *L.A. Confidential* (1997) and *Mystic River* (2003), released *42*, a biopic on Robinson that zooms in on his first year with the Brooklyn Dodgers. Several years later, Ken Burns, Sarah Burns, and David McMahon released a four-hour documentary in two parts on Robinson. Unlike *42*, *Jackie Robinson* (PBS, 2016) is detailed and comprehensive, covering his entire life and exploring his often oversimplified life after he retired from major league baseball in 1956. To be fair, *42* could not have done what the long-drawn-out documentary did.

Robinson's widow, Rachel Robinson, served as a consultant for *42*, which received her stamp of approval. "I love the movie," she said, "I'm pleased with it. It's authentic and it's also very powerful."[65] Like many biopics, *42* was advertised as being "based upon a true story."[66] As could be predicted, there are more than a few historical inaccuracies in *42*. The slight errors, however, are not as problematic as other dimensions of the film. The film should be used cautiously as a starting point for conversations about Robinson's life and broader trends in the history of US race relations during the period immediately after World War II.

Narrated by Andre Holland (who played the *Pittsburgh Courier* sports-writer Wendell Smith, who traveled with Robinson in 1946 and 1947 and recommended Robison to Branch Rickey), *42* opens with original footage depicting African Americans' contributions of World War II. "African Americans had served this country gallantly," Smith noted, "They returned home from fighting to free the world from tyranny only to find racism, segregation and Jim Crow laws still waiting at home. Segregation was the law and no group was more scrupulous in its observance of custom than organized baseball." This is the only historical context that the viewer is provided with regarding this pivotal period in US history. Without offering any scenes from Robinson's early years, the film then picks up with Branch Rickey discussing his legendary "plan," his quest to find an ideal "Negro ballplayer" who could play for the Brooklyn Dodgers. "New York is full of Negro baseball fans; every dollar is green," Rickey, played by Harrison Ford, retorted and prophesized. "I don't know who he is, or where he is, but he's coming."[67]

---

65   Rahshaun Haylock, "Rachel Robinson Reflects on Role in Making *42*," foxsports.com, August 15, 2013 .

66   Brian Helgeland, dir., *42*, with Chadwick Boseman, Harrison Ford, Nicole Beharie, and Andre Holland, Burbank, CA: Warner Bros. Pictures, 2013, film.

67   Ibid.

From this moment, *42* becomes a film that is as much about Robinson's first years with the Dodgers as it is about Rickey's altruistic mission. The nonconforming general manager is portrayed as being a pragmatist, but also as a civil rights-minded white savior of some sort.

Viewers are definitely exposed to how Robinson struggled on a daily basis to remain calm and cerebral in the midst of heightened, fanatical racism. But we learn very little about Robinson the person. Though the concept of "black love" manifested in the heartfelt relationship between Robinson and his wife Rachel ("Rae") is effectively depicted, we do not see Robinson interacting with his family or the black community at large that revered him so dearly.

One of Robinson's main roles in *42* is that of a whipping post for white racism. We are inundated with scenes revealing the extent of Jim Crow segregation and visceral white racism. Jackie and Rachel had to live with a black family during training camp in Florida with the Montreal Royals (the top farm club of the Dodgers in the International League) and they were eventually run out of town in the middle of the night by white racists who oppose the integration of the MLB. In another scene, a bigoted police officer in DeLand, Florida, interrupts a Royals's game, demanding that Robinson leave the field. Throughout the film, Robinson is belittled by fans and members of opposing teams. Pitchers throw at his head and we see how in August 1947 a St. Louis, Cardinals player slid into him at first base with his spikes in the air and cut Robinson's thigh. Such incidents really happened.

The most blatant racism that Robinson faced in the film was when Philadelphia Phillies manager Ben Chapman called him all types of racist epithets—from the n-word to "porch monkey" to Bojangles to shoe shine to spade—while the stoic Robinson was at bat. This episode, dubbed by one sports journalist "one of the most intense scenes in the film," was also accurate. In a 2013 interview, Chapman did not hesitate to admit that he berated Robinson in this way. "Sure I did. Everyone used those kind of words back then," he nonchalantly avowed.[68] Another scene that exemplified the type of abuse that Robinson faced occurred when his teammate Pee Wee Reese received a piece of hate mail and shared it with Rickey. Unmoved, the fearless Dodgers manager showed his concerned shortstop folders of death threats that were sent to Robinson since he started playing with the Dodgers. At least one of the letters that was zoomed in on was a replica of a famous death threat that Robinson received.

A prevailing theme that received equal attention to white racism in *42* is interracial cooperation and whites' changing racial attitudes. While it is evident in the film that Rickey was driven by his desire to win and make money, he is ultimately portrayed as being an outspoken advocate for African American civil rights. In one instance, he chastises the coach of the Montreal Royals, Clay

---

68   Allen Barra, "What Really Happened Ben Chapman, the Racist Baseball Player in 42?" *The Atlantic*, April 15, 2013.

Hopper, for his racist remarks. "Clay, I realize that attitude is part of your heritage; that you practically nursed race prejudice at your mother's breast, so I will let it pass." Rickey rejoined in defense of his black virtuoso Robinson, "But I will add this: you can manage Robinson fairly and correctly or you can be unemployed." In another instance, Rickey goes after Phillies general manager Herb Pennock when he told him not to bring "that nigger" to play against the Phillies in Philadelphia. Once again, Rickey responded as an activist would have. "It means you're going to meet God one day, Herb, and when he inquires why Robinson wasn't on the field in Philadelphia and you answer because he was a Negro, it may not be a sufficient reply."[69] In this case, Rickey drew upon a biblical interpretation of black equality. Rickey is also depicted as being a fatherlike figure to Robinson. While watching Helgeland's film, one might wonder: What was the nature of Robinson's relationships with his parents?

In one of the most famous scenes in the film that was featured in trailers, during their first meeting Rickey tutors Robinson on how to interact with a hostile white America. Foreshadowing Martin Luther King Jr., Rickey shouted at Robinson: "I want one who has the guts not to fight back! . . . Your enemy will be out in force, but you cannot meet him on his own low ground . . . Like our Savior, you must have the guts to turn the other cheek." Later in the film, after popping up in a game against the Phillies during which Chapman was verbally abusing Robinson, Rickey consoles him in private, instructing him on how to deal with white racism. "You're in this thing," Rickey tells him, "You don't have the right to pull out from the backing of people who believe in you, respect you and who need you."[70]

As is the case in other films about African Americans integrating sports teams like Disney's popular *Remember the Titans* (2000), many of Robinson's white teammates are portrayed becoming sensitive to the racism endured by black Americans because of their interactions with him.

Resistance from black characters in the film is understated. Robinson's most effective rebuttals to racism are revealed through his breathtaking baseball skills and his private conversations with his wife and Rickey. Rachel is on the one hand Jackie's helpmate, yet she is also given some agency. In one scene when she and her husband are in an airport in New Orleans, she deliberately crosses the color line by using the "white only" restroom.

Making roughly a quarter of what *42* did at the box offices, Stephen Hopkins's *Race*, a biopic on Jesse Owens, is similar to *42*.[71] Like *42*, *Race* was advertised as being based upon a true story. Just as Rachel Robinson served as a chief consultant for *42*, the Owens family, the Jesse Owens Foundation, and the Jesse Owens Trust sanctioned *Race*. Owens's daughters had full script approval.

---

69   Helgeland, dir., *42*.

70   Ibid.

71   Stephen Hopkins, dir., *Race*, with Stephan James, Jason Sudeikis, Jeremy Irons, Carice van Houten, and William Hurt, Toronto, Canada: Forecast Pictures, 2016, film.

One of his daughters said: "We're so happy it's truthful. It is his life at that time. Because it's truthful there should be no doubt in anybody's mind."[72]

As Helgeland did with Robinson, Hopkins focuses on several critical years and episodes in Owens's miraculous career. Moreover, *42* and *Race* give equal treatment to valiant white male gurus—Branch Rickey and Larry Snyder, respectively—as they accord to their black protagonists. Unfortunately, both directors fail to probe into the minds of these icons, both of whom were intellectuals in their own right. We witness their athletic prowess and the obstacles that they faced and overcame but learn little about their deeper thoughts and beliefs.

Race begins in Cleveland, Ohio, in the fall of 1933, on the eve of Owens's departure for Ohio State University (OSU) to run track. Before leaving, Owens spends time with his family. His mother and father are clearly sources of inspiration and support. As it is the case in *42* with Jackie and Rachel, in *Race*, we are exposed to "black love" through Jesse and Minnie Ruth Solomon, who he marries in 1935. When he left for OSU, they had a daughter, Gloria, who was born in 1932. In the film, Owens had a brief affair with a woman he met in a speakeasy, but eventually he reconciled with Ruth. The film reveals how segregation and racial prejudice existed in Ohio: he sits in the "colored only" section in the bus en route from Cleveland to Columbus, he receives disbelieving glares from whites on OSU's campus, he lives off campus in the segregated black community, and members of the OSU football team hurl racial epithets at him in the locker room. The most preposterous, yet real, example of segregation occurs at the end of the film when Owens was not allowed to enter the main doors of the Waldorf Astoria in New York City for a reception honoring his accomplishments at the 1936 Summer Olympics.

Just as *42* features Rickey as much as Robinson, *Race* puts a spotlight on the longtime OSU track and field coach Larry Snyder. He is portrayed as being a moderate advocate of African American civil rights and a racial progressive. When they first meet, Snyder is like a drill sergeant who cares little for his new recruit. "You belong to me," he shouts at Owens as if he was a slave. Like Rickey schooling Robinson about how to deal with racism in *42*, in one scene Snyder instructs Owens on how to overcome racist verbal attacks. "You can't get distracted," he advises Owens. "You gotta learn to block it all out."[73]

Later in the film, when Owens is training with the US Olympic team in Germany, a coach calls him "boy" and Owens lashed back. When the coach demands that Owens be forced to apologize to him, Synder steps in and defends Owens. Hopkins gives the impression that Owens was motivated to win four gold medals for Snyder, who was unable to do this during his own career. In a sense, Owens becomes an extension of Snyder. The coach becomes a surrogate

---

72 Christian Red, "Jesse Owens Biopic Race True-to-Life Say Daughters of Track Legend," nydailynews.com, February 19, 2016.

73 Stephen Hopkins, dir., *Race*.

father figure to Owens, who is seeking to live through his child. At the end of the film, Snyder performs his final act of racial benevolence on behalf of the helpless Owens. When Owens is forced to enter the backdoor at the Waldorf Astoria for an event in his honor, Synder goes off on the doorman, calling the policy "bullshit" in the presence of onlookers. Owens, on the other hand, does nothing and walks to the back door of the hotel with his head down.

What are the viable teachable moments in *Race*? For viewers who know nothing about Owens, the film does an excellent job of recreating his remarkable performance at the 1935 Big Ten track and field finals (where he set three world records) and his more widely known phenomenal victories at the 1936 Summer Olympics. The film also offers food for thought for rethinking Leni Riefenstahl's film *Olympia* and the role that US Olympic Committee President Avery Brundage played in supporting the games in Nazi Germany.

A scene in which a representative of the NAACP visits Owens and encourages him to boycott the Olympics because of the mistreatment of African Americans had great potential. This debate within the black community could have been further unpacked. As it is often the case with biopics of this nature, *Race* ends in a cliché way: viewers are provided a list of brief historical facts and original images of Owens.

CONCLUSION

More than seventy years ago, historian, educational theorist, and longtime curator at the Schomburg Center for Research in Black Culture L. D. Reddick surveyed how blacks were represented in American films. "Movie houses," as opposed to schools and colleges, he argued, were among the most influential "educative" forces "on the public mind." Reddick surveyed one hundred "important" films that consisted of "Negro themes and Negro characters." Though he identified noticeable shifts in how African Americans were depicted in films after *Gone With The Wind*, he concluded that African Americans were usually misrepresented and that three-quarters of the films were "anti-Negro" in orientation. His remedies were straightforward: the production of Hollywood films that more accurately portrayed black life and the further development of the black filmmaking industry beyond Oscar Micheaux's pictures. Reddick also suggested specific steps for policing and transforming mainstream Hollywood. Among his recommendations, which included boycotting "anti-Negro films," he urged the creation of "local committees for cultural democracy" that would be in charge of helping to monitor the portrayal of blacks in mainstream films. He hoped that scholarship could shape the cinematic images of African Americans. "Such committees should undertake sufficient research to document, chapter and verse, the generalization that the Negro is inaccurately and unfairly presented on screen," Reddick outlined, "The widest dissemination ought to be given to this information so that the movie-going public, movie critics, actors, screen writers and producers will be aware of these facts."[74]

Much progress has been made in Hollywood since Reddick conducted his study. Be that as it may, we can still learn from his observations.

Hollywood film directors will continue to produce films on events and personalities from the African American past for profit and in some cases to encourage moviegoers to rethink history in worthwhile ways. Scholars, film critics, bloggers, and especially historians will continue to debate the merits of such historical dramatizations. Those who teach American and African American history must be aware of how the US motion picture industry interprets the past because, after all, many of their students will shape what they think they know about the past based upon these portrayals.

In 1987, comedian, actor, and director Robert Townsend released his film *Hollywood Shuffle*, a creative and persuasive satire that pointed out the stereotypical roles that African American actors were relegated to in the US television and film industry. In one memorable scene, Townsend (playing the main character Bobby Taylor, an aspiring black actor) daydreams while waiting for an audition. His daydream becomes a revealing skit, a five-minute commercial for "Hollywood's first Black Acting School" where students can learn to play slaves, cooks, servants, and rapists by taking classes like "Jive Talk 101," "Shuffling 200," and "Epic Slaves 400." At the dawning of the new millennium, Spike Lee released his satire *Bamboozled* in which money hungry producers successfully launch a fictional blackface television show, *Mantan: The New Millennium Minstrel Show*. Using satire, Townsend and Lee were criticizing the television and film industries for their contemporary portrayal of black people, highlighting that African Americans have routinely been forced to play roles that harken back to the days of slavery.

Black comedians have also critiqued representations of blacks in mainstream Hollywood films dealing with African American history. In the early to mid 1990s, Paul Mooney (who played an NAACP leader in Townsend's film who called upon black people to stop playing "Sambo" roles) and Martin Lawrence both lampooned how Morgan Freeman portrayed black men in Bruce Beresford's *Driving Miss Daisy* (1989). Several decades later during an interview with hip-hop radio personality Davey D, Mooney and Dick Gregory, who teamed up for "The Godfathers of Comedy" tour, ridiculed how African Americans were portrayed in *The Help* and *Red Tails*. In 2013 a skit called "Slave Fight" on Comedy Central's *Key & Peele*, Keegan-Michael Key and Jordan Peele played the roles of slaves who were required to fight to the death by their masters. Though they did not mention Tarantino or his film by name, Key and Peele parodied the controversial "Mandingo fighting" scene in *Django Unchained* by

---

74   L. D. Reddick, "Educational Programs for the Improvement of Race Relations: Motion Pictures, Radio, The Press, and Libraries," *Education for Racial Understanding*, Summer 1944, 367, 368, 369, 381, 382.

having their characters devise a plan to escape their predicament. More recently, Chris Rock (who detailed how Hollywood was a "white industry") argued that the recent films on African American historical subject matter, especially *12 Years a Slave*, challenged viewers to think critically about US history and race.

While some writers and directors like Tate Taylor and Quentin Tarantino have incorporated humor and even comedy into their recent black historical dramas, black comedians like Mooney and Rock have revisited episodes in African American history with humor being at the center of their interpretation. Like the directors of films on the black past, they interpret African American history creatively. Unlike their director counterparts, they have much more latitude in representing the black past. As comedians, they are not accused of misrepresenting what was actually said and done in the past, and they can always fall back on the argument that they were just making a joke, that they were being funny and should not be taken seriously.

The next chapter probes into such issues by unpacking how a diverse group of black comedians in the twenty-first century has used their craft to revisit key periods in African American history that filmmakers have been preoccupied with: namely slavery and the civil rights era.

4

"Everything Is Funny?"

Humor, Black History, and African American Comedians

"It has come to my attention that lyrics from my contribution to a fellow artist's song has deeply offended your family. As a father myself, I cannot imagine the pain that your family has had to endure," Dwayne Michael Carter Jr. (aka Lil Wayne) wrote in an open letter to the family of Emmett Till in early May 2013. "Moving forward, I will not use or reference Emmett Till or the Till family in my music, especially in an inappropriate manner." The Grammy-winning artist added: "I have tremendous respect for those who paved the way for the liberty and opportunities that African Americans currently enjoy." The talented Holly Grove, New Orleans emcee was apologizing for his offensive verse on the song "Karate Chop" on Future's album *Honest* that was leaked online months earlier. After spitting the lyrics "Beat that pussy up like Emmett Till" on this popular track, it sounds as if Young Weezy laughed in a self-congratulatory manner, as is often his custom after his tongue-in-cheek rhymes.

Was this master of metaphors actually attempting to be witty? Did he honestly think that African Americans without his warped sense of humor would not interpret these lyrics as being off-putting and disrespectful? We will probably never know exactly what Wayne was thinking when he came up with and decided to record this play on words. Perhaps it was his alien or Martian alter ego that was responsible. What is clear-cut is that the Till family (who did not accept his apology) and others in the black community found nothing humorous about his lyrics in "Karate Chop." As a result of the Till family's and others' outrage, the song was re-released without Wayne's verses and he lost his multi-million-dollar endorsement arrangement with Mountain Dew.[1]

Several months later, hip-hop mogul Russell Simmons—who praised Wayne a year earlier, commenting that "what Lil Wayne does speaks to the next generation"—also issued an apology for denigrating another perhaps more sacred African American historical icon. "In the whole history of Def Comedy Jam, I've never taken down a controversial comedian. When my buddies at the NAACP called and asked me to take down the Harriet Tubman video from the All Def Digital YouTube channel and apologize, I agreed," Simmons wrote in a

---

1 R. J. Cubarrubia, "Lil Wayne Apologizes for 'Inappropriate Emmett Till Lyric," *Rolling Stone*, May 1, 2013 ; Tanzina Vega, "Lil Wayne Puts Mountain Dew in Crisis Mode," *New York Times*, May 7, 2013, C1.

brief statement posted on globalgrind.com in August 2013.[2] The "Harriet Tubman Sex Tape," a three and a half minute YouTube video that he initially thought was "politically correct" and "the funniest thing" he had ever seen, graphically depicted a fictional Harriet Tubman conning a slave master into making a sex tape so that she could blackmail him into supporting her efforts to liberate slaves. Countless people tweeted and blogged their disapproval of Simmons's notion of humor at the expense of a revered abolitionist called "Moses" for helping many bondspersons escape the yoke of slavery through the heralded Underground Railroad.

In 2014, the interdisciplinary journal *Meridians: Feminism, Race, Transnationalism* published a special issue on Tubman in honor of the 100th anniversary of her death on March 13, 1913. Indeed, the volume was especially relevant in light of "the public discussions that erupted in response to this controversial video." The contributors to this volume hailed from the scholarly disciplines of English, history, African American Studies, and women's and gender studies and offered innovative ways to think about Tubman's life and legacy in the twenty-first century. Several brief essays in the second segment of this special issue, "Reclaiming and Defending a Legacy," collectively denounce Simmons's digital short, concluding that it was "disgusting," "highly offensive," and "harmful," trivialized rape, and belonged more to porn that it did to the genres of satire or parody. For these scholars, the "Harriet Tubman Sex Tape" was a "failed comedic video."[3] There were, however, various interpretations of what Simmons's jest signified. For instance, Treva B. Lindsey and Jessica Marie Johnson provide a detailed blow-by-blow synopsis of the YouTube clip and dubbed it a "bold but failed comedic venture" and a "failed mapping." Nonetheless, they also encouraged scholars to use it as a "point of departure for critical considerations of the complexities of the erotic life of enslaved blacks."[4] Janell Hobson, on the other hand, concluded: "In order for a satire or parody to work (whether it's funny or not), there has to be a kernel of truth to the punch line. This atrocious video bases its insults on historical lies."[5]

This would not be the last time that Tubman would be the subject of parody. On September 25, 2015, Comedy Central's *Drunk History* released "Harriet Tubman: Superspy" narrated by a tipsy Crissle West, a writer, comedian, and co-host of the podcast *The Read*. Though fantastical, West's representation of Tubman—convincingly played by Academy Award-winning

---

2   Russell Simmons, "I Get It And I Respect It . . . The Harriet Tubman Video Has Been Removed," globalgrind.com, August 15, 2013 .

3   Janell Hobson, "Harriet Tubman: A Legacy of Resistance," *Meridians* 12: 2, 2014, 2; Janell Hobson, "The Rape of Harriet Tubman," *Meridians* 12: 2, 2014, 162.

4   Treva B. Lindsey and Jessica Marie Johnson, "Searching for Climax: Black Erotic Lives in Slavery and Freedom, *Meridians* 12: 2, 2014, 171, 176, 182.

5   Janell Hobson, "The Rape of Harriet Tubman," *Meridians* 12: 2, 2014, 163.

actress Octavia Spencer—did not spark the controversy that Simmons's did.[6]

Coinciding with the beginning of Obama's second presidential term, Lil Wayne's and Russell Simmons's unsuccessful exercises of wittiness and cleverness can be situated within the larger context of how African Americans, especially professional comics and satirists in the late twentieth and twenty-first centuries, have used humor, jokes, parodies, and comedy to revisit and explain (*away* in some cases) slavery, Jim Crow segregation, racism, and past racial injustice and anti-black violence. This phenomenon is nothing new.

Since the antebellum era, African Americans have used humor as an empowering coping mechanism. As longtime comedian and civil rights activist Dick Gregory noted in 2002: "Comedy was the original form of entertainment that black families created in order to survive."[7] According to film and media studies scholar Bambi Haggins, black comedy, "in its literal and literary constitutions, has always overtly *and* covertly explored the trials, tribulations, and triumphs of African American communities."[8] Leading theorist of black humor and comedy Mel Watkins adds:

> And even when it acknowledges despair, black American humor transcends the present situation: it nimbly moves on to a vision of a brighter future or insistently counters the disparaging picture at hand with the image of an underdog (blacks themselves) with superior attributes. More subtly . . . by its expressive tone it may transform a negative situation or stereotype into a positive one by exposing its essentially ludicrous nature.[9]

The title of this chapter comes from a statement that a young Chris Rock made in a 1989 interview. Long before he became a famous comedian, Rock began telling jokes about controversial and taboo subjects, including racial inequality and the perpetual mistreatment of black people in the United States.

---

6   In "Harriet Tubman: Superspy," Crissle West creates a tale of how Tubman became a spy for the Union during the Civil War, led the Combahee River raid, and helped liberate many slaves. In the sketch, Tubman frequently curses and speaks in twenty-first-century African American English. "She helped the Union win the war. She freed like 1,000 slaves in her lifetime. She was just dope as hell." West completed her tale, "God, black people have been through so much shit." See "Harriet Tubman: Superspy," *Drunk History*, Comedy Central, Season 3, Episode 4, September 22, 2015. Unlike Simmons's video, West's piece did not denigrate Tubman. If anything, it hyperbolized her historical significance. This episode was praised by many online websites. The senior editor of *Huffington Post's* "Black Voices" said that the sketch was "hilarious" and "comedic perfection." Similarly, the online magazine for black women, *Clutch*, called West's and Spencer's sketch "awesome."

7   Dick Gregory, "Foreword," in *African American Humor: The Best Black Comedy from Slavery to Today,* ed. Mel Watkins, xi, Chicago: Lawrence Hill Books, 2002.

8   Bambi Haggins, *Laughing Mad: The Black Comic Persona in Post-Soul America*, New Jersey: Rutgers University Press, 2007, 2.

9   Mel Watkins, *On the Real Side: A History of African American Comedy*, Chicago: Lawrence Hill Books, 1999, 39.

By the early 1990s, he incorporated jokes revolving around black history into his stand-up specials. In defense of his style, in a revealing interview when he was merely twenty-three years old, he said: "You can't deny the truth of the statements," referring to his observations on contentious subject matters, including racism. "You know, you laugh and you think about it a little bit . . . *Everything is funny*."[10] Because I probe into varying comedic interpretations and commentaries on black history, I converted Rock's statement into a question for the title of this chapter. Rock certainly changed over the years. But, he, like other black comedians and satirists, has remained committed to an underlying belief that "everything is funny," or at a minimum, potentially funny, especially when dealing with African American history. Like Rock, many black comedians, before and after him, have skillfully incorporated clever, yet often inaccurate and over simplistic, discussions of slavery, racism, and past racial injustices in their stand-up performances. In particular, I consider how comedians Rock, Paul Mooney, Dave Chappelle, and Martin Lawrence; Comedy Central's *Key & Peele* hosts Keegan-Michael Key and Jordan Peele; creator of the *Boondocks* animated series Aaron McGruder; *Saturday Night Live* cast members, mainly Kenan Thompson and Leslie Jones; and other comics and satirists have parodied dimensions of black history.

Contributing to a rich history that Watkins, Haggins, and others have unraveled, many twenty-first century black comedians are highly skilled at chewing over painful episodes from African American history in entertaining and even therapeutic manners. While the violence faced by African Americans during the era of Jim Crow segregation and the civil rights movement is a familiar subject for black comedians, slavery is perhaps the most popular subject for black history material. "Though slavery is not a joke," scholar Lisa Woofork has suggested, "it is a source for much African American humor."[11]

I analyze how a group of black comics, satirists, humorists, and, for lack of a better term, jokesters have used their craft and positions as public spokespersons to put forward intriguing and sometimes controversial commentaries on the black past. Are certain dimensions of African American history off-limits to comedians and satirists? Can one go "too far" in "pushing the envelope?" If so, how do we judge what going "too far" entails? Did, for instance, Chappelle go too far in 2003 when he, as the blind "black white supremacist," donned a KKK robe? Does joking about serious episodes from the black past (for example, slavery, Jim Crow segregation, lynching and racial violence) trivialize African American history? Who has been compelling and inept and why? Such inquiries guide this chapter.

---

10   Michael J. Dennis, dir., *Who Is Chris Rock?*, Brooklyn, NY: Syncopation Studios, 1989.

11   Lisa Woofork, *Embodying American Slavery in Contemporary Culture,* Urbana: University of Illinois Press, 2008, 194. For various black comedians' views about slavery, see "Take My Overseer, Please!" in Darryl Littleton, *Black Comedians on Black Comedy: How African-Americans Taught Us to Laugh,* New York: Applause Theatre & Cinema Books, 2006, 3–8.

"KNOW YOUR HISTORY": PAUL MOONEY'S VISION OF BLACK HISTORY

A close friend of and writer for comedic legend Richard Pryor and a "high school pal" of co-founder of the Black Panther Party Huey P. Newton, Paul Mooney has been in the entertainment industry for more than four decades. He has said that he was "born as a stand-up comic in 1970 on the stage of Ye Little Club," a small nightspot in Beverly Hills, California where comedian, actress, and writer Joan Rivers practiced her craft. In late January 2016, freelance writer David Peisner penned an essay that probably saddened and angered many of Mooney's loyal fans. In "The Curious Decline of Paul Mooney," he discusses Mooney's declining health and cited several recent examples of poor performances, concluding that his "legacy is in danger of being sullied by an increasingly disheartening series of appearances."[12]

Mooney is no longer at the top of his game, but he remains one of the most outspoken black comedians when it comes to the wide-reaching subjects of race, racism, and the status of black people in the United States. Mooney also affirmed cross-generational interactions within the community of black comedians by working closely with Keenen Wayans, Robert Townsend, Dave Chappelle, and Eddie Murphy. Despite the incidents that Peisner calls attention to, Mooney has been relevant during the new millennium. His last major stand-up show that has been available for several years on Netflix was released in 2014, *Paul Mooney: Piece of Mind.*

During the twenty-first century before his alleged decline, Mooney has been at the center of more than a few controversies that revolve around his criticism of black celebrities, his attacks on George W. Bush, his excessive use of the n-word, and his unwavering critiques of racism and white American culture. In all of his stand-up shows, he reminds his audience that he is a renegade. Like his character Junebug, Pierre Delacroix's father, in Spike Lee's masterpiece *Bamboozled* (2000), he takes great pride in this. Rejecting "racial neutrality," in his 2009 memoir Mooney explained his approach: "I am who I am. I'm the first to bring a 'just between us' voice to the stage, to any stage, any audience, white, black or mixed." He continued, "I try to keep it real, I always have. But not many white people like it 'real.'"[13] While performing in Dallas, Texas in 2010, he mocked his black listeners who might have been startled or even embarrassed by his dissing of white people: "Massa, Paul's goin' get us in trouble."[14]

Although he collaborated with his younger more crossover counterparts, he has not achieved the mainstream status that the other comedians explored in this chapter have, probably because of his uncompromising in-your-face style in confronting racism and white privilege. As he famously said, "I'm not Hollywood.

---

12   David Peisner, "The Curious Decline of Paul Mooney," vulture.com, February 2, 2016 . This essay originally appeared in the January 25, 2016, issue of *New York Magazine*.

13   Paul Mooney, *Black Is the New White: A Memoir,* New York: Gallery Books, 2009, 16, 18.

14   *Paul Mooney: It's the End of the World,* Dallas, TX: AMS Pictures, 2010.

I'm neighborhood." As a result, he is, in his words, "unheard-of by white people" and is "the real unknown comic." In fact, Mooney contends that he received more "street recognition" from being on the *Chappelle's Show* than he "had ever gotten."[15]

Central to Mooney's comic modus operandi is his construal of black history. By the dawning of the 1970s, he began foregrounding race and African American history into his performances. Speaking in the present tense while reflecting on his early years as a comic, Mooney noted: "At Ye Little Club, I always drop some history into my act. It's knowledge. There's always a message in my comedy." He added, "I'm reading a lot of African history, black history, all kinds of history, so I start working it into my act."[16] While critically exploring US racism and bluntly confronting his white listeners who he has studied carefully, Mooney routinely offers his enterprising interpretations of African American history, often drawing direct connections between the past and the present.

In *Race*, his first major comedy album recorded in San Francisco during the immediate aftermath of the 1992 Los Angeles riots, he focused on analyzing white people, their collective racial psyche, and their general perceptions of black people. He observed that whites enjoy listening to jokes about black people but feel uncomfortable and threatened when they were clowned on, especially by black people. After dismissing the portrayal of Morgan Freeman's character Hoke Colburn, the driver for a wealthy white Jewish woman in Atlanta from the late 1940s through the 1970s in *Driving Miss Daisy* (1989), Mooney concluded: "I don't like that coonin', happy slave bullshit." Mooney had no desire to return to the days when black people were coerced into being subservient to whites. "I'm not going back," he said, "I'm stayin' right here in the '90s where I can tell you white people to kiss my black ass!" Infuriated by what his ancestors endured during the antebellum era, he told the whites in the audience that they can return to their history with pride, whereas black people, like him, can only go back to when they were "in chains." He argued that whites loved it when blacks were slaves. Highlighting a great paradox, he recounted that slaveholders allowed their slaves to live in close proximity to them, working in the house, making their food, and even breast-feeding their children. When freedom came, however, this all changed, he noted, and segregation and hatred toward black people became the norm.[17]

Evoking slavery, Mooney also introduced his joke about Philadelphian Betsy Ross, who is credited with making the first American flag in 1776. Even though she was a Quaker, Mooney joked that she did not make the flag, that it was really made by one of her slaves, "some big fat Aunt Jemima." He then impersonated the familiar "mammy" archetype. How Mooney and scores of other black male comedians often imitate and portray black women is

---

15   Mooney, *Black Is the New White*, 238.
16   Ibid., 115, 141.
17   Paul Mooney, *Race*, Step Sun Music/Tommy Boy, 1993, CD.

undoubtedly problematic, rooted in sexist and misogynist frames of reference. Though Mooney's joke belittled a white historical icon and spoke to the broader issue of the often unacknowledged labor that black people performed during the antebellum era, he did, in the process, deprecate black women.[18] This rendition of black womanhood, moreover, contradicts his veneration of his straightforward, no-nonsense grandmother whose wisdom he cited in later performances. Mooney was largely raised by his maternal grandmother. "I could never endure the racism and prejudice in Hollywood if not for the strength and character she gives to me."[19]

The new millennium was a devastating time for Mooney. His son Symeon was murdered in 2001, and Richard Pryor died in 2005. Mooney persevered. In the twenty-first century, he expanded his discussions of black history in his stand-up shows, often repeating jokes that he created in the 1990s and earlier. In one routine in his creative 2002 *Analyzing White America*, Mooney explained that black people were not impacted by the pervasive post-9/11 racial profiling because of their history of being socialized by violent racial oppression. "Thank you white America for making us tough," he said, "White folks made us tough, 'cause they been terrorizing us for five hundred years. Siccing dogs, putting water hose, lynchin' us. We used to terrorists, this ain't no big deal to us." Mooney joked about blacks' ubiquitous culture of survival. "We will get through this, just like we got through slavery . . . We will hum our way through slavery." He then hummed a Negro spiritual. Mooney continued to joke about slavery by retelling his story about Ross's mythical slave sewing the first American flag, referencing the fabled Willie Lynch letter, and arguing that racism will forever persist in America "'cause white folks owned us and they will never get over it."[20]

In drawing upon painful times when blacks overcame unimaginable forms of oppression, Mooney, similar to black leaders in various time periods who sought to inspire black people, was celebrating black historical resilience.

Released about one week before Obama officially announced that he was seeking the Democratic nomination for president, in *Know Your History: Jesus is Black; So Was Cleopatra*, Mooney observed that Jesus, with his hair of wool, was black, that ancient Egypt was a black African civilization, that icons like Cleopatra were black Africans, and that human beings originated in Africa. He celebrated the African physical features that black Americans inherited. In positing these arguments, Mooney validated an Afrocentric perspective, a point of view that was certainly validated in the black community in Harlem, New York, that he called home. In this special, Mooney also compared the plight of black people with a stereotypical depiction of Mexican Americans and

---

18   Ibid.
19   Mooney, *Black Is the New White*, 38.
20   *Paul Mooney: Analyzing White America*, starring Paul Mooney with Joe Inscoe, Bridget Gethins, and Katie Fleckenstein, Los Angeles, CA: Shout! Factory, 2006.

challenged the myth that black people are lazy by drawing upon the labor that African Americans did during slavery. "We were forced to come here . . . to work for free. For 500 fucking years. Free! So if black people choose to sit on their ass," he yelled, "so be it!" He added: "We built, we gave everything to this country."[21]

He then recounted how slaves built the White House from 1792 until 1800. To spite blacks, Mooney said whites named the official residence of US presidents the *White* House. Mooney returned to the topic of slavery in *It's the End of the World* (2010). When discussing the many "scary" diseases like Alzheimer's disease, dyslexia, and arthritis that had recently caught the attention of the US mainstream media and medical profession, Mooney joked: "Where was all these diseases when we needed it, during slavery?" Taking on the persona of a slave and embodying his enslaved ancestors, he said: "I could have used that shit! I'se a slave massa? I forgot . . . Massa, I can't pick cotton, my arthritis." He later speaks for slaves in telling the whites in the audience that ghosts do not exist. "If there were ghosts," he quipped, "slaves would come back and beat your ass, you know that?! So only the white ghosts come back?"[22]

Mooney's last major recorded stand-up special was released in 2014, *Piece of Mind*. Recycling some old material while addressing current events, the seventy-three-year-old Mooney was in prime form. He did not miss a beat. For the first ten minutes of the show, he talked about whites' widespread contemporary appropriation of black culture, a way of life with deep historical roots. In looking back at black history in general, he conjured up Harriet Tubman and Madam C. J. Walker when joking about white Hollywood's portrayal of black people and subject matter, he historicized the character named Annie who has become the spokeswoman for the Popeyes Louisiana Kitchen (cleverly identifying her as possibly being Uncle Ben's daughter, Aunt Jemima's niece, or Mrs. Butterworth's granddaughter), he justified why he did not like dogs because whites used to "sic them on him," and he referenced slavery in passing, indicating that blacks were not the first to be used as slaves in America.

He directed his comments about slavery to the blacks in the audience: "Don't you black people think that you were the first person the white man put out there to pick cotton . . . There was a huge audition for that." Oversimplifying historians' explanations, he explained that Native Americans, Chinese, and whites did not fit the bill. "God picked us to be the slaves 'cause we can handle it." If whites had been slaves, he qualified, it would have "ended in twenty minutes." Again, Mooney made sense of slavery by playing up blacks' abilities to plod on and by indirectly transforming slavery into a spiritual badge of honor or challenge from God.

---

21   Bart Phillips, dir., *Know Your History: Jesus Is Black; So Was Cleopatra*, starring Paul Mooney, Chatsworth, CA: Image Entertainment, 2007.

22   *Paul Mooney: It's the End of the World.*

Unlike in previous performances, in *Piece of Mind* Mooney also incorporated discussions of the civil rights era. To begin with, he maintained that whites were fond of blacks who turned the other cheek during the 1950s and 1960s, but feared Obama because he had the spirit of *Root's* Kunta Kinte in him and "looked like Malcolm X and talked like Martin Luther King." He then painted a stereotypical picture of black activism during the civil rights era that depicted blacks as being passive and wholeheartedly committed to King's philosophy of nonviolence. He humorously compared those of his generation with "little hip hoppers," African American millennials. "They ain't like us," he said, "They ain't scared to die. They ain't scared of no goddamn dogs." He warned whites about mistreating today's young blacks in the same manner that many whites in the South did more than fifty years ago. "White folks," he continued, "tell 'em they can't ride in the bus . . . Go tell 'em . . . Ain't gon' be no bus . . . No singin', they don't give a damn . . . Bring your German Shepherds. They got pit bulls."[23]

In this case, Mooney drew upon a normative interpretation of blacks who believed in nonviolence in order to reveal how young blacks' responses to racial violence has changed. Mooney, who was a teenager during the civil rights movement, undoubtedly knew that not all civil rights activists embraced nonviolence and that nonviolence was a complex strategy. He admired leaders from this period and considered Martin Luther King Jr. to be "a prophet." He deliberately oversimplified the history of the civil rights movement to underscore his point about today's black youth. While performing, Mooney does something that other black comedians, especially Chris Rock and Martin Lawrence, often do when discussing US race relations and African American history: though he tells jokes, he also lectures in a serious, believable tone and manner. In this sense, he, like others, meshes comedy with informed social commentary. Describing his material, Mooney insisted: "It's the truth."[24]

"TRUTH IN JEST?": CHAPPELLE'S SHOW TACKLES THE BLACK PAST

For several years, Mooney wrote for and appeared in sketches on *Chappelle's Show*. "Paul Mooney is a genius, brilliant, a legend, and a force to be reckoned with," Chappelle wrote in 2009, "Paul Mooney was *too black for Hollywood!*"[25] Chappelle came of age as a comic when the parameters of being "too black for Hollywood" had expanded. Though he was in a range of films in the late 1990s and had an HBO stand-up special in 2000 (*Dave Chappelle: Killin' Them Softly*), Chappelle's career as a racial satirist took off with the very popular *Chappelle's Show* that ran in three seasons from January 22, 2003, until July 23, 2006.

23   Chet A. Brewster, dir., *Paul Mooney: Piece of Mind*, starring Paul Mooney, Los Angeles, CA: Szymon Say'z, 2014.

24   Mooney, *Black Is the New White*, 141.

25   Dave Chappelle, "Foreword," in Mooney, *Black Is the New White*, 2, 3.

Chappelle left the show in May 2005. Scholars have been intrigued enough by Chappelle's comedic genius, interpretations of race, and influence on popular culture to make him the focus of extensive scholarship.[26] In what follows, I focus on how he has rescripted and parodied slavery and the civil rights era in a collection of sketches in *Chappelle's Show*.

In the first season, Chappelle harkened back to slavery and the civil rights movement. Airing early in Black History Month in 2003, the sketch *"Roots" Outtakes* advertised a "one-of-a-kind" DVD collection celebrating the 25th anniversary of the classic 1977 miniseries that included "never before seen" outtakes. The cover of the DVD features Chappelle as Kunta Kinte in shackles, resembling the 2001 25th anniversary edition with LeVar Burton on the cover. Chappelle parodied two of the most popular scenes in the miniseries. In one scene, the character of Kunta Kinte is holding up Kizzy before a star-filled night sky in the tradition of his ancestors and she urinates on him, as newborns often do, and he drops her. "I'm sorry. I told ya'll not to give me a real baby. Pissing all over me," the fictional Kinte says while laughing. In another scene, an elderly Asian man is leading the singing of a group of slaves who, chained together, are being transported to a plantation. The preposterousness of this image is self-evident. The last scene lampoons perhaps the most famous incident in *Roots* that left impressions on its black viewers for generations. Kinte, played by Chappelle, is being whipped and instructed to admit that his name is Toby and not Kunta Kinte. After he is told that his name is Toby and is whipped a second time by the slaveholder, Chappelle the actor, who felt part of the lash, yells: "Damn! Steve, what I say about hittin' so hard, man?!"[27] Then, to the amusement of the other actors, an angry yet jovial Chappelle runs over to the man brandishing the whip (the actor named Steve), throws him to the ground, shakes hands with a few of the black actors playing slaves, helps Steve up, and then returns to where he was being whipped to continue the shoot as if nothing happened.

Graphic whipping scenes in films about slavery are common. Like the horrific whipping scene in Steven Spielberg's *Amistad* (1997) when the victim's blood splatters across Cinque's (Djimon Hounsou's) face during the voyage from Cuba to the United States, viewers are usually horrified by such images. These scenes also often anger black viewers who perhaps wish that the victims could have retaliated. By comically attacking the slaveholder, Chappelle symbolically gets some type of revenge on slavery.

---

26   Since 2007, five dissertations have been completed on Chappelle and in 2007, public intellectual Jelani Cobb published a book bearing the title *The Devil and Dave Chappelle: And Other Essays*. Though unpublished, one of the most provocative studies on *Chappelle's Show* is Lisa Glebatis Perks, "Sketch Comedy of Errors: *Chappelle's Show*, Stereotypes, and Viewers, PhD dissertation, University of Texas—Austin, 2008. Also see K. A. Wisniewski, ed., *The Comedy of Dave Chappelle: Critical Essays*, Jefferson, NC: McFarland, 2009, 9.

27   "*Roots* Outtakes," *Chappelle's Show*, Comedy Central, Season 1, Episode 3, February 5, 2003.

In a sketch in the next episode on February 12, 2003, "Reparations 2003 Follow-Up," Chappelle tangentially deals with slavery. Chappelle introduces the sketch on a fictional *The Phil Donahue Show* with a monologue reflecting upon his experiences. He said:

> Not only am I for affirmative action, I will take it a step further. I want my reparations for slavery. That's right. I'm trying to get paid for the work of my forefathers. Done and done. The only thing I would say is if we do ever get our reparations, which I doubt, but if we do we Black people got to get together to come up with a plan for the money. This is a consumer based economy. You can't just give Black people all this money and turn them loose on the streets. That could be a potential disaster.[28]

He then showed one of his sketches on reparations. Dressed in white face make-up, like Eddie Murphy did in his 1984 *SNL* mockumentary "White Like Me" and the Wayans brothers would in *White Chicks* (2004), Chappelle opened the skit playing the character of white news reporter Chuck Taylor who announced that black people just received reparations from the US government. Assuming that his viewers know what reparations entails, he does not offer a definition of this deeply rooted struggle. In the skit, Chappelle infers that black people would change drastically if awarded reparations.

In Chappelle's imagination, black basketball players would quit the NBA, and ordinary black people would spend their money frivolously and would insult their white employers. In addition to playing Chuck Taylor, Chappelle also plays a Harlem dice player named Tron who, when asked how he was going to spend his money, jests that he would reinvest it into the black community. Even Colin Powell, Chappelle says while playing Taylor, would "bitch slap" Vice President Dick Cheney. Chuck Taylor ends his commentary by warning white Americans: "White people, run for cover."[29]

In the second season, Chappelle returned to the subject of slavery in his revenge skit "The Time Haters—Great Misses—Uncensored," a sketch that he considered to be too controversial to air during the regular season. Along with three other haters, Chappelle, playing the character Silky Johnson, travels back in time to a slave plantation. Upon their arrival, a startled slaveholder with a whip in hand approaches them and demands, "What the hell are you niggers doing out here?" Johnson replies, "We are the Time Haters. We travelled all the way back through time to call yuh a cracker." The confident slaveholder warns Johnson to be careful of how he speaks to him. Buc Nasty, played by Charlie Murphy, retorts: "Actually you better watch your mouth white boy, before I

---

28   "Dave on 'Donahue'—Uncensored," *Chappelle's Show*, Comedy Central, Season 1, Episode 4, February 12, 2003.

29   "Reparations 2003 Follow-Up," *Chappelle's Show*, Comedy Central, Season 1, Episode 4, February 12, 2003.

shove these gators up your ass and show yo' insides some style." By this point, the slaveholder is getting angry and pulls out his whip to attack the Time Haters. Full of fear, one of the Time Haters, Beautiful, runs away to Johnson's dismay and Johnson says to the slaveholder, "Nice whip. This here is a pistol. Reach for the sky, honky!" One of the slaves asks Johnson what the word "honky" means and Johnson digresses into a brief history of the "racial epithet," situating it in the 1970s with *The Jeffersons* sitcom. He then informs the slaves that "in the future, all black people will be free!" One of the slaves then asks him, "When's we gonna be free?" to which Johnson replies, "That is a good question my man. How about now-ish?" Johnson then shoots the slaveholder in the chest and this clip is replayed five times. After the brief skit, Chappelle notices that the whites in his audience may not have found the skit as funny as he did and he comments, "If I could, I'd do it every episode."[30]

As Spike Lee did in the "ice slop" scene in *Miracle at St. Anna's* and Quentin Tarantino did at the end of *Django Unchained* when Django blew up the Candie Land plantation, Chappelle got revenge for oppressed African Americans during trying times. The image of a slaveholder being killed over and over again most likely gave his black viewers in particular some sense of satisfaction. Chappelle certainly felt vindicated by this.

In addition to slavery, Chappelle reimagined the civil rights era in two major sketches. "'Frontline'—Racist Hollywood Animals—Uncensored" is a mock PBS documentary that explores racism in Hollywood. "What we uncovered may shock you," says the host Kent Wallace while introducing the investigation. The sketch then shifts to a discussion of the career of Rin Tin Tin IV, a German Shepherd who starred in *The Adventures of Rin Tin Tin* during the 1950s. Viewers are then introduced to Justin Wilkes, an African American man from Alabama who was active during the civil rights movement. According to Wilkes, played by Chappelle, Rin Tin Tin was a racist dog who worked with the Selma, Alabama police department. Wilkes recounts the story of how he was attacked by Rin Tin Tin while he was protesting in Selma in 1957 in front of a Woolworth's. As Wilkes shares his memories, actual footage of young African Americans being sprayed with water hoses and attacked by police dogs is shown. A still image of a police dog biting an African American man on his backside taken from actual footage is shown and Wilkes says that that is him. "What you callin' 'classic civil rights footage,' I call me getting' bit on my ass by a German Shepherd," Wilkes responds to the *Frontline* host, who seems to doubt his claim. Wilkes proves his point by visiting a doctor who was able to locate Rin Tin Tin's dental records and make the match. After Wilkes's case was publicized, Kent Wallace points out, other African Americans shared similar "allegations against iconic animals, breaking decades of silence." It is revealed that Mr. Ed called a

---

30 "The Time Haters—Great Misses—Uncensored," *Chappelle's Show*, Comedy Central, Season 2, Episode 11, March 31, 2004.

black female actress the n-word and was owned by the KKK and that Flipper was used by racists to terrorize blacks who attempted to integrate swimming pools. At the conclusion of the sketch, an advertisement for the next Frontline episode is previewed: racist Hollywood cars, including *The Dukes of Hazard's* "General Lee" and *Night Rider's* KITT.[31]

Though comical, Chappelle prompts us to think about German Shepherds that were routinely use to terrorize black people during the civil rights movement. Other skits would later bring up the issue of dogs being trained to dislike black people, such as "The Bowtie" episode in Larry David's *Curb Your Enthusiasm* (season 5), in which comedian Wanda Sykes accuses David of adopting a racist dog, and the 2012 "Racist Dog" sketch on *Key & Peele*, in which a dog that barked at Key and Peele while they were jogging is shown in KKK garb addressing other racist dogs.

Like sketches involving the crack addict Tyrone Biggums, "Profiles in Courage: Toilet Pioneers" is one of Chappelle's cruder performances. The five-minute-and-forty-second-long parody begins with the well-dressed white male host of the show introducing the segment about one man, former steel mill worker Cyrus Holloway from Hartsville, Alabama (played by Chappelle), who "made history" with one act of heroism as Rosa Parks did in early December 1955.

Standing in a room filled with photos of civil rights era icons, the host of "Profiles in Courage" contextualizes Holloway's actions by highlighting the significance of 1954. While he correctly identifies *Brown v. Board of Education* as taking place, he errs by saying that the Montgomery Bus Boycott began in this year. Viewers are then introduced to an elderly Holloway who, in the tradition of documentaries like the popular *Eyes on the Prize* series, shares his story. When he was at work one day, he recounts, he ate a roast beef sandwich for lunch and had to use the bathroom. Located in the basement of the steel mill, the "colored toilet" wasn't, in Holloway's words, "fit for a Christian." In a similar manner that viewers of civil rights era documentaries are bombarded with images of segregated drinking fountains, movie theaters, and other public facilities, we are shown a picture of the "disgusting" toilet that was reserved for blacks. In an act of defiance and desperation, Holloway decided to use the white restroom. As he conveys, he decided to take a monumental risk in order to avoid the dreaded "mud butt" (soiling himself). The host returns, noting that Holloway took "what would be known as one of the most significant dumps in American history."[32]

Notified by one of his white co-workers, the police barged in on Holloway in the white bathroom stall, set a German Shepherd on him, sprayed him with

---

31   "'Frontline'—Racist Hollywood Animals—Uncensored," *Chappelle's Show*, Comedy Central, Season 1, Episode 8, March 12, 2003.

32   "Profiles in Courage: Toilet Pioneer," *Chappelle's Show*, Comedy Central, Season 2, Episode 13, April 14, 2004.

a water hose, and arrested him. Holloway was then taken to jail and charged with "desecration of a white facility with Negroid feces." The sentence for this crime was nine years in prison. According to the host, the news of Holloway's actions spread across the nation, launching a movement. Reverend Charles Welton, played by Charlie Murphy, was among those activists to descend upon the scene. "Why can't my turd float next to yours?" Welton asked while addressing a group of African Americans who were sitting on toilets staging what was called "the nation's first shit-in." With their pants down, the protesters were attacked by police officers with nightsticks to which Welton responded, "No my brothas and sistas, do not run. Turn your butt cheeks towards the aggressor and let them clean your butt cheeks with the cascade of water. This is a good thing, my brothas and sistas." Viewers are then informed by the host of the show that the mythical American Legal Society took the case to the Supreme Court who ruled in Holloway's favor. In his ruling, the Justice solemnly declared: "It is my opinion that no matter what the color of your skin, your feces will be brown," he added, "No matter what the hue of your poo, it will undoubtedly stink."[33]

The sketch ends with Holloway leaving the courtroom after the verdict to take his "first free dump." He is even joined in the bathroom stall by members of his church choir who are singing the famous Negro spiritual "Down by the Riverside." Holloway farts along with the singing.

Chappelle has confessed that juvenile jokes about farting and defecation amused him as a young adult. It would not be surprising if those African Americans who came of age during the civil rights movement were offended by this sketch that equated a "shit-in" with a "sit-in." While his skit may have caricatured the mythical Cyrus Holloway, it did point out the absurdity of segregation laws.

Chappelle has recently made a comeback of some sorts. At the end of 2017, he released standup comedy specials on Netflix. Towards the end of his third Netflix special, *Dave Chappelle: Equanimity*, Chappelle retold his version of the murder of Emmett Till.[34] Taking on an authoritative voice, he called his story a "history lesson" and assumed a somber tone when speaking. For Chappelle, however, the specific "facts" about the case were not essential. For instance, he claimed that Till's body was tied to a wheel when it was thrown into the river, that he was abducted by a group of white men, and that the image of his corpse was reprinted in all major newspapers. Though he summarized the crux of the Till case, specific "facts" were not important to Chappelle and we should not have expected them to be. After all, he is a comedian, not a professional historian. At the same time, he underscored the significance of this case, deeming Till's mother a "fuckin' gangster" for turning her son into a martyr and helping

---

33   Ibid.
34   Stan Lathan, dir., *Dave Chappelle: Equanimity*, Netflix, December 31, 2017.

propel the modern civil rights movement. In a strange twist, he also intimated that Carolyn Bryant's lies lead to a turn of events that sparked a larger movement that enabled him to be here today.

One could say that the multitalented comedian, actor, director, and producer Martin Lawrence was perhaps destined to incorporate African American history while practicing his craft. His parents named him after Martin Luther King Jr., and Lawrence was very proud of this. After appearing in a handful of films and television shows, his career as a stand-up comedian took off when he became the host of Russell Simmons's HBO *Def Comedy Jam* that premiered in 1992. He starred in his show *Martin* (1992–1997) and in more than a dozen Hollywood films from 1995, when the original *Bad Boys* was released, until *Big Mommas: Like Father, Like Son* (2011). Lawrence performed in one major stand-up comedy special in the twenty-first century that incorporated discussions of black history, *Martin Lawrence Live: Runteldat* (2002). He also discussed episodes from black history in his first stand-up comedy special that was released nearly a decade earlier, *You So Crazy*.

Several minutes into *You So Crazy*, Lawrence jumped into a discussion of racism and spoke directly to the blacks and whites in the audience. "It fucks me up when *some* white people don't accept black people in America, 'cause you brought us to this motherfucker. We was chillin' in Africa," Lawrence noted. He then joked that Africans were tricked into boarding slave ships and enduring the Middle Passage. After stressing that he believes that "America is the best country in the world," he says that, if drafted, he would not "go to war" for the United States, that he would fake being disabled and advise other black men to do the same. It is clear that he came to this conclusion because of the racism that African Americans endured and were still facing. He stressed that racism still existed, exemplified by the Rodney King case. He joked that King "kept getting up," explaining that this was a reflection of the black historical struggle in general. "We don't stay down for nobody," Lawrence proclaimed, "Rodney had that Kunta Kinte spirit." Like Paul Mooney, he then impersonated Morgan Freeman in *Driving Miss Daisy* and flips the script by placing himself in that role. Suffice it to say that he, like Mooney, would not have put up with Miss Daisy's treatment of him as a black driver. He was revisiting the past with his late twentieth-century sensibilities.[35]

In *Martin*, Lawrence often paid tribute to African American history and culture, and in 1999, he starred in a comedy-historical drama that addressed an important dimension of black life in the South during the era of Jim Crow

---

35 Thomas Schlamme, dir., *You So Crazy*, HBO Independent Productions, 1994.

segregation. In Ted Demme's *Life*, Lawrence and Eddie Murphy, playing small-time New York hustlers, are wrongly convicted of murder in Mississippi while attempting to buy a truckload of alcohol.[36] They were sentenced to life in a brutal, all-black prison camp where they are forced to perform tedious, hard manual labor. One of the most popular dialogues in *Life* is known as the brief "You Gonna Eat Your Cornbread?" scene. There are several scenes in this film that can serve as windows into the convict labor system that many black men were exploited by during the first half of the twentieth century. One of their early failed escapes is particularly powerful. As they are aimlessly making their way through the woods at night in a quest for freedom, they are being chased by armed guards and barking hound dogs. Just after they climbed through a fence, they were hit in the back of their heads by a guard's rifle butt. In the next scene, they are returning to the prison camp, chained, like runaway slaves. The images are moving.

Recorded in DAR Constitution Hall in Washington, DC, *Runteldat* was a comeback performance of some sort for Lawrence.[37] Central to this performance is his revisiting of what happened to him in 1996 when he was arrested on Ventura Boulevard in Los Angeles for brandishing a gun. His opening dialogue was humble, serious, and humorous. "No one is immune to the trials and tribulations of life. No one. We all have ups, and we all have downs," he said in reference to his run-ins with the police and his near-death experiences. Throughout the energetic performance, a sharp Lawrence repeated that we need to live life to the fullest "until the wheels fall off." At the same time, toward the end of the show, he confessed that he was high when he was arrested and accepted full responsibility for all of his mistakes. This show was clearly very therapeutic for Lawrence; it seems that knowledge of black history helped him put his own personal "trials and tribulations" into perspective. In the remainder of the show, he smoothly blended together routines about post-9/11 life in America, raising children, getting older, married life, and of course sex, one of his favorite subjects. He also integrated a dialogue on black history.

After joking about the threat of terrorism, the unsuccessful search for Bin Laden, and the omnipresence of blacks on the television show *Cops*, Lawrence celebrated the struggles of his foreparents during the civil rights movement in a much different way than Chappelle would later do. He gave a shout-out to the *Eyes on the Prize* documentary series that he recently watched. "This program will make you cry," he said solemnly, "I'm serious. It's a beautiful thing." As he did in *You So Crazy* before critically discussing US race relations, he underscored: "I'll tell you. I love America. This is the best country in the world . . . But I'm a black man and I ain't forgot what the fuck we black have

---

36   Ted Demme, dir., *Life*, Universal Studies, 1998.

37   David Raynr, dir., *Martin Lawrence Live: Runteldat*, starring Martin Lawrence, Hollywood, CA: Paramount Pictures, 2002.

been through in America, know what I'm sayin'?! We ain't gonna just act like shit is all right." Lawrence then praised those featured in *Eyes on the Prize* who "put their lives out there so that we can be in the forefront." He asked his predominantly black audience to think about "segregation and civil rights and all those things," to reflect upon what Martin Luther King Jr. and Malcolm X stood for.

Rejecting the King–Malcolm dichotomy that was still somewhat prevalent in 2002, he surmised: "Martin and Malcolm were sayin' the same thing. They just had different opinions and approaches to it." Lawrence then joked about King's nonviolent disposition that he understood and respected in the context of his times. "But if you like me," he qualified to the audience's collective burst of laughter, "then one time you would have loved to hear Martin say, 'Another one of you motherfuckers hit me with a rock, I'll beat your bitch ass. You motherfucker. Fuck that, Coretta, these niggas think I'm soft.'"[38] The audience clearly resonated with Lawrence's humorous rewriting of black history. Like Kenan Thompson, Jamie Foxx, Aaron McGruder, Jordan Peele, and others, he empowered King with a twenty-first-century voice, a voice that he impersonated quite well.

"THE MOST IMPORTANT THING IS TO BE FUNNY": CHRIS ROCK

Years before they appeared as brothers in the comedy *Death at a Funeral* (2010), Lawrence opened up for one of Rock's performances. According to Rock, his colleague (both were born at the apex of the civil rights movement) had the building "shaking," and he was "terrified" to follow his act. Lawrence and Rock are similar in that they both pace intensely during their shows, have starred in more than a few blockbuster movies, and spice up their comedy routines with pensive social commentary about race and the black condition. By the time that he released three major stand-up specials at the turn of and into the twenty-first century (*Bigger and Blacker*, 1999; *Never Scared*, 2004; and *Kill the Messenger*, 2008), Chris Rick was a seasoned comedian.

During the "Age of Obama," a period that Rock insists has led to "white progress" and not "black progress," he was recognized as being one of the most renowned comedians of his peer group. The then Senator Obama even gave a shout-out to Rock in one of his more controversial presidential campaign speeches.

On Father's Day in 2008 at the Apostolic Church of God in Chicago, Obama chastised the many black fathers who "have abandoned their responsibilities, acting like boys instead of men"; he shared his experiences of being raised by a single mother and called upon the black community to solve this problem by turning within. Though he began his sermon on a solemn note,

---

38   Ibid.

about five minutes into his speech he made his audience laugh by saying: "Any fool can have a child. That doesn't make you a father." Throughout the remainder of this oration, Obama code-switched and "style-shifted." He even revealed his skills as an amateur stand-up comic by paraphrasing Rock's infamous 1996 "Niggas vs. Black People" routine from *Bring the Pain*. "I don't know if you guys remember, Chris Rock had a routine." Obama continued, "He said too many of our men, they're proud, they brag about the things they're supposed to do. They say, 'Well, I'm not in jail.' Well, you're not supposed to be in jail. Don't brag about that."[39] Obama's Chris Rock impression, minus the n-word of course, was met with laughter and applause. Like comedians who know that they have struck a cord with their audience, Obama laughed at his own rendition of Rock's ridiculing of black men. In his most recent stand-up performance, *Tamborine*, Rock returned a different type of shout-out to Obama.[40] Reflecting on Obama's presidency, Rock said that black people should thank George Bush for paving the way for the first black president to be elected. Rock reasoned that because of what Bush did to the country, white Americans were ready to elect a black president. "I think people overlook George Bush's contributions to black history," Rock joked, "George Bush is a black revolutionary. Malcolm X, Rosa Parks, George Bush."

Epitomized by his hosting the Academy Awards in 2005 and 2016 and earning four Emmy Awards and three Grammy Awards, by the new millennium Rock had gained unprecedented mainstream success. Like other black comedians before him who came of age in post–civil rights era America (most recently Kevin Hart), he has enjoyed great crossover appeal. This Brooklyn (Bedford–Stuyvesant) native and high school dropout, however, did not earn mainstream recognition at the expense of downplaying his blackness or shying away from tackling polarizing issues related to American race relations. Some of his critics have argued that his "Niggas vs. Black People" routine lampooned and demonized poor black men, verged on minstrelsy, and legitimized white racists' thoughts about black people. In this routine, Rock even remarked, "Boy I wish they'd let me join the Klu Klux Klan. Shit I'd do a drive-by from here to Brooklyn. I'm tired of niggas, man."[41]

Nonetheless, since the 1990s when his career began taking off, Rock has never shied away from controversial issues pertaining to race and the African American experience. After he was a cast member on *Saturday Night Live* from 1990 until 1993, appeared in many movies (including *CB4*, which he wrote and co-produced), and starred in several stand-up specials, *The Chris Rock Show* that ran from February 7, 1997, until November 25, 2000, featured comedy sketches and more serious discussions on contemporary racism. Whether they

39   "Barack Obama's Speech on Father's Day," youtube.com, uploaded on June 15, 2008.
40   Bo Burnham, dir., *Tamborine*, Netflix, February 14, 2018.
41   Keith Truesdell, dir., *Chris Rock: Bring the Pain*, starring Chris Rock, New York: HBO, 1996.

were entertainers, athletes, political pundits or spokespersons, public intellectuals, or social activists, Rock always had black people as guests on every episode. In season 1 in the February 21, 1997, episode, he introduced two "Black History Month Minute" skits with Eartha Kitt and Stanley Crouch. In several other episodes, Rock created skits dealing with contemporary debates with concrete historical antecedents. In 1999, for instance, he interviewed people in South Carolina about whether the Confederate flag should be allowed to fly and ran an ad for the "Malcolm X Games." The next year, he interviewed ordinary people about their thoughts on reparations.

In his early comedy albums and stand-up specials in the 1990s, he subtly reflected on dimensions of African American history. Recorded in Atlanta, Georgia in 1991, *Born Suspect* is Rock's first major solo comedy album. In his "My Father" routine, he poked fun at his father's "old school" worldview. Rock offered humorous impressions of his father and explained why he thought that Run-DMC was "ignant" (ignorant). Referring to the gold chains that Run-DMC used to sport, Rock's father (imitated by Rock) asked him, "And what's that thing around they neck?" To which Rock replied, "Rope chain, dad." Rock's father then retorted, "I told you them boys was ignant. What nigga in his right mind wants a rope around his neck?"[42] Following this punch line, there was an outburst of laughter and applause followed by a silence suggesting that the predominantly black audience caught his reference to lynching. For Rock's father, Christopher Julius Rock II (who was born in Charleston, South Carolina in 1932 and whose parents shared with him stories of black life in the South), the symbols of lynching were powerful, albeit as expressed in the "My Father" routine in a comedic way.

Three years after *Born Suspect* appeared, HBO released *Chris Rock: Big Ass Jokes*. Though slightly less than one-half hour in length, Rock skillfully moves from topic to topic and includes several references to black history. During a segment on Americans' perceptions of healthy verses unhealthy food, he quips that what black people affectionately call *soul food* was "not black food," it was "some nasty shit they fed to the slaves." He added: "You think a ham hock tasted good the first time the white man gave it to us? We put some seasonin' on it and made it work." Rock was giving props to his enslaved ancestors' ingenuity. In another bit, Rock joked about how blacks had it rough during the days of Jim Crow segregation. "Now a brother was at the back of the bus in the '60s. In the '20s, a brother must have been inside the engine of the bus," Rock declared. He then engaged in what some may call minstrelsy by adding: "On a carriage belt, chasing a piece of chicken."[43] Rock then pretended that the microphone was a piece of chicken and imitated a black man running frantically on the belt in pursuit of the chicken.

---

42 Chris Rock and Kevin Harewood, producers, *Born Suspect*, starring Chris Rock, New York: Atlantic, 1991.

43 Keith Truesdell, dir., *Chris Rock: Big Ass Jokes*, starring Chris Rock, New York: HBO, 1994.

In *Bring the Pain* (1996), when talking about dropping out of high school and the insignificance that passing the general educational (GED) test had for him, he shared a story about his later academic struggles. Poking fun at black college students who might believe that courses in black history and African American studies are easy for them because they are, after all, black, Rock shared a funny story about taking a black history course at a community college.

"Let me take some shit I know, so I took a black history class," Rock recounted, "I got to know this, I'm black, right, right?" He then confessed that he failed the class. "A black man failing black history. Ain't that some shit. Cuz you know, fat people don't fail cooking," Rock replied. He went on to explain that he failed the class because he did not know anything about Africa; in high school he learned nothing about his African heritage. The only thing that he knew about Africa was that it was far away. He pointed out: "So you know that boat ride was real long. The boat ride was so long there still slaves on the way here." Similar to his passing reference to lynching in *Born Suspect*, in this instance Rock alludes to a tragic genocide from the black past, the horrific Middle Passage that resulted in the deaths of millions of Africans. Like many African American youth, a young Rock, who attended predominantly white schools, only learned about a handful of black icons.

For him, black history equated to Martin Luther King Jr. He relates how King became his "answer to everything" pertaining to black history. He then drew attention to the irony of the numerous streets and boulevards named after King throughout the nation. While King "stood for nonviolence," he underscored, "if you are on Martin Luther King Boulevard, there some violence going on."[44] Rock's joke speaks to the racial segregation that still persists in America and the fact that the vast majority of the streets named in honor of King are located in poor black neighborhoods. He also noted that King had been commercialized. "One way you can tell Martin Luther King's birthday is now a real holiday is that it's become a good reason for stores to have sales." He added, "I had a dream I could get an ice-cold Coca Cola." In another routine from the 1990s, he joked about King's size: "If he was four or five inches taller and had more muscles on him, his message might have been totally different. We might all be dead right now."[45]

By the late 1990s and the new millennium, Rock expanded his repertoire, addressing events and personalities from the annals of black history in a variety of manners. African American history is important to Rock. It seems that early in his career, he expected African Americans to know something about their past.

In 1999, Rock's heralded *Bigger and Blacker*, an HBO special recorded live at the famous Apollo Theater in Harlem, New York, was released.[46] In this

---

44   Truesdell, dir., *Chris Rock: Bring the Pain*.
45   Chris Rock, *Rock This!* New York: Hyperion, 1997, 27, 46.
46   Chris Rock, *Bigger and Blacker*, produced by Prince Paul and Don Newkirk, Dreamworks, 1999.

stand-up performance, Rock kicked around a range of issues, including school shootings orchestrated by white youth and gun control, the lack of appreciation for black fathers who take care of business, the Bill Clinton–Monica Lewinsky scandal, gays in the military, racial profiling, male–female relationships, sex, AIDS, medical care in the United States, Robitussin ("Tussin") as his father's cure-all, and, of course, racism.

He began his dialogue on racism by pointing out that while many different groups are "yelling racism" in the United States, no group "got it worse than the American Indian." Alluding to a history of genocide in early North America (a theme that Mooney addressed earlier than Rock), he joked about how Native Americans are nearly invisible in American society. "You know how bad the Indians got it?" Rock asked, "When's the last time you met two Indians?" After chastising white people who complain that they are "losing the country" because of affirmative action and "illegal" immigration, he introduces his character, the "old black man," a persona with whom his predominantly black audience is intimately familiar. He also lets the whites in the audience know that they too have met this type of black man, someone they think is so "nice" but really "hates your guts."[47]

Rock explains why the "old black man" harbors ill feelings toward whites and is justifiably racist toward white people. Transcending the argument that only whites can be racist because racism involves access to institutional power, Rock announces that the "old black man" is the most racist person in America.

"There's nothing more racist than an old black man. You know why? 'Cause an old black man went through some real racism. He did not go through that I-can't-get-a-cab shit," Rock continued with laying out a punch line, "He was the cab. A white man just jump on his back, 'Main Street. Left nigger! Left, you fucking nigger!" He also explained how black men who came of age most likely during the era of Jim Crow segregation wore "the mask" that Paul Lawrence Dunbar discussed in his famous 1896 poem. He called attention to the code-switching that African Americans who were employed in service jobs engaged in to survive. "Whenever the old black man sees an old white man, the old black man always kisses the old white man's ass," Rock recounts, "As soon as the white man gets out of sight, he's like: 'Cracker-ass cracker! I'll put my foot in the crack of your ass, cracker-ass cracker!" Rock adds, "The white man come back. 'Howdy sir."[48]

Several dynamics are at play in this routine. One, Rock was reminding the younger African Americans in the Apollo that night that racism, though it was alive and kicking at the turn of the twenty-first century, was much worse and more overt during the era of Jim Crow segregation. In a routine from the 1990s, Rock used another example to get this point across. "People always talk about

---

47   Ibid.
48   Ibid.

the good old days," Rock observed, "You think that there was less crime in 1929? Maybe so. But back then, a white man could lynch a black man . . . and get a seven-dollar fine."[49] Two, he was letting his white listeners know that older black men who seem to be cheerful and deferential are often processing their interactions with white America in different ways than they would think. Three, to rounds of laughter, Rock effectively captured how blacks, most likely before the end of the civil rights movement, developed practical strategies of coping with the racial norms of their times while also privately fighting back in the small and gratifying ways that they could.

In *Bigger and Blacker*, Rock lamented the current state of black leadership. "We ain't had a black leader in a while. In a long time. Somebody that moves you. You know, we had Martin Luther King, Malcolm X," Rock maintained, "and ever since then, a bunch of substitute teachers." He then juxtaposed King and Malcolm with Al Sharpton, Jesse Jackson, and Louis Farrakhan, implying that the contemporary black spokespersons are not in the same league as their predecessors. He also joked about how emcees Tupac and Biggie Smalls are routinely but inaccurately viewed by the hip-hop generation in the realm of black leadership, as icons who were assassinated like black freedom fighters from the past. What was Rock's solution to the void in black leadership? Pat Riley. "He may not get us to the mountaintop. But he'll get us to the playoffs," Rock remarked. Implying that African Americans had lost their historical vision of what genuine leadership means, he added: "And that's all we want."[50]

Five years after *Bigger and Blacker*, Rock's HBO comedy special *Never Scared* was recorded at DAR Constitutional Hall in Washington, DC.[51] While many probably remember his routines about how his "only job in life is to keep" his daughter "off the (stripper) pole," the problematic lyrics of Lil Jon and the East Side Boyz's "Get Low," the racialized differences between being rich and wealthy, the trials of married life, or black men's love of rims ("they spinning"), in this show Rock offered some of his most extensive stand-up routines on episodes from black history, both contemporary and more distantly located.

On June 7, 1998, a forty-nine-year-old man named James Byrd Jr. was horrifically murdered by three white men in Jasper, Texas, a lynching-by-dragging that was reminiscent of lynchings during the "nadir" period of the black experience when lynchings were commonplace. About fifteen minutes into *Never Scared*, Rock criticized how the US government was "trying to," in his mind, "scare us" with its warnings about al-Qaeda. While he announced that he loves his country, he qualified his admiration of the United States. "I ain't scared

---

49   Rock, *Rock This!* 33.
50   Rock, *Bigger and Blacker*.
51   *Chris Rock: Never Scared*, dir., Joel Gallen, with Chris Rock, New York, New York: HBO, 2004.

of Al-Qaeda," Rock proclaimed. "Did Al-Qaeda drag James Byrd down the street 'til his eyeballs popped out of his fucking head? No. I ain't scared of Al-Qaeda. I'm scared of al-cracker!"[52] Like generations of black Americans from previous eras and echoing Martin Lawrence's opposition to being drafted in *You So Crazy*, Rock pointed out the problem of (white) America calling upon black people to join in patriotic fervor when racism and anti-black violence still persist.

Rock also offered his interpretation of slavery within the context of affirmative action, which, in his estimation, was at the time "the most divisive issue in America." Wearing the hat of a scholar, Rock provided a concise definition of this policy, highlighting how slavery impacted generations of African Americans following the passage of the Thirteenth Amendment (1865). "Affirmative action was put into place to offset policies that the United States government implemented during slavery that affect us today. Now, when I talk about slavery," Rock emphasized, "I'm just talking about a period when black people had no rights. So you talk about the 1600s to about 1964. You know, give or take a few years, depending on when your town decided to act right." Though he did not mention the passage of the Civil Rights Act in 1964, it is not a stretch to assume that he used this landmark as an ending point for overt forms of black oppression like slavery. In responding to his own question about what specifically occurred during the antebellum era that still impacted blacks in 2004, he responded: "A lot of shit happened during slavery that affects us every day." Rock proceeded to impart to his audience a mini-lecture on slavery in the tone of a scholar, yet, in the black comedic tradition, laced with hyperbole and factual inaccuracies. This approach was not entirely new for Rock. In the late 1990s, Rock made a similar observation about the impact of slavery on blacks' thinking. Explaining why blacks distrusted American "institutions," he surmised: "Hmm. I think it all started with slavery." Rock continued, "Slavery affected the black psyche . . . We're like battered wives ordered to stay with their husbands. No wonder we're so fucked up."[53]

Reinforcing the notion that calculated slave breeding was the norm, in *Never Scared* Rock declared that the "biggest, strongest slaves" were bred in order to make "strong super slaves." He added: "They bred the slaves, and this is why black people dominate every physical activity in the United States of America, okay?"[54] Rock's statement sounds very similar to sentiments uttered by sports commentator James George "Jimmy" Snyder Sr. (aka "Jimmy the Greek") who in 1988 was fired by CBS for remarking in an interview on Martin Luther King Jr. Day, believe it or not, that black athletes were "better" than white athletes[55] because "the slave owner would breed his big black (man) to his big

---

52   Ibid.
53   Rock, *Rock This!*, 15.
54   *Chris Rock: Never Scared.*
55   Jay Sharbutt, "Jimmy 'The Greek' Is Fired by CBS," *Los Angeles Times*, January 17, 1988.

woman so that he could have a big black kid." He added: "That's where it all started."[56] Obviously, as a black comedian performing a routine before a predominantly black audience, Rock had the license, cultural capital, and authenticity to say what he did.

While Rock's "big, strong slaves" were admired for their ability to work, the "smart ones" were feared and killed. "That's right," a confident Rock proclaimed, "that was the policy of the United States government, to kill smart black people, that's right. So the real smart motherfuckers had to hide the fact that they were smart, okay?" Adopting the familiar voice and mannerisms of the stereotypical slave and bugging his eyes like so many black performers did during the vaudeville years, Rock then goes on to narrate a story about a literate yet ignorant sounding slave who was driving a buggy and approached an intersection with a stop sign. Instead of stopping, which would indicate to whites that he could read, he "wipes out" and "almost kills somebody." Rock then fluidly returns to the controversy over affirmative action, concluding that these sets of laws and policies are useful mechanisms to right past wrongs against black people, like preventing them from learning how to read and write during the era of slavery. For Rock, the historical oppression of black people impacted their future lives, up until the present. "Don't get me wrong," Rock explained, "I don't think that I should get accepted into a school over a white person if I get a lower mark on a test. But if there's a tie? Fuck 'em! Shit, you had a 400-year head start, motherfucker."[57]

In more recent years, Rock has returned to this subject of white privilege in the midst of black oppression. In a lengthy interview in late 2014 with *New York Magazine* that was featured as the cover story, Rock mentioned that he enjoyed *12 Years a Slave* "because it just didn't feel the need to make people feel comfortable" and argued that "we treat racism in this country like it's a style that America went through." His most controversial statement was that white people needed to own up to the actions of their predecessors and ancestors. "Yeah, it's unfair that you can be judged by something that you didn't do," Rock said in reference to slavery and perhaps Jim Crow segregation, "but it's also unfair that you can inherit money that you didn't work for."[58]

One of Rock's most recent public comments on black history were viewed by millions of Americans who watched the 88th Academy Awards ceremony that he hosted at the Dolby Theatre in Hollywood, Los Angeles, on February 28, 2016. Rock reflected on those blacks—namely Spike Lee and Jada Pinkett Smith—who called for a boycott of the Oscars by historicizing their concerns. As he did in his "old black man" routine in *Bigger and Blacker*, Rock reminded today's black entertainers that early periods in the African American experience were much more challenging than the present times. In his opening monologue, Rock observed:

---

56   *Chris Rock: Never Scared.*
57   Ibid.
58   Frank Rich, "In Conversation: Chris Rock," *New York Magazine*, December 1, 2014.

Now the thing is, why are we protesting? That's the big question, why this Oscars? It's the 88th Academy Awards, which means this whole 'no black nominees' thing has happened at least 71 other times. You got to figure that it happened in the '50s in the '60s, you know in the '60s one of those years Sidney [Poitier] didn't put out a movie. I'm sure there were no black nominees one of those years and black people did not protest.

Why? Because we had real things to protest at the time. Too busy being raped and lynched to care about who won best cinematographer. When your grandmother is swinging from the tree, it's really hard to care about Best Documentary Foreign Short.[59]

Lynching and rape were among the most inhumane and barbaric forms of anti-black violence that were not uncommon during the "nadir" period and the era of Jim Crow segregation. By evoking these genocides, Rock was flagrantly trying to get his point across that black people have more important things to be concerned with than whether actors and actresses who look like them are nominated for Oscars.

On November 1, 2014, Chris Rock hosted *Saturday Night Live* (*SNL*). In addition to his seven-minute monologue, or stand-up routine, he appeared in several sketches. About a month later in a cover story in *The Hollywood Reporter* in which he described Hollywood as being "a white industry," Rock shared his thoughts about how *SNL* had changed since he was on the show in the early 1990s. "But there's been progress. I was on *Saturday Night Live* a few months ago, we did a sketch where I was Sasheer Zamata's dad and she had an Internet show," Rock narrated, "Twenty years ago when I was on *Saturday Night Live*, anything with black people on the show had to do with race, and that sketch we did didn't have anything to do with race."[60]

While Rock's observation that the roles of black *SNL* cast members have changed since he was on the show (or even since Garrett Morris's days of being the first and only African American cast member from 1975 until 1980) has some validity, in the twenty-first century, the fewer than ten African Americans who appeared on *SNL* with some regularity continued to be featured in skits dealing with race. At a minimum, the skits that they have performed in are most profoundly determined by their blackness. Take, for example, Kenan Thompson, who began his career on *SNL* in 2003. He has played 150 characters whose black identity more often than not shapes the sketches that he is in. Over the years, his most popular characters have included Charles Barkley, Star Jones, Bill Cosby, Whoopi Goldberg, Steve Harvey, and Reverend Al Sharpton. His only major character that is not defined by race is the bartender that he played in the 2013

---

59 Derek Wong, "Watch Chris Rock's Opening Monologue at the 2016 Oscars," oscar.go.com, February 28, 2016.

60 Chris Rock, "Chris Rock Pens Blistering Essay on Hollywood's Race Problem: 'It's a White Industry,'" *The Hollywood Reporter*, December 13, 2014.

and 2014 seasons. Thompson has played several black historical icons, including B. B. King, Desmond Tutu, Louis Armstrong, Maya Angelou, and, most recently, Martin Luther King Jr.

TWENTY-FIRST-CENTURY PARODYING OF MARTIN LUTHER KING JR.

In the 2015 *SNL* sketch "Martin Luther King, Jr. Learns About the Country's Equal Rights Progress," the ghost of King, played by Kenan Thompson, drops in on a high school student (played by Pete Davidson) who is up late writing a paper on King's legacy. The student, who like many millennials knows very little about King, updates the fictional King about how American race relations have changed and how he has been memorialized since he died. He tells him that streets and a federal holiday have been named in his honor and that a new film, *Selma*, explores his contributions to the civil rights movement. While the notion of progress, as epitomized by having a black president, is shared with the apparition of King, the sketch cleverly points out how social activism and protest strategies have changed since the civil rights movement. Although the King family probably would not have approved of this parody, it was not contentious and did not trivialize King in the same manner that Jamie Foxx did in the 2000 *SNL* sketch "A Martin Luther King Day Moment" that satirized King's "I Have a Dream" oration.

In Foxx's rendition of King, he is delivering an early version of his famous speech. "I have a dream," Foxx opens his speech, "I keep having this dream and I guess that it is what you would call a reoccurring dream. I'm at my old high school and I'm naked. And I'm taking the class that I never went to. The dream is very stressful to me." He then rambles on about this strange dream for about a minute. While Thompson's impersonation of King is not as disrespectful as Foxx's, throughout the sketch, Thompson does playfully re-invoke King's last major speech delivered on the day before he was assassinated, "I've Been to the Mountaintop." After each update that Thompson's King receives about the present state of the struggle for social justice, he pessimistically responds that Americans are "still climbing that mountain."[61]

Between Foxx's and Thompson's skits, other satirists have parodied King in comedy sketches. Countless amateur comedians and impersonators have uploaded onto YouTube spoofs on King's "I Have a Dream" oration.

One of the most famous King satires is Aaron McGruder's animated *Boondocks* episode "Return of the King" that originally aired the day before the King federal holiday in 2006. According to scholar Deborah Elizabeth Whaley, this episode significantly helped boost the ratings of McGruder's cartoon series. Much anticipated, "Return of the King" is considered one of McGruder's more

---

61   "A Martin Luther King Day Moment," *Saturday Night Live*, Season 25, nbc.com, January 8, 2000; "Martin Luther King, Jr. Learns About the Country's Equal Rights Progress," *Saturday Night Live*, Season 40, nbc.com, January 17, 2015.

controversial skits. Shortly after it was first aired, the Reverend Al Sharpton called upon Cartoon Network to issue an apology for belittling King's legacy and to pull all of McGruder's episodes "that desecrate black historic figures." Sharpton was particularly offended by McGruder's use of the n-word and while he claimed that he respected the cartoonist's craft, for him, "Return of the King" was "over the line."[62] Other older African Americans chastised the then thirty-two-year-old McGruder. Longtime *USA Today* columnist DeWayne Wickham, for instance, agreed with Sharpton. While he appreciated how McGruder's fictional King criticized "the failings of some blacks" to live up to the ideals of his dream, Wickham argued that by having King use the n-word so liberally he "pushes the slain civil rights leader into the swamp of self-loathing speech." Wickham was concerned that "some people might not get the point he's trying to make," that "most will not see—or hear—anything beyond King repeatedly calling his people 'nigger.'"[63]

McGruder defended his Peabody Award-winning sketch. On January 16, 2006, he was interviewed by Cynthia McFadden on *Nightline*. McFadden began by asking McGruder about his use of the n-word in the sketch. With a smile on his face, this astute hip-hop generationer let her know that in the *Boondocks* he uses "nigga." "We never use the n-word on my show," he underscored. McGruder acknowledged the challenging role of satirists, noting: "It's kind of our job to be out there on the edge." In response to a question about what King would be doing today, McGruder commented that King would not "fit in" with the "modern context." If King had been alive in 2000, he would have been seventy-one years old and would have evolved with the times in his own way. McGruder's presentist response freezes King in time. McFadden ends by asking McGruder what King means to him. McGruder's response was concise and introspective. Armed with a BA in African American Studies from the University of Maryland, he cited black nationalist historian John Henrik Clarke and admired King because "he died for what he believed in." Suffice it to say that McGruder handled himself with great poise, successfully disempowering his critics.[64]

Though discussions of "Return of the King" died down several months after it originally aired, in January 2015 it made it into the news again. Without permission from school administrators in her district, a second-grade teacher in Cedarville, Arkansas, showed McGruder's King episode to her students in celebration of Martin Luther King Jr. Day. More than a few parents were outraged. In this case, Wickham's criticism was valid.

---

62   "Sharpton Criticizes 'Boondocks' for N-word Use," *The Associated Press*, January 25, 2006.

63   DeWayne Wickham, "'Boondocks' Steps Over the Line in Its Treatment of King," *USA Today*, January 31, 2006.

64   See ABC broadcast, "Pushing the Envelope: An Interview with Aaron McGruder (host Cynthia McFadden), *Nightline*, January 16, 2006.

McGruder's satire of King remains the most thought-provoking piece of its kind. In "The Return of the King," *Boondocks'* protagonist Huey Freeman revises the history of King.[65] According to Huey, King was not assassinated on April 4, 1968. He fell into a coma and woke up in late October 2000. Huey explains that "Kingmania" ensued at first. However, after the resurrected King appeared on a television show and said that he would "turn the other cheek" in dealing with terrorism, he was labeled an al-Qaeda sympathizer and his newly found popularity disappears, as evidenced by people calling him all sorts of names when he is out and about and the lack of people who attended a book signing for his *Dream Deterred* that prior to his decline was entitled *Dream Deferred*. Huey and his grandfather, Robert Freeman, meet up with King at his book signing and King joins the Freeman family for dinner.

McGruder creatively rewrites another famous episode in US history by having King and Robert Freeman recount how Robert was active in the Montgomery Bus Boycott, sitting next to Rosa Parks when she refused to give up her seat. With this, McGruder was symbolically challenging "great woman history" by acknowledging the many other African Americans who engaged in similar activities as she did but did not receive the credit. Cedric the Entertainer's character, Eddie, did a similar thing in the 2002 comedy *Barbershop* (2002) when he mentioned others who refused to give up their seats in segregated buses. Huey befriends King, fills him in on what has happened to black America while he was in a coma, and convinces him to start a new political party. Finding it difficult to communicate with young African Americans, King hires an "urban promotions firm" to help publicize his new party's first major meeting. When King and Huey arrive at the church where the meeting is, which looks more like a club than a church, they are shocked by what they see: groups of different black people trying to get in the spotlight. A fed up King ascends to the podium and shouts: "Will you ignorant niggas please shut the hell up?!"

King then proceeds to deliver a passionate speech:

Is this it?! This is what I got all those ass-whuppings for?! I had a dream once. It was a dream that little black boys and little black girls would drink from the river of prosperity, freed from the thirst of oppression. But lo and behold, some four decades later, what have I found but a bunch of trifling, shiftless, good-for-nothing niggas. And I know some of you don't like to hear me say that word. It's the ugliest word in the English language, but that's what I see now, niggas. And you don't want to be a nigga. Cause niggas are living contradictions! Niggas are full of unfulfilled ambitions! Niggas wax and wane, niggas love to complain, niggas love to hear themselves talk but hate to explain! Niggas love being another man's judge and jury! Niggas procrastinate until it's time to worry! Niggas love to be late! Niggas hate to

---

65   Aaron McGruder, "Return of the King," *Boondocks*, Season 1, Episode 9, Cartoon Network, January 15, 2006.

hurry! Black Entertainment Television is the worst thing I've ever seen in my life! Usher, Michael Jackson is NOT a genre of music! And now, I'd like to talk about Soul Plane . . . I've seen what's around the corner! I've seen what's over the horizon! And I promise you, you niggas have nothing to celebrate! And, no, I won't get there with you. I'm going to Canada.[66]

McGruder's fictional King's oration was a great success. His message resonated with black people across the nation who began to heed his call, change their ways, and engage in protests reminiscent of the uprisings during the Black Power era.

I agree with Deborah Elizabeth Whaley that McGruder's "satire is ever the more vital in serving as the medium through which" young African Americans "might find enjoyment to raise their consciousness to a critical level."[67] I do not agree with Wickham, who suggested that most viewers would miss the clever subtext of McGruder's sketch—that African American culture has in many ways suffered during the post-civil rights era, that the sacrifices of freedom fighters from King's time have been underappreciated, and that, at bottom as it has often been conjectured, King and his contemporaries might be turning in their graves because of the contemporary state of African American life.[68]

At the same time, through the character Huey (named after Black Panther Party co-founder Huey P. Newton), McGruder demonstrated that some millennials have not forgotten their history like his brother Riley, who mistakes King for actor Morgan Freeman. When Cedric the Entertainer was criticized for what he said about Rosa Parks and Jesse Jackson in *Barbershop*, in an interview with CNN he commented that he was happy that black historical subject matter was being discussed outside of Black History Month, that this controversial dialogue succeeded in encouraging younger blacks to rethink what they had been told about these black historical icons. Similarly, with "Return of the King," McGruder generated discourse and debates about King beyond mid-January.

In 2012, Comedy Central's *Key & Peele* produced two major sketches on King that did not have the impact of McGruder's long piece, nor were they as impactful as those done on *SNL*. In "Martin Luther King, Jr. vs. Malcolm X at the Theater," Jordan Peele and Keegan-Michael Key play King and Malcolm respectively in a play. They divert from the script and compete for their audience's approval by reiterating their divergent philosophies. The respectful competition resembles a battle between two emcees. In the end, both succeed in winning over the appreciative African American audience. In another sketch,

---

66   Ibid.

67   Deborah Elizabeth Whaley, "Graphic Blackness/Anime Noir: Aaron McFruder's *The Boondocks* and the Adult Swim," in *Watching While Black: Centering the Television of Black Audiences*, edited by Beretta E. Smith-Shomade, New Brunswick: Rutgers University Press, 2012, 187–206.

68   Wickham, "'Boondocks Steps Over the Line in Its Treatment of King."

Key plays Reverend Robert Jones, a mythical civil rights preacher and colleague of King, who is burdened by the responsibility of delivering a speech following King's famous "I Have a Dream" oration at the March on Washington on August 28, 1963.

Like the *SNL* sketch that Foxx played King in, "Speaking After Martin Luther King, Jr. Pt. 1" is shot in grainy black and white.[69] To add further authenticity to this sketch, original footage from the march is used. In fact, Peele, who plays King for several seconds, and Key's Reverend Jones character are superimposed with figures who originally flanked King in 1963. The skit has a sense of realness that is reminiscent of the 2001 controversial commercial by Alcatel Americas that had King delivering his "I Have a Dream" speech at the Washington Monument by himself. The audience was completely cut out from the footage. This commercial, one journalist noted, was a "'Forrest Gump'–like spin." Many spoke out against this commercialization of King. The former chair of the NAACP, Julian Bond, commented: "I guess this is just proof that in America even the most sacred icons of the civil rights movement are not immune to exploitation and commercialization."[70] More recently, during the 2018 Superbowl, Dodge ran an ad for their Ram trucks that used excerpts from King's "Drum Major Instintct" speech that he delivered in Atlanta, GA on February 4, 1968. Perhaps because it did not appear on prime time television, did not center King, and did not use extensive quotes from his speech, this *Key & Peele* parody did not spark controversy. On the other hand, it received nods of approval from online social media outlets such as the *Huffington Post* and various comedy websites.

"Speaking After Martin Luther King, Jr. Pt. 1" begins with the fictional King played by Peele concluding his speech by declaring the famous lines, "Free at last, free at last. Thank God Almighty, we are free at last." Viewers are then shown footage of those in attendance. A nervous Reverend Jones then steps up to the podium after he is introduced. Before he begins his speech, he covers the microphone and whispers to those near him, "How I'm supposed to follow that? I can't, nobody can follow that." He then says, "That was the best speech that I have heard in my entire life. Ever. I have never heard a better speech." Full of fear, he then says that King covered much of what he planned to talk about in his speech "A Vision for the Future." After he jokes, "I am not saying Dr. King copied my speech." The audience perceives him to be saying that King may have plagiarized from him and the original footage from the March on Washington that is shown reveals listeners being disappointed with Jones's attempt to be funny. Desperate, Jones pulls out his note cards only to find nothing of use. He then introduces a solution to the "race problem" in the United States. "How 'bout we let black people enslave white people," he suggests. This too is met with

---

69   *Key & Peele*, Comedy Central, Season 2, Episode 2, October 3, 2012.
70   Paul Farhi, "King's 'Dream' Becomes Commercial," *Washington Post*, March 28, 2001.

disapproval from his white and black listeners. In another act of desperation, he tells all the "Negroes" to hug a white person. Viewers are then shown actual footage of black civil rights protesters being chased by the police. Jones has sparked a riot. The sketch ends with Jones being sprayed by a water hose while everyone near the podium runs for cover.

In 2010, Peter Shukoff and Lloyd Ahlquist created the popular YouTube video series *Epic Rap Battles*. In 2013, they released "Gandhi vs. Martin Luther King, Jr.," starring Key as Gandhi and Peele as King. As of mid-2016, this brief video received more than sixty million views. Gandhi begins the battle by celebrating his greatness and subtly accusing King of plagiarism and being distracted with extramarital affairs. King responds by reminding Gandhi that he won the Nobel Peace Prize and has been memorialized in American culture. The video ends with King attempting to enter into a truce with Gandhi, who responds with "I don't give a fuck." Those sensitive to how historical icons are commemorated would probably be troubled by how Shukoff and Ahlquist treat their heroes.

Similar to *Epic Rap Battles* is Comedy Central's *Drunk History*, which premiered on July 9, 2013.[71] In the first season, the series had a very brief and inept sketch in which Martin Luther King Jr. and J. Edgar Hoover had a meeting in Hoover's office during which King attempted to suggest that they should become "better teammates." Hoover responded by celebrating the efforts of the FBI. Later, King received a call from an unidentified Malcolm X look-alike friend who asked him what his meeting with Hoover was like. King responded by saying that Hoover was an old crazy man. Little did King and his friend know that Hoover was listening to their conversation through a wiretap. Hoover was shocked to hear King dissing him. The point of this skit is unclear. Maybe the producers of *Drunk History* were trying to introduce its viewers to the fact that Hoover monitored King closely through the FBI.

REIMAGINING BLACK HISTORY ON SATURDAY NIGHT LIVE

In the twenty-first century, there have been a handful of sketches pertaining to African American history that feature the black *SNL* cast members, namely Tracy Morgan, Kenan Thompson, Maya Rudolph, Finesse Mitchell, and Jay Pharoah. Moreover, the topic of slavery has been the subject of several *SNL* sketches in the new millennium. Actor and comedian Tracy Morgan was a cast member on *SNL* from 1996 until 2003. One of his most famous characters was Brian Fellow, the host of "Brian Fellow's Safari Planet." Yet, in 2000, he played the role of a mythical "Uncle Jemima"—the drunkard husband of the caricature Aunt Jemima—in a minute and a half long commercial parody advertisement for "Uncle Jemima's Pure Down-Home Mash Liquor." Actor and comedian Tim

---

71 Steve Heisler, "Drunk History," July 9, 2013, tv.avclub.com.

Meadows, who was a regular cast member on *SNL* from 1991 until 2000, is also in the skit playing Sammy, a friend of Uncle Jemima's.

The skit begins with a drunk Uncle Jemima walking with a cane and talking to an imaginary bird. Though the specific historical context of the commercial is unclear, based upon how Morgan is dressed, how he talks, and his apparent residence on a farm or plantation of some sort, the sketch conjures up memories of slavery. Uncle Jemima is marketing a 190-proof liquor that is guaranteed to get someone drunk for less money. The bottle of the product closely resembles Aunt Jemima's pancake syrup but has the image of an elderly African American man named Frank Brown, who was the face for Uncle Ben's rice. Uncle Jemima justifies his product by saying that he is selling what he knows best. He dismisses his wife's criticism of him. "Now, she says that sellin' booze is degradin' to our people," Morgan says with an exaggerated slave dialect, "I always say that black folk ain't exactly swellin' up with pride on account of you flippin' flapjack!" He then insults his wife with a plea to his potential buyers: "Hook a brotha up. Buy some of my pure mash liquor and let's show that old bitch there's more to this world than just makin' pancake." At the end of the commercial, we get a glimpse of Aunt Jemima (played by Morgan) who with a big grin on her face lets her husband know that the "pancakes is ready" to which Uncle Jemima responds, "I just want to make liquor."[72]

While this commercial is a parody that pokes fun at the stereotypical portrayals of black men as "uncles" and black women as "mammies" with mild cynicism, Morgan does reinforce these denigrating archetypes that are still prevalent in American culture.

In a 2006 *SNL* sketch on Colonial Williamsburg, Maya Rudolph and Kenan Thompson play reenactors who play slaves. Rudolph is called "mammy" by an overenthusiastic performer played by the host John C. Reilly. Because he is committed to providing the visitors with as much historical accuracy as possible, he speaks to the black people playing slaves as if he is really a slaveholder. The black performers, Rudolph and Thompson, reveal their anger with Reilly, epitomized at the end of the sketch when Thompson threatens to beat him down in the parking lot.[73]

SNL had fun parodying *12 Years a Slave*. In "12 Days Not a Slave" that aired in late October 2013, Jay Pharoah plays Cecil, a former slave who was just emancipated, yet knows nothing about how to handle his freedom, a freedom that in the beginning of the sketch is credited to Lincoln's 1863 Emancipation Proclamation, as is often the case. In essence, Cecil is portrayed as being totally unaware of how to act as a newly freed man in the presence of white people. He thinks that he is on an equal footing with his white counterparts, epitomized in his attempt to order a drink at a saloon and talk to white women. His white

---

72   See "Uncle Jemima's Pure Mash Liquor," *Saturday Night Live*, Season 25, nbc.com, February 5, 2000 .

73   See "Colonial Williamsburg," *Saturday Night Live*, Season 32, nbc.com, October 21, 2006

Canadian friend Zackary, a spin-off of Northrop's white ally Samuel Bass played by host Edward Norton, schools him about how to cope with his freedom. "My God," Cecil says at the end of the sketch, "I guess I really never realized the price of being free."[74] For those who have written about the meaning of freedom to African Americans in the immediate wake of emancipation, Cecil's behavior is a gross aberration.

In March 2014, *SNL* had a skit, "*12 Years a Slave* Auditions," in which Steve McQueen (played by Kenan Thompson) discussed the challenges of casting whites who could play slaveholders. In the presence of Jay Pharoah and Sasheer Zamata, who were playing the roles of members of the film production crew, the politically correct white male actors who auditioned were uncomfortable playing the roles of pro-slavery racists. In the end, only one of the white actors, a racist at heart who really did not need to act to play the role of a nineteenth-century racist, was comfortable acting as a slaveholder.

On the first day of Black History Month in 2014, Pharoah, Zamata, and Thompson performed their hilarious and much tweeted skit "28 Reasons to Hug a Black Guy." The sketch begins in a high school classroom with a teacher introducing a presentation for Black History Month, a song, that the three black students in the class have prepared. Pharoah begins the rap by paying tribute to three of the most widely discussed black historical icons during this annual commemoration, Rosa Parks, Martin Luther King Jr., and Harriet Tubman. "Black history, our forefathers pave the way," Pharoah rhymed, "Here's twenty-eight reasons to hug a black guy today. Number one, we deserve a chance." Then, in unison with angry looks on their faces, Pharoah, Zamata, and Thompson shout: "Two through twenty-eight: slavery!" Before this line, the teacher and white students in the class were smiling and bobbing their heads to the music. When slavery was mentioned and became the hook and mantra, the students looked sad and guilt-ridden. Pharoah followed with a verse explaining how black history is not taught in high school, so he had to do research for the presentation. "Did a lot of research, slavery kept coming up," he spit. Then, acting as a hype-man, Thompson clamored to his white classmates in the tradition of call-and-response, "When I say slavery, you say sorry!"[75]

This skit adroitly speaks to several tendencies. In many high schools throughout the nation, African American history is only acknowledged during Black History Month, and black students are often expected to be the resident experts on or translators for the black experience. Along with the civil rights movement and perhaps the Harlem Renaissance, slavery predominantly shapes US high school discussions of black history and this often makes black students feel uneasy. It can be painful for young African Americans to revisit, in the case

---

74   "12 Days Not a Slave," *Saturday Night Live*, Season 39, nbc.com, October 26, 2016.
75   "28 Reasons to Hug a Black Guy," *Saturday Night Live*, Season 39, nbc.com, February 1, 2014.

of slavery, the oppression of their ancestors. As Chris Rock reflected while reminiscing on his traumatizing years in a white public school, "It was hard being the only black kid in my class. Whenever they would do that lesson on slavery, everyone would turn around and look at me."[76] White students, on the other hand, tend to have mixed feelings toward slavery, ranging from guilt to denial to shock to disbelief to everything in between. The skit is also refreshing because it suggests that young African American high school students have a sense of black historical consciousness.

In 2014, two black women, Sasheer Zamata and Leslie Jones, joined the *SNL* cast. With very few exceptions, the sketches that they have appeared in have focused on race, black women, and black popular culture. Zamata, for instance, first appeared on *SNL* in January 2014 and, beginning with her *comme ci, comme ça* impersonation of Rihanna, consistently played the black female character lingering in the background. She left the show in May 2017. The much more experienced Leslie Jones, on the other hand, has been given major roles when compared to Zamata. Her identity as a strong, assertive, and self-confident black woman usually prevails in the more than one hundred sketches that she has performed in. Five months before she made her official debut on *SNL*, she performed a controversial monologue on the popular "Weekend Update" segment hosted at that time by *SNL* writer Colin Jost.

Known as the "slavery skit" and the "No. 1 Slave Draft Pick," Leslie Jones's commentary prompted a social media firestorm. Many African American bloggers in particular debated and in many cases condemned Jones's jokes about slavery. Jones's monologue was discussed by many online mainstream newspapers and newsmagazines. In the first week of May, articles like the *New York Daily's* "Leslie Jones Sparks Outrage with Slavery Skit on 'Saturday Night Live'" and *People's "Saturday Night Live*: Leslie Jones's Slavery Skit and 5 More Controversial Moments" were common. Of the numerous Jones's haters, digital senior editor of *Ebony* magazine Jamilah Lemieux was among those most offended. She called Jones's performance a "grossly offensive skit about slave rape" and "something far more offensive to Black women than Kenan Thompson in a dress." If this was what it meant to have an increased African American female presence on *SNL*, Lemieux was concerned. She also found Jones's defense of her sketch to be weak and predictable and concluded that Jones "should be ashamed of herself." She added: "Black women are so often the butt of the joke. If any of us deserve to be protected from such, it is our ancestors who endured the indignity and dehumanization of slavery."[77]

What did Jones say that nauseated Lemieux and caused such a frenzy of reactions on social media? Introduced by Colin Jost as being *SNL's* in-house

---

76   Rock, *Rock This!* 46–47.

77   Jamilah Lemieux, "Once Again, No One is Laughing at 'SNL': Jamilah Lemieux on Leslie Jones' Controversial Slavery Routine," ebony.com, May 5, 2014.

"image expert," Jones began her two-and-a-half-minute long routine by addressing actress Lupita Nyong'o being on the cover of *People* magazine's annual "World's Most Beautiful" issue. Jones acknowledged Nyong'o's beauty, but stressed to Jost that she also had her strengths and assets. She told him that she could protect him if his life was threatened by three Crips "who about to whip [his] ass" in a parking lot at night. Validating her own beauty and unique attributes of black womanhood, she then shifted her discussion to slavery, passionately arguing that "back in the slave days" she would have been a prized possession. She trumpeted that she would have made the "most useful" list for sure. Jones said: "The way we value black beauty has changed. I'm single now, but back in the slave days, I would have never been single. I'm 6 feet tall and I'm strong. Look at me, I'm a Mandingo." In response to Jost asking her if she wanted to be a slave, she responded: "I do not want to be a slave. I don't like working for all you white people now and you pay me." She then offered her most controversial statements:

> But back in the slave days, my love life would have been better. Master would have hooked me up with the best brotha on the plantation and every nine months I'd be in the corner popping out super babies. I'd just keep popping them out. Shaq. Kobe, LeBron, Kimbo Slice, Sinbad. I would be the number one slave draft pick. All of the plantations would want me . . . Now, I can't get a brotha to take me out for a cheap dinner. Can a bitch get a beef bowl?!!⁷⁸

Jones did not waste any time responding directly to Lemieux and her other critics in the black community. Several days after her monologue, she sent out close to twenty tweets in which she unapologetically defended her routine and explained why she said what she did. She called the scuttlebutt "ridiculous" and flat-out rejected Lemieux's claim that her skit had anything to do with rape. With humor and razor-edged candor, her goal was to place herself within the context of the "slave days." In fact, based upon her general knowledge of African American history, she viewed her commentary as being historically accurate. "What part of this joke that wasn't true?" Jones retorted in a tweet, "I would have been used for breeding straight up. That's my reality." Jones did have a point. Based upon her stature, something that she has often joked about (she opened her 2010 stand-up special "Problem Child" by saying "I know ya'll already noticed that I'm a big bitch . . ."), during the "slave days" that she spoke of she would have most likely been viewed as being "useful" to slaveholders as not only a laborer but also a slave woman who could reproduce. Jones further justified her skit as most comedians conveniently would have: "I'm a comic it is my job to take things and make them funny to make you think."

---

78 "Weekend Update: Leslie Jones on Lupita Nyong'o," *Saturday Night Live*, Season 39, nbc. com, May 3, 2014.

She also offered a relevant gendered analysis, suggesting that if Chris Rock or Dave Chappelle had told her joke, it would have been called "brilliant." Jones could have been more precise in her reference to Rock, one of her greatest supporters who recommended her to SNL's Lorne Michaels. After all, a decade earlier in Never Scarred, Rock joked about slave breeding in a much more problematic manner than Jones who, unlike Rock, used herself and her own body as the focus of the joke. Guaranteeing the historical accuracy of his assessment of slavery, Rock did not receive the same type of criticisms and personal attacks that Jones did.

It is also worth noting that two years before Jones's skit, the first season of Key & Peele had a skit, "Auction Block," in which the duo played slaves who were being sold in Savannah, Georgia, in 1848. Given the horrific nature of slave auctions often characterized by the breaking up of families and intrusive inspections, those who were offended by Jones's skit should have had problems with this one as well. When they first step onto the auction block, Key and Peele whisper to each other that they will lead revolts if they are sold. Then, after four slaves are sold for between $2 and $9 (absurd prices for slaves) instead of them, they begin to get jealous and angry because they are apparently not sought after by buyers. In an effort to justify their worth, they then advertise themselves to their potential buyers as if it is their goal to be purchased. The portrayal of slaves as happy and "docile" is equally as detrimental as reinforcing stereotypes about the enslaved black woman as an over-sexed breeder. Unlike Jones, Key and Peele were not asked to expand upon what their intentions were with their sketch.

In a long 2016 article in the New Yorker based upon an interview with her, Jones opened up more about the origins of her slavery skit. Andrew Marantz wrote:

One night, after a bad date, she came home alone, smoked a joint, and turned on the TV. She told me, "A slave movie was on and, out of bitterness, this ridiculous idea popped into my head: during slave times, I never would have been single." She wrote a joke based on the premise, but felt it was too personal to perform. "It wasn't a commentary on slavery," she said. "It was about my pain—about how hard it is, as a black woman, to get black dudes to date you. The first time I told it"—to a mostly black audience in L.A.—"it massacred to the point where I went, 'There's something real here.'" She told it several more times, in clubs and on TV.[79]

If Jones had reserved her "slavery skit" for the black audiences that she first pitched it to, it would have most likely never become the subject of debate within the black community. The fact that she performed this sketch on the SNL before a predominantly white audience changed its meaning in a similar manner to

---

79   Andrew Marantz, "Ready for the Prime Time," New Yorker, January 4, 2016.

how Bill Cosby's 2004 "Pound Cake" speech and other tirades against poor African Americans that were publicized by the mainstream white press upset so many black social commentators.

CONCLUSION

Going back to the early twentieth century, we can identify those standout African American comedians and satirists who undeniably transformed their craft and future generations. For most of those discussed in this chapter, Richard Pryor was a guiding light and guru. It is too early to predict who will be the next Chris Rock, Dave Chappelle, or Aaron McGruder. It would be a reach to identify an African American millennial comedian who will significantly shape the future of black comedy, especially as it pertains to comedy focused on race and black history. The next generation of African American comedians and satirists will inevitably be molded by their times, their heroes, role models, and mentors and the generations to which they belong. Perhaps because they were born during the civil rights–Black Power movement and came of age during a distinct post-Soul black consciousness movement, Rock, Lawrence, Chappelle, McGruder, and others were more stimulated to address racial inequality and African American history in their art.

The closest heir to the throne of black comedy at this point, if there is such a thing, is arguably Kevin Hart. He has recently been called the "hottest stand-up comic in America." His *What Now?* tour broke some records and made history. Born in 1979 and highly influenced by hip-hop culture, he has already appeared in many movies, he created the popular BET parody *Real Husbands of Hollywood*, he launched a Sirius XM channel, and he has starred in many major stand-up specials. Unlike many of the comedians discussed in this chapter, Hart's stand-up comedy is not contentious, nor is it focused on the contemporary state of blacks in American society. He did not address or joke about race or African American history in his *I'm a Grown Little Man* (2009), *Seriously Funny* (2010), *Laugh at My Pain* (2011), *Let Me Explain* (2013), or *What Now?* (2016). In one sense, Hart embraces what Paul Mooney has described as "racial neutrality." As Mooney reflected in 2009, "If they want to gain a wide crossover audience, black comics have to be careful what they say."[80]

Hart seems to have deliberately avoided "race-based" humor in order to win over as many white fans as possible. Though it has been considered racial satire by some, the comedy *Get Hard* (2015), co-starring Hart and Will Ferrell, reinforces many stereotypes about African Americans for laughs. Hart defended Etan Cohen's film, claiming that it ultimately helps challenge prevailing misconceptions about black people through the evolving relationship between his character Darrell Lewis and James King (played by Ferrell). In response to a tweet

---

80 Mooney, *Black Is the New White*, 16.

criticizing how he depicted black people in his films, he tweeted back: "When are black people going to stop being so hard on their own kind . . . We can't do better until we support each other . . . I make movies for everyone."[81] In 2016, Katt Williams (who joked about black history a bit in his 2018 Netflix stand-up special *Great America*) accused him of being a "puppet," a code word for a safe black comedian who has won whites' approval. While Williams has made many outlandish statements, even calling Chris Rock a "Stepin Fethchit," his diss of Hart could be reasonably compared to Paul Mooney calling Bill Cosby "the perfect Negro" for white American audiences.

When Hart has talked about black history, his observations are simple and conventional. For instance, in a brief 2012 BET Black History Month tribute, Hart overviewed the life of Richard Pryor, concluding: "Richard Pryor paved the way for me to be a star. And I thank him for being a black history hero."[82] Several years later during Black History Month, he tweeted a joke to his millions of followers: "For Black History Month I feel like all black people should get free cable. Just for one month," he jested, "we should get all of the channels lmao."[83]

Hart appeared on the cover of the August 13, 2015, issue of *Rolling Stone* magazine. In the lengthy essay that included an interview with the rising star, Hart explained his approach of "racial neutrality." He underscored that he was "not a political guy" and that he avoided talking about pressing issues like the numerous deaths of black men at the hands of the police because "it's not a joking matter. There's no joking there. I would not touch it."[84] Unlike Chris Rock, Martin Lawrence, or Dave Chappelle, Hart does not deliberately sound off to his audiences about serious matters concerning black life in America. The closest that Hart has recently come to being "political," as he put it, was at the 88th annual Academy Awards ceremony. Before introducing The Weekend, he freestyled a bit. "I want to take a moment to applaud all my actors and actresses of color that didn't get nominated tonight," Hart continued

> I want them to understand that tonight should not determine [the worth of] the hard work and effort that you put into your craft . . . At the end of the day, we love what we do and we're breaking major ground doing it. These problems of today will become the problems of the old. Let's not let this negative issue of diversity beat us.[85]

Hart's kumbaya comments were strikingly different from Rock's observations at the same event. In essence, Hart was telling black people to be patient

81   Jackie Willis, "Kevin Hart Goes on Twitter Rant After He's Accused of Making 'Stereotypical' Black Movies, etonline.com, January 29, 2016.

82   "News: Kevin Hart: Black History Month," BET Season 2012, February 1, 2012.

83   "BET Black History Month: Know Your History," youtube.com, February 7, 2013 ; twitter.com/kevinhart4real.

84   Jonah Weiner, "Kevin Hart's Funny Business," *Rolling Stone*, July 29, 2015.

85   Ashley Williams, "Kevin Hart Takes Moment During 88th Academy Awards to Applaud Actors of Color," hiphollywood.com, February 29, 2016.

for change. Hollywood, he implied, will continue to open more doors to African American actors and actresses. As Hart continues his remarkable career, it is possible that he may incorporate discussions of race and black history into his stand-up performances. As public figures with a large audience base, comedians like Hart have the potential to sway, if only for a few moments in passing, how their fans think about a range of issues. The comedians discussed in this chapter have demonstrated the potential effect of their craft as an enterprising platform for making sense of and reenvisioning black history.

5

"So Long in Coming"

Political and Legal Attempts to Right Past Wrongs

It is not only in remembering that shameful past that we can make amends and repair our nation, but it is in remembering that past that we can build a better present and a better future. And without remembering it, we cannot make amends and we cannot go forward . . . The United States government did something that was wrong—deeply, profoundly, morally wrong . . . The American people are sorry—for the loss, for the years of hurt. You did nothing wrong, but you were grievously wronged . . . I apologize and I am sorry that this apology has been *so long in coming.*

—President William Jefferson "Bill" Clinton, 1997

An emotional President Bill Clinton offered the remorseful remarks above in a monumental speech on May 16, 1997, approximately one year before he expressed regret for how the United States benefitted from the slave trade while visiting Rwanda during his newsworthy tour of Africa.[1]

In his historic "Apology for Study Done in Tuskegee" delivered in the East Room of the White House, Clinton officially said on behalf of the US government that he was sorry for the infamous Tuskegee Study of Untreated Syphilis in the Negro Male that was conducted by the US Public Health Service from 1932 until 1972. Directing his apology to the survivors and their descendants as well as to the black community as a whole, the 42nd President of the United States called the study "profoundly, morally wrong" and "so clearly racist." In issuing this ceremonial atonement for an unethical study that ended twenty-five years earlier, Clinton was not stepping out on a limb or taking any racialized political risks.

As a direct result of Tuskegee Study, more than two decades before Clinton offered his penitence, Congress had passed the National Research Act that lead to the creation of the National Commission for the Protection of Human Subjects of Biomedical and Behavioral Research and the release of the landmark Belmont Report. The US government had also already paid some restitution to the study's surviving subjects and to the heirs of those patients who died, and established the Tuskegee Health Benefit Program. Furthermore, in 1981, historian James H. Jones first released his path-breaking classic *Bad Blood: The*

---

1   William J. Clinton, "President William J. Clinton's Remarks," in *Tuskegee's Truths: Rethinking the Tuskegee Syphilis Study*, ed. Susan M. Reverby, 574–77, Chapel Hill: University of North Carolina Press, 2000 (emphasis added).

Tuskegee Syphilis Experiment, and, on the eve of Clinton's apology, the popular, award-winning HBO television drama on the experiment, *Miss Evers' Boys,* debuted starring Alfre Woodard and Laurence Fishburne. Clearly, by the late 1990s, the Tuskegee Study already had been widely publicized and condemned by many.

On behalf of the US government, during a private memorial service that was made public on C-CPAN and was covered in the mainstream media, Clinton was simply repenting for an obvious tragedy that, unlike slavery, was part of America's more recent past. That said, several years before the new millennium, he became the first US president to admit guilt and seek forgiveness for past atrocities committed against a group of African Americans.

"The United States will be willing to acknowledge past errors where those errors have been made," remarked President Obama in 2009 in Port of Spain, Trinidad and Tobago at the opening ceremony of the Summit of the Americas.[2] Obama's declaration abroad apparently did not extend to his own country's past mistreatment of black Americans. While Obama has opined that the legacy of slavery and Jim Crow segregation has impacted the contemporary status of African Americans, he did not issue an apology to black people for past racial injustices in the elaborate manner that Clinton did with his denunciation of the Tuskegee Study. Unsurprisingly, no American president has ever formally apologized for slavery. Such a move would, after all, potentially provide more ammunition for advocates of reparations, and no American president wants to open that can of worms.

Like others before him, Obama had ample opportunities to apologize for slavery on many symbolic occasions, most notably in December 2015, when he commemorated the 150th anniversary of the 13th Amendment at the US Capitol. He condemned slavery like his predecessors by calling it "antithetical" to American ideals; as expected, however, Obama did not go to the next level by formally apologizing for the US government's championing of slavery. Instead, as he had previously done, he pointed out that "the scars of our nation's original sin are still with us today."[3]

One of Obama's major apologies to an oppressed group was one that he bestowed upon Native Americans. On December 19, 2009, he signed the Native American Apology Resolution into law that, among other things, "apologized on behalf of the United States to all Native Peoples for the many instances of violence, maltreatment, and neglect of Native Peoples by citizens of the United States." This act of palliation, as many of its critics have pointed out, was not only "watered down, not making a direct apology from the government," but it was

---

2   Barack Obama, "Remarks by the President at the Summit of the Americas," Hyatt Regency, Port of Spain, Trinidad and Tobago, April 17, 2009, whitehouse.gov.

3   Barack Obama, "Remarks by the President at Commemoration of the 150th Anniversary of the 13th Amendment," US Capitol, Washington, DC, December 9, 2015, whitehouse.gov.

not a public admission of guilt spoken from the mouth of the president himself and, as such, it fell short of constituting a genuine apology and slipped under the radar.[4] One wonders if, while signing this document, Obama noticed that he could have replaced *all Native Peoples* with *African Americans* and it would have been equally applicable.

To be fair, before he became president, Obama was more forthright in his appraisal of the past oppression of African Americans. On June 13, 2005, then Senator Obama (D-Illinois) offered a candid and heartfelt statement in support of the Senate's momentous Resolution 39 that apologized for its past failure to enforce anti-lynching legislation. He was "proud" that his country was "taking a step that allows us—after looking at the 4,700 deaths from lynchings, the hate that was behind those deaths, and this Chamber's refusal to try to stop them—to finally say that we were wrong." He declared that there was "a power in acknowledging error and mistake." Obama, who underscored that this confession and apology were *finally* being made, then went a step further by calling upon the Senate to do "something concrete and tangible to heal the long shadow of slavery and the legacy of racial discrimination."[5] Though deliberately vague, this rhetoric sounds very much like that of reparations activists.

It is not surprising that during his first presidential campaign Obama did not reiterate what he argued years earlier or show any sympathy toward the reparations movement. During the 2008 presidential campaign, Senator John McCain (R-Arizona) told at least one reporter that he stood behind a resolution apologizing for slavery. Obama understandably remained silent on this issue during his quest to become America's first black president.

Yet, in a statement celebrating Juneteenth, on June 19, 2009, President Obama did allude to the Senate's monumental apology for slavery and segregation. Many in the mainstream social media were overenthusiastic in claiming that the newly elected president had openly praised the Senate's apology. Obama highlighted the historic nature of this resolution, but did not explicitly celebrate it as he did when he was a senator speaking about the Senate's 2005 apology for failing to pass anti-lynching legislation. "African Americans helped build our nation brick by brick and have contributed to her growth in every way, even when liberties were denied to them." Obama continued, "In light of the historic unanimous vote in the United States Senate this week supporting the call for an apology for slavery and segregation, the occasion carries even more significance."[6]

---

4 Rob Capriccioso, "A Sorry Saga: Obama Signs Native American Apology," *This Week From Indian Country Today*, January 20, 2010 .

5 Barack Obama, "Statement of Barack Obama on Anti-Lynching Apology Resolution," Senate Apology to Victims of Lynching, U.S. Senate, C-SPAN 2, June 13, 2005.

6 Barack Obama, "Statement from President Obama on the Occasion of Juneteenth," The White House, Office of the Press Secretary, June 19, 2009, whitehouse.gov.

A month later while the then newly elected US president was at Cape Coast Castle in Ghana during his tour of Africa, he called the slave trade a "great evil" but did not touch upon the history of slavery in the United States or apologize in any way for the slave trade as Clinton had done more than a decade earlier. A week later on a special edition of *Anderson Cooper 360°*, a private interaction that was televised once and is now available on YouTube, Obama was uncharacteristically plainspoken about slavery, commenting: "I think that the experience of slavery is like the experience of the Holocaust. I think it's one of the things you don't forget."[7] In comparing slavery with the Holocaust, which East Germany apologized for in April 1990, Obama was certainly putting forward a controversial assertion. With this simple observation, he validated the arguments of generations of black radical activists who, like Civil Rights Congress founder William L. Patterson, viewed episodes of black history through the lens of genocide. Obama echoed reparations activist and lawyer Randall Robinson who, at the dawning of the new millennium, called slavery and Jim Crow segregation the "black holocaust." Obama also perhaps even subtly intimated that he believed that an apology for slavery, a "holocaust," was warranted.

Pulitzer Prize-winning reporter Timothy Egan called upon Obama to apologize for slavery in a 2015 column in the *New York Times*. By apologizing for slavery, Egan touted, the "first black man to live in the White House, long hesitant about anything bold on the color divide, could make one of the most simple and dramatic moves of his presidency."[8] Egan's commentary, which earned him interviews on CNN with Don Lemon, was not only preachy and self-righteous, but also quite naïve. Because he is a black man, Obama could not have issued public and official apologies to the black community for past injustices as smoothly as Clinton and other white politicians. He was well aware that if he made racial reconciliation a part of his domestic policy, he would have been accused of being partial to African Americans and demonized even more. At the same time, as many of his African American detractors have argued, at the end of his second term he could have been more outspoken about African Americans' rights. Obama's approach to past atrocities committed against African Americans is analogous to his diverse and situational representations of African American history in general.

Months before Obama delivered his remarks commemorating the 150th anniversary of the 13th Amendment, Senator Bernie Sanders (D-Vermont) told radio host Joe Madison ("The Black Eagle") in an interview on Sirius XM's Urban View channel that an apology for slavery from the president of the United States was warranted. "As a nation we have got to apologize for slavery, and of course the president is the leader of the nation," the fiery Sanders testified.

---

7   "President Obama's African Journey," *Anderson Cooper 360°*, CNN, July 18, 2009 .
8   Timothy Egan, "Apologize for Slavery," *New York Times*, June 20, 2015, A19.

Perhaps in a desperate effort to win over undecided black voters (as McCain was probably attempting to do in 2007 by verbally backing a resolution apologizing for slavery), about a year later, shortly before the 2016 Democratic National Convention, Sanders reiterated what he told Madison. In early April 2016, he announced to members of Philadelphia's United Methodist Church that if elected president, he would issue a formal apology for slavery. "A lot of things that we have done in this country that are shameful, we've gotta recognize that," Sanders noted.[9] He added that he would also endorse reparations by investing in low-income black communities.

In a sense, Sanders's approach was a familiar one. As it has been pointed out, the essence of his sentiments and promises to black America was not new. American politicians had already entertained and delivered such apologies. While former Presidents Clinton and George W. Bush condemned the United States's participation in slavery while on tours of Africa, in 2007, the legislature of the Commonwealth of Virginia expressed "profound regret" for the state's past support of slavery. Soon thereafter, a group of other states followed suit and the Senate unanimously passed a resolution apologizing for slavery that included a predictable disclaimer prohibiting the gesture from being used for any claims against the US government.

During the late twentieth century and the twenty-first century, a variety of US politicians and policymakers—governors, senators, congressmen, and Presidents Clinton and Bush—as well as lawmakers and other state and city officials have symbolically and often strategically apologized for past atrocities committed against African American people, granting posthumous pardons to African American historical icons and the victims of legalized racial repression and injustices in the courts. Equally as thought-provoking, for a variety of reasons, from the conviction of Medgar Evers's murderer in 1994 into the twenty-first century, the murders of many African Americans, especially civil rights activists, were reinvestigated, memorialized, and deemed wrong.

What constitute apologies for atrocities and wrongdoings committed against African Americans? What language is used in apologies to African Americans? What is the nature of these ceremonial expressions of regret that have gained momentum in the twenty-first century? What do such cases convey about US elected officials' notions of retributive justice and the past oppression of black people? What are the deeper meanings and implications of these apologies, reinvestigations, and pardons and reckonings with dark times in America's past? These are the types of questions that the remainder of this chapter explores.

---

9   Francesca Chambers, "Sanders: 'Yes' I'd apologize for slavery and I'd make reparations by investing in low-income communities," dailymail.co.uk, April 6, 2016 .

CONTEXTUALIZING AFRICAN AMERICAN-RELATED APOLOGIES

One of the first major book-length studies on the multiple "essentials, forms, and functions of apology" was published by sociologist Nicholas Tavuchis in 1991. In his often-cited study *Mea Culpa: A Sociology of Apology and Reconciliation*, Tavuchis commented that scholarship on "the social import of apology" was grossly underdeveloped and that journalists' musings were among the most vital sources for "concrete descriptions" of this complex phenomenon. Tavuchis considered many of the modes as well as the varied "meanings, nature, and functions of apology" that future scholars active in what can now loosely be called *apology studies* have since elaborated upon.[10]

Scholarship on what have been called public "historical apologies" and "political apologies" blossomed during the twenty-first century, coinciding with a noticeable increase in public apologies made by political leaders throughout the world to victimized populations and their descendants for past mistreatment. For more than a decade, political scientist Graham G. Dodds has been maintaining a prodigious "working list" of significant political apologies "for significant public wrongs" committed throughout the world. Focusing on the post–World War II era, specifically the late twentieth century and the new millennium, the most recent incarnation of the list includes close to 650 entries.[11] Recently, African American studies scholar Ashraf H. A. Rushdy has convincingly argued that we are living in a "guilted age" that, contrary to popular belief, is not merely a late twentieth and twenty-first century phenomenon. Today's "guilted age," he contends, is part of a broader trend that emerged during the immediate aftermath of World War II.[12] Nevertheless, the twenty-first century has justifiably been dubbed "The Age of Apology" by more than a few scholars. Though there is a great deal of debate and hyperspecialization in apology studies, there is a consensus that during the last quarter century there has been a proclivity on the part of political leaders to apologize for past wrongs and repression. "There seems to be almost universal recognition that a society will not be able to successfully pass into the future until it somehow deals with its demons from the past," human rights scholars Rhoda E. Howard-Hassmann and Mark Gibney observed in 2008.[13]

Situating the mushrooming of the "apology phenomenon" in the 1990s, in his accessible and wide-reaching book *On Apology*, psychiatrist Aaron Lazare

---

10   Nicholas Tavuchis, *Mea Culpa: A Sociology of Apology and Reconciliation*, Stanford, CA: Stanford University Press, 1991, 3, 9.

11   Graham G. Dodds, "Chronological List of Political Apologies," humanrightscolumbia. org, April 19, 2016 .

12   Ashraf H. A. Rushdy, *A Guilted Age: Apologies for the Past*, Philadelphia: Temple University Press, 2015, xii, 1–3.

13   Rhoda E. Howard-Hassmann and Mark Gibney, "Introduction: Apologies in the West," in *The Age of Apology: Facing Up to the Past*, ed. Mark Gibney, Rhoda E. Howard-Hassmann, Jean-Marc Coicaud, and Niklaus Steiner, 1, Philadelphia: University of Pennsylvania Press, 2008.

has suggested that apologies began proliferating during the twenty-first century for a range of reasons, including the tendency to view the new millennium as a "time for new beginnings," increased globalization and global awareness, the expansion of the digital era, shifting balances of power around the world, and publicized instances of mass human destruction. Scholarship on reparations to African Americans for slavery and America's reckonings with and memorializations of its blemished racial past has flourished since the publication of Randall Robinson's landmark *The Debt: What America Owes to Blacks* (2000). Yet, with few exceptions, scholarship on wide-ranging historical and political apologies and reconciliation tend to marginalize the African American experience.

In her study *The Politics of Official Apologies*, political scientist Melissa Nobles alerted her readers that "African American-related apologies (and non-apologies) are not among the book's main cases."[14] Those apology scholars who have addressed African American-related apologies have tended to use Clinton's apology for the Tuskegee Study and the Senate's apology for slavery and Jim Crow segregation as their primary case studies, often using these examples to highlight how certain racial minorities in the United States have been verbally redressed. In many cases, the specific language deployed in these apologies is not thoroughly analyzed. As this chapter demonstrates, it is important to scrutinize what was actually said and written as well as the broader context that shaped the apologies or non-apologies.

Some twenty-first century scholarship on apologies can be useful in framing and conceptualizing African American-related apologies. To begin with, it is necessary to establish what I mean by the term *apology*. There are a bewildering number of definitions for this concept. Lazare has offered several characterizations that are applicable to African American-related apologies and nonapologies. "'Apology' refers to an encounter between two parties in which one party, the offender, acknowledges responsibility for an offense or grievance and expresses regret or remorse to a second party, the aggrieved," Lazare asserted. "Each party may be a person or a larger group such as a family, a business, an ethnic group, a race, or a nation. The apology may be private or public, written or verbal, and even at times, nonverbal." Lazare reasonably subdivided the "apology process" into four main components: "1) the acknowledgement of the offense; 2) the explanation; 3) various attitudes including remorse, shame, humility, and sincerity; and 4) reparations."[15]

Drawing upon Lazare's ideas, I focus on public verbal and written historical apologies to African American individuals and groups from political leaders (for example, city and state officials, governors, senators, congressmen,

---

14 Melissa Nobles, *The Politics of Official Apologies,* New York: Cambridge University Press, 2008, 39.

15 Aaron Lazare, *On Apology,* New York: Oxford University Press, 2004, 23, 25.

and presidents) who spoke on behalf of US cities and states and, in the case of presidents, the nation. In doing so, these purveyors of "political" or "official" apologies embraced a collective sense of responsibility. In effect, they were representing those who elected them, even if some of their constituents did not agree with their sentiments. Philosopher Janna Thompson has offered an excellent definition of political apologies that applies to my discussion. In 2008, she wrote:

> A political apology is an official apology given by a representative of a state, corporation, or other organized group to victims, or descendants of victims, for injustices committed by the group's officials or members. For some political leaders apology has become a standard way of coming to terms with past injustices and victims' demands for redress. But official apology is by no means an uncontroversial or universally accepted practice, and its present popularity may not last.[16]

I am also concerned with what Lazare has called "failed apologies" or "pseudoapologies" and what Melissa Nobles termed "non-apologies." These kinds of apologies are not uncommon when dealing with past crimes committed against African Americans. Nonapologies are of course those that have not come to fruition, such as a presidential apology for slavery. Failed, pseudo, or quasi apologies are those that are advertised as being apologies but, for a variety of reasons, are not genuine and are often employed merely as symbolic gestures by those giving and performing them. They can also be declarations that have been misconstrued as being real apologies.

History is an essential dimension of the apologies and reckonings with the past that are discussed in this chapter. The apologies that I unpack are what Rushdy has called *historical apologies*—apologies for events or crimes "from the distant past."[17] When exploring African American-related apologies, Nobles's observations about the historical nature of apologies for the past are relevant. "Apologies, after all, ratify certain reinterpretations of history. National histories are re-examined; justifications are looked at anew; aspects of history that were ignored draw focus; and actions that were denied are acknowledged." Nobles adds:

> Apologies, then, are admissions of past injustice that can be, in turn, pressed into service, providing justification for change in the content and direction of state policies. It is these central features of acknowledgement and judgement that make apologies attractive to some and objectionable to others.[18]

---

16   Janna Thompson, "Apology, Justice, and Respect: A Critical Defense of Political Apology," in *The Age of Apology*, ed. Gibney et al., 31.
17   Rushdy, *A Guilted Age*, xiii.
18   Nobles, *The Politics of Official Apologies*, 29, 30.

Keeping these general ideas in mind, in what follows, I look into a selection of African American-related apologies and conclude by discussing a phenomenon related to politico-historical apologies: posthumous pardons granted to and sought for African Americans who were the casualties of miscarriages of injustice.

"IT IS THE RIGHT THING TO DO"

In June 2014, national correspondent for *The Atlantic* Ta-Nehisi Coates revived discussions about reparations in American popular culture, especially among younger black intellectuals, with his lengthy essay "The Case for Reparations." Not only did he sample the title of his essay from Boris I. Bittker's 1973 book on reparations and Robert Westley's important 1998 essay, but Coates also recycled some of the numerous underlying arguments of reparationists. This gifted writer and thinker who was dubbed the heir to James Baldwin by Toni Morrison did, however, add more provocative and personalized case studies of "everyday" African Americans to the mix, translate reparations for a broader, liberal readership, and offer the perspective of a hip-hop generationer on a hotly contested issue that many of today's black public intellectuals do not tackle.

In addition to highlighting the present disparities between blacks and whites caused by slavery, Jim Crow segregation, and widespread discriminatory practices, Coates also argued that reparations were not only about "recompense for past injustices" but also should include "a national reckoning" and a "revolution of the American consciousness." He did not argue that an apology was the first step toward reparations. For Coates, the United States needed to openly acknowledge and express genuine remorse for its past mistreatment of black people. This "settling with old ghosts" was central to his twenty-first-century vision of reparations.[19]

Reparationists began calling upon the US government to compensate African Americans for the unpaid labor of their ancestors more than one century before Coates's widely read essay appeared, as demonstrated by Callie House's National Ex-Slave Mutual Relief, Bounty and Pension Association founded in 1897. In addition to House's crew, the roll-call of reparations activists prior to the end of the Black Power era is long, including for instance, former enslaved Tennessean Jourdon Anderson, Frederick Douglass, radical Reconstructionist Thaddeus Stevens, Cornelius J. Jones, Marcus Garvey, Queen Mother Audley Moore and her Reparations Committee of Descendants of United States Slaves, Malcolm X, the Republic of New Africa, Christopher Alston, James Farmer, the National Black Economic Development Conference, and the National Black Political Assembly.[20]

---

19 Ta-Nehisi Coates, "The Case for Reparations," *The Atlantic*, June 2014.

20 For an excellent history and collection of diverse essays on the reparations movement, see Raymond A. Winbush, ed., *Should America Pay?: Slavery and the Raging Debate on Reparations*, New York: HarperCollins, 2003.

Several years after the founding of the National Coalition of Blacks for Reparations in America (N'COBRA), in January 1989 Congressman John Conyers (D-Michigan) made history by first introducing H. R. 40—which has never moved to the floor of the House—to "acknowledge the fundamental injustice, cruelty, brutality, and inhumanity of slavery in the United States" and to establish a commission to study the effects of slavery and subsequent forms of systematic discrimination and racial oppression. Conyers did not include an apology as a starting point for an investigation into the viability of reparations, but implicit in H. R. 40 was that slavery, sanctioned by the US government from 1789 until 1865, was wrong—a crime against humanity—and therefore warranted an apology.

As law professor and reparations scholar Alfred L. Brophy has pointed out, many reparationists do not accept apologies as adequate remedies and compensation for past racial injustice, but they "can be part of a meaningful program of repair and reconciliation." Apologies for slavery and racial discrimination, he reasoned, have been very burdensome to secure because they give "signals about blame and responsibility for the consequences of that crime." In spite of this, "'apologetic justice' has gained substantial followers, perhaps in large part because of the limited expense."[21]

The reluctance to issue apologies to African Americans for slavery in particular becomes crystal clear when looking at the efforts of former State Representative and US Ambassador to the United Nations Agencies for Food and Agriculture Tony Hall (D-Ohio). On June 12, 1997, Hall made history by introducing House Concurrent Resolution 96, "Apologizing for Those Who Suffered as Slaves Under the Constitution and Laws of the United States Until 1865." Three years later when he reintroduced a similar resolution, he explained that he was prompted to craft such an official apology because he heard, in passing, that the US government had never formally expressed regret for slavery.

> So I went to the Library of Congress and discovered . . . no one in the government of the United States ever apologized for slavery. I set out to correct this glaring omission in history, and in 1997, I introduced my simple resolution without much fanfare.[22]

To be sure, Hall's resolution—for which he received some hate mail—was simple and straightforward: "Resolved by the House of Representatives, That Congress apologizes to African-Americans whose ancestors suffered as slaves under the Constitution and the laws of the United States until 1865." Hall's resolution had only twenty co-sponsors and was widely opposed and passed

---

21   Alfred L. Brophy, *Reparations Pro and Con,* New York: Oxford University Press, 2006, 11, 13, 170.

22   "Resolution Apologizing for Slavery," Hon. Tony P. Hall of Ohio in the House of Representatives, Wednesday, July 12, 2000.

over. Steadfast in his convictions, Hall was outspoken in his belief that Congress owed African Americans an apology. He elaborated on this when he was recognized by his colleagues for five minutes on June 18, 1997. "When a brother wrongs a brother, he apologizes. This is the foundation for beginning again. This is the price for restoring trust. This is the only way to start over," Hall pronounced. "It is a simple gesture. It carries deep meaning. And it is the right thing to do." In essence, in line with Lazare's "apology process," he considered an apology for slavery to be a starting point for "reconciliation" and "healing."[23]

In justifying Congress's apology to African Americans, Hall compared such a gesture to apologies that Pope John Paul II made for violence during the sixteenth century Counter-Reformation, British prime minister Tony Blair's apology to the Irish for how they were mistreated during the potato famine, and even East Germany's historic apology to Jews for the Holocaust. Hall also reminded his colleagues that Congress recently apologized to Japanese Americans, native Hawaiians, and uranium miners and those impacted by nuclear testing in Nevada. Echoing Conyers, Hall argued that "African-Americans still suffer from the lingering effects" of slavery and that the "hatred and racial divisions from slavery are very much alive."[24]

Though he qualified his apology by asserting that his colleagues in Congress did not directly "perpetuate slavery," he stressed that their predecessors did indeed encourage this inhumane institution and, therefore, "the Congress as an institution does bear responsibility." Anticipating his critics' reactions, Hall raised the issue of why this revisiting of black history would be substantial and not merely symbolic. "If it was so meaningless," he asked, "why has the resolution erupted such a fire storm of controversy throughout this Nation? If apologizing were so easy, then why is this resolution so difficult?"[25] The answer to Hall's question, as he and those supporting him were fully aware, is self-evident. An apology for slavery would have constituted an admission of guilt and could have been used as fuel for the reparations movement.

Many African Americans and reparations activists stood by Hall's side and praised his efforts. Members of the Congressional Black Caucus agreed that an apology would have symbolic value and could serve as a logical starting point for a larger struggle. They also called for more concrete interventions and reforms to help address the problems that were the foundations of the apology. For them, it was clearly a point of departure.

Hall's resolution was unsurprisingly met with much resistance. Former Speaker of the US House of Representatives Newt Gingrich (R-Georgia) was one of the most high-profile outspoken dissenters. "Any American, I hope, feels

---

23 Tony P. Hall, "Resolution Apologizing for Slavery" (House Concurrent Resolution 96), Congressional Record H3890-H3891, 105th Congress, 1st Session (June 18, 1997).
24 Ibid.
25 Ibid.

badly about slavery," Gingrich commented. "We can go back and have all sorts of apologies. But will one more child read because of it? The emotional symbolism as an avoidance of problem-solving strikes me as a dead end." Gingrich added: "Finding new, backward oriented symbolic moments so we can avoid real work doesn't strike me as a strategy that's going to solve the country's problems."[26] Gingrich even told African Americans to visit the Lincoln Memorial and to read his "second address" if they wanted to see a "great apology for slavery."[27] Gingrich's reactions to Hall's resolution are revealing at various levels. His claim that a simple apology would in some way stand in the way of practical programs to address racial inequalities that stem from slavery and Jim Crow segregation is especially dumbfounding.

In 2000 during Juneteenth, Hall reintroduced his slavery apology resolution as H. Con. Res. 356 and offered some more extensive remarks. Citing the sentiments of several "ordinary" African Americans, in his comments he argued that Congress needed to apologize for slavery because it would serve as a starting point for healing, "restoring lost trust, and a necessary step in moving in the right direction." As he did three years earlier, he pointed out that Congress had recently apologized for similar injustices and that various nongovernmental organizations were courageously stepping forward to apologize for their involvement in slavery. Hall concluded his remarks by accentuating that the legacy of slavery still shaped white privilege, US race relations, and black Americans' collective status and summoned the US government to "be big enough to admit its mistakes." He declared: "I believe this apology is faithful to our past, and essential to our future."[28]

H. Con. Res. 356 was much more detailed than its 1997 predecessor. Beginning by acknowledging the inhumane nature of US slavery, it called upon Congress to recognize and admit the immorality of slavery, to apologize to African Americans for what was done to their ancestors, and to commit to rectifying the "misdeeds of slavery done in the past." Like Conyers's H. R. 40, H. Con. Res. 356 called for the creation of a commission to study the impact of slavery. It also requested reforms in how slavery was taught in the public school system, the funding of research related to slavery, and the creation of a national African American history and slavery museum. Hall's resolution addressed each phase of Lazare's ideal "apology process."

The timing of Hall's resolution was fitting. Arguably the most influential book on reparations for African Americans was published in 2000, Randall Robinson's monumental *The Debt: What America Owes to Blacks*. Robinson's

---

26   Associated Press, "Speaker Scoffs at Proposal for an Apology for Slavery," *New York Times*, June 14, 1997, 10.

27   Sam Fulwood, "Gingrich Rejects Apology for Slavery," *The Los Angeles Times*, June 14, 1997.

28   "Resolution Apologizing for Slavery," Hon. Tony P. Hall of Ohio in the House of Representatives, Wednesday, July 12, 2000.

treatise made a splash, jettisoning the issue of reparations into the mainstream, especially within black middle-class leadership circles. In a sense, he helped publicize the sentiments of more militant reparations spokespersons like Conrad W. Worrill, Dorothy Tillman, Imari Abubakari Obadele, and many others. In January 2001, *The Debt* was *Essence* magazine's #1 best-selling nonfiction title. Afrocentrist Molefi Kete Asante concisely summarized the impact of Robinson's landmark work:

> Randall Robinson's *The Debt* has been one of the most popular and important books written on the subject so far because he has captured the warrants for reparations in very clear and accessible language.[29]

Historian Robin D. G. Kelley heralded Robinson's "moving and bold testimonial," observing that "his is one of the few voices willing to call out the traitors and name names."[30]

Robinson did not mince words in advocating for reparations or in describing blacks' collective suffering. "No race, no ethnic or religious group," Robinson insisted, "has suffered so much over so long a span as blacks have, and do still, at the hands of those who benefited, with the connivance of the United States government, from slavery and the century of legalized racial hostility that followed." For him, reparations were the only viable solution for solving America's "race problem" and alleviating the suffering of the masses of African Americans. According to the founder of TransAfrica Forum, reparations were necessary because the vast majority of African Americans still suffered because of "America's racial holocaust" and "the vicious climate that followed it." Robinson did not offer a detailed, step-by-step framework for how reparations could be best engineered and carried out. But, he did stress that the US government and Americans in general needed to stop denying the "crime" and ignoring history. Ultimately, he made a plea for, at a minimum, a "full-scale reparations debate." In reference to American society as a whole, he vented: "First, it must own up to slavery and acknowledge its debt to slavery's contemporary victims." Robinson added, "Once and for all, America must face its past, open itself to a fair telling of all of its peoples' histories, and accept full responsibility for the hardships it has occasioned for so many."[31]

Robinson criticized the leadership of President Clinton for helping maintain a climate that was not supportive of reparations. Clinton, in Robinson's

---

29   Molefi Kete Asante, "The African American Warrant for Reparations: The Crime of European Enslavement of Africans and Its Consequences," in *Should America Pay?*, ed. Winbush, 3.

30   Robin D. G. Kelley, "'The Debt' Calls for America to Pay Up," *Emerge* 11: 4, February 2000, 105.

31   Randall Robinson, *The Debt: What America Owes to Blacks*, New York: Dutton, 2000, 8, 9, 107, 243.

estimation, did "discernably little for black people," created policies that "contributed to the disproportionate incarceration of blacks," and avoided dealing directly with issues like reparations by initiating an ineffective advisory board on US race relations.[32] Robinson reprimanded black voters for blindly following Clinton and the Democratic Party, for accepting his symbolic gestures and rhetoric without scrutinizing his policies toward them or African peoples throughout the world.

CLINTON'S APOLOGIES TO BLACK AMERICA

It should come as no surprise that US presidents have not regularly issued apologies for mistakes that they themselves have made during their administrations or for the wrongs committed by their predecessors. Among the most famous presidential apologies since the second half of the twentieth century include Gerald Ford's apology for the internment of Japanese Americans during World War II, Richard Nixon's apology for Watergate, Clinton's acknowledgment of misleading the American people about the Monica Lewinsky case, and George W. Bush's expression of regret concerning Hurricane Katrina and his contentious apology for the abuse of Iraqi prisoners at Abu Ghraib.

US presidents and elected politicians have issued apologies to Japanese Americans, Native Hawaiians, and Native Americans, but they have been very hesitant and conservative when dealing with African Americans. The first major public apology issued to African Americans from the mouths of politicians emerged in the late twentieth century during the Clinton administration. Symbolic gestures such as his public reckonings with America's past maltreatment of African Americans in part influenced social commentators like Dwayne Wickham to argue that Clinton had a "special bond with blacks."[33]

When viewed within the broader context of American presidents' interactions with black America, Clinton forged a unique relationship with African Americans. Under the guise of racial reconciliation, he symbolically revisited tragedies from the black past. In the assessments of Randall Robinson, law professor Randall Kennedy, and others, Clinton's dealings with black America are instructive when looking at how he expressed regret for his country's past abuse of African Americans. In Kennedy's mind, Clinton was a "shrewd politician" and "absent from his record is any episode in which he risked considerable political capital on behalf of a fight for racial justice that would benefit black people."[34] Indeed, Clinton was very cautious when commenting on the brutal past ill-treatment of African Americans.

---

32   Ibid., 100–104.

33   Dwayne Wickham, *Bill Clinton and Black America*, New York: Ballantine Publishing Group, 2002, 5.

34   Randall Kennedy, "Is He a Soul Man? On Black Support for Clinton," *The American Prospect*, March–April 1999, 26–30.

Several days after signing off on an executive order creating the President's Advisory Board on Race, on June 15, 1997, Clinton was interviewed on CNN Late Edition by Emmy-award winning journalist Frank Sesno. The topic was California's Proposition 209 and affirmative action in more general terms. After posing a slew of questions focusing on affirmative action, Sesno asked Clinton his thoughts about apologizing for slavery. Clinton was tactical in his response, noting that he'd "like some time to think about it." He did, however, indicate that he believed that official apologies like the one that he offered a month earlier for the Tuskegee Study could be symbolically "very important." When pushed by Sesno to indicate if he was "in favor" of an apology for slavery, Clinton came close to supporting it:

> I'd like some time to think about it. What I will say, though, is that surely, every American knows that slavery was wrong and that we paid a terrible price for it and that we had to keep repairing that. And surely, every American knows that the separate but unequal system we had for 100 years after slavery was wrong. And surely, every American knows that the discrimination that still exists in this country is wrong. And just to say that it's wrong and that we're sorry about it is not a bad thing. That doesn't weaken us. Now, whether this legislation should pass, I just need time to think about that.[35]

Clinton's musings on an apology for slavery did not go unnoticed. On June 16, 1997, the *Washington Post* published a piece under the headline: "President Mulls National Apology for Slavery." In the months following his interview with Sesno, Clinton was pressed in several interviews to elaborate on this matter, and he responded by reiterating that he was still contemplating this complicated subject. He did, however, make it clear that he was not in favor of reparations in part because the amount of time that had transpired since slavery. He also divulged that he would let his Advisory Board on Race counsel him on this issue. At the same time, in early August 1997, White House Press Secretary Michael D. McCurry revealed that an apology for slavery was not an important issue to Clinton:

> The President has really, in a way, put that issue aside and said that's not going to be the focus of his race initiative; nor is it the place he believes we should really start the kind of discussion he is looking for, one that's aimed at bringing Americans together.[36]

"No other President in the history of this Nation has had the courage to raise the issue of race and racism in American society in such a drastic way,"

---

35   "Transcript of interview with President Bill Clinton: CNN Late Edition with Frank Sesno," cnn.com, June 15, 1997 .

36   Steven A. Holmes, "Idea of Apologizing for Slavery Loses Steam, at Least for Now," *New York Times*, August 6, 1997.

enthusiastically wrote members of the President's Advisory Board on Race in reference to Clinton in their final report completed in September 1998.[37] Slightly more than a year earlier, Clinton signed Executive Order 13050 to establish this group of seven experts on aspects of the generically defined concept of "race" from outside the federal government. They were appointed to advise Clinton about issues broadly dealing with "race and racial reconciliation." Based upon the various functions ascribed to the advisory board, an apology for slavery could have very easily been a germane topic of discussion. However, some of the specific terminology describing their role suggests that Clinton was not interested in substantively revisiting the legacy of slavery or Jim Crow segregation. When dealing with history, the board was nudged to focus on increasing "the Nation's understanding of our *recent* history of race relations." Of course, by the late 1990s, Jim Crow segregation and especially slavery would not have really been considered "recent." Chaired by renowned historian John Hope Franklin, the advisory board did, however, decide to expand Clinton's notion of "recent" history.

In September 1998, the board submitted a report to the president that included their observations and recommendations. They acknowledged the incontrovertible: that "the long history of slavery" in the United States laid the foundations for the contemporary "racial hierarchy" in the United States. "Our point is that our history has consequences, and we cannot begin to solve 'the race problem' if we are ignorant of the historical backdrop," they wrote. In a section on the African American experience, the board highlighted how slavery impacted the United States and particularly black Americans. Most likely at Clinton's urging, they were not in favor of a formal apology for slavery from the president or Congress. "We conclude that the question of an apology for slavery itself is much too narrow in light of the experience of blacks over the course of this Nation's history," Clinton's advisory board wrote. They reasoned that an apology was not necessary because it would not solve the problem. What were needed in their estimation were "forceful steps to eliminate the consequences of this awful history of racism." For them, an apology, if offered at all, did not necessarily need to be made by the president or Congress, but instead by "all" Americans and could not "be adequately expressed in words but in actions."[38] As simple and straightforward as it could have been, a political apology for slavery was absent from the advisory board's numerous recommendations.

On March 24, 1998, Clinton issued a strange sort of apology for slavery that was covered in US and foreign newspapers. In response, the *New York Times* ran

---

37   John Hope Franklin, Linda Chavez-Thompson, Susan D. Johnson-Cook, Thomas H. Kean, Angela E. Oh, Robert Thomas, and William F. Winter, *One Americas in the 21st Century: Forging a New Future*, The President's Initiative on Race, The Advisory Board's Report to the President, September 1998.

38   Ibid.

the following headline: "In Uganda, Clinton Expresses Regret on Slavery in U.S." During his twelve-day visit to Africa, he visited Ghana, Uganda, South Africa, Botswana, Senegal, and Rwanda; while in Uganda, Clinton decided to apologize for the fact that the United States had "not always done the right thing by Africa." After admitting that the United States ignored the needs of African countries during the Cold War era, Clinton confessed that "European-Americans received the fruits of the slave trade." He added, "And we were wrong in that, as well."[39]

Clinton's quasi apology for the participation of European Americans in the slave trade specifically before the founding of the United States is interesting at many levels. It was incomplete, in many respects a nonapology. For one thing, he made it seem as if the United States did not participate in the slave trade following the ratification of the US Constitution. He did not mention that Article 1, Section 9 of the US Constitution prevented Congress from enacting any laws to prohibit the importation of enslaved Africans into the United States prior to 1808. In other words, he did not broach the fact that from 1789 until 1808, his predecessors supported the slave trade, and that well into the second half of the nineteenth century, an illegal slave trade flourished in parts of the country. Second, Clinton did not, as many in the media implied, apologize for slavery that blossomed in the United States from 1789 until 1865. Third, his quasi-apology was not official. Not only were his remarks about the slave trade perfunctory and part of a speech on the US relationship with Uganda, but he did not apologize for the slave trade while he was on US soil. He unconvincingly and mildly condemned how his country benefitted from the slave trade in a country that was not directly impacted by this phenomenon. Such an apology would have been better suited in his remarks in Ghana or Senegal. In his brief speeches at Gorée Island on April 2, 1998, he described the Middle Passage as being "murderous" and called slavery "one of the most difficult chapters" of US history, but his comments were milder than those made a week earlier in Uganda.

Beyond his pseudo apologies for slavery, Clinton expressed regret over several specific episodes in which African Americans were wronged. During World War II, no black soldiers were awarded the Medal of Honor. By the early 1990s, the US Army decided to revisit and take steps in correcting this oversight and in 1993 sponsored a study at Shaw University "to determine if there was a racial disparity in the way the Medal of Honor recipients were selected." The research team concluded that black soldiers were discriminated against when these awards were originally given out, and it identified ten who they considered worthy of this esteemed honor. Then, in 1996, "Congress passed legislation lifting the statute of limitations that otherwise barred presentation of the

---

39   William J. Clinton, "Remarks at the Kisowera School in Mukono, Uganda, March 24, 1998," presidency.ucsb.edu.

medals."[40]

On January 13, 1997, Clinton awarded the Congressional Medal of Honor to seven African American World War II veterans, only one of whom was still living at the time, because they were "denied the nation's highest honor" when they deserved to receive it. In doing so, as he pointed out, he sought to "finally" right a wrong committed by former President Harry Truman. "Today we fill the gap in that picture and give a group of heroes . . . the tribute that has always been their due," Clinton announced. "Now and forever, the truth will be known about these African Americans who gave so much that the rest of us might be free."[41] Months later, Clinton celebrated the fortieth anniversary of the integration of Little Rock Central High School; among other comments, he asserted that "reconciliation" was "important." During Black History Month in 1999, Clinton officially and fully pardoned African American Lieutenant Henry O. Flipper, who was dishonorably discharged from the US Army in 1882 for reasons that were found to be unjustified when reviewed in the 1990s. In his brief remarks, Clinton called the event "117 years overdue" and "too long to let injustice lie uncorrected," admitted that the US government did not treat African Americans justly, and underscored that the ceremony sought to "correct the error."[42]

Viewed within the broader context of his previously discussed reckonings with America's checkered racial past, Clinton's official apology for the Tuskegee Study on May 16, 1997, stands out. Clinton directly apologized to five of the eight surviving participants, essentially "guinea pigs" for the US Public Health Service's experiment.

Herman Shaw, one of the survivors who spoke at the ceremony, may have expressed the sentiments that many African Americans of his generation held regarding apologies for past racial injustice when he said: "We are delighted today to close this very tragic and painful chapter in our lives . . . The wounds that were inflicted upon us cannot be undone." In support of Clinton's apology, he added:

> In my opinion, it is never too late to work to restore trust and faith . . . This ceremony is important because the damage done by the Tuskegee Study is much deeper than the wounds any of us may have suffered.[43]

Members of the Tuskegee Syphilis Study Legacy Committee were also in

---

40   "African American World War II Medal of Honor Recipients," history.army.mil; Alan M. Anderson, "Medal of Honor Reexamination Boards," in *Ethnic and Racial Minorities in the U.S. Military: An Encyclopedia*, ed. Alexander M. Bielakowski, Santa Barbara, CA: ABC-CLIO, 2013.

41   William J. Clinton, "Remarks on Presenting the Congressional Medal of Honor to African-American Heroes of World War II," January 13, 1997.

42   William J. Clinton, "Remarks on the Posthumous Pardon of Lieutenant Henry O. Flipper," February 19, 1999, presidency.ucsb.edu .

43   "Statement of Herman Shaw: Living Participant in the Tuskegee Syphilis Study," May 16, 1997, The White House, Washington, DC, health-equity.pitt.edu.

attendance at this historic event. This organization was instrumental in influencing Clinton to issue this apology. Founded in the mid-1990s, this group had its first major meeting early in 1996, and in May it produced a final report. Outraged that no public apology was ever made "by any government official," one of their main goals was to convince Clinton to apologize to the survivors of the study, their families, and the broader Tuskegee community. The committee viewed an apology as being the "first step toward healing the wounds inflicted." The committee also pointed out that in 1995 Clinton apologized for the US government's sanctioning of human radiation experiments for a thirty-year period (the same amount of time the Tuskegee Study lasted). The committee concluded:

> The Committee urges President Clinton to apologize on behalf of the American government for the harms inflicted at Tuskegee. The apology should be directed to those most directly harmed: to the elderly survivors of the Study, to their families, and to the wider community of Tuskegee and its university. Also included within the apology should be all people of color whose lives reverberate with the consequences of the Study. As the highest elected official of the United States, the President should offer the apology for the Study which was conducted under the auspices of the United States government. The significance of a presidential apology was recognized recently when the President apologized to those harmed by Cold War radiation experiments as a way to regain confidence of the American people. In the context of President Clinton's stated desire to bridge the racial divide, this apology provides the opportunity to begin to heal the racial wounds that persist in this country. Given the ages of the living participants and the period of time since the Study was disclosed, we believe that the apology should be offered swiftly.[44]

The Tuskegee Syphilis Study Legacy Committee stressed that a presidential apology alone was not enough. In calling for the creation of a center located at Tuskegee University, the committee sought to preserve "the national memory of the Syphilis Study for public education and scholarly research." They also highlighted the initiation of several other "concurrent programs" that would help rectify the enduring harm that was done by the Tuskegee Study.

In his brief remarks, Clinton acknowledged that the Tuskegee Study—which took place, in his words, "when our nation failed to live up to its ideals, when our nation broke the trust with our people that is the very foundation of democracy"—was "deeply, profoundly, morally wrong." By remembering this tragedy, he noted, the country could "go forward." He apologized directly to the survivors whose "rights were trampled upon" and to Tuskegee residents, the Tuskegee University community, and African Americans as a whole. "We can

---

44   "Final Report of the Tuskegee Syphilis Study Legacy Committee—May 1996," exhibits. hsl.virginia.edu.

look you in the eye and finally say on behalf of the American people, what the United States government did was shameful, and I am sorry," Clinton declared. Clinton considered the apology to be a "first step" in working towards rebuilding African Americans' trust in the US government. He concluded his remarks by describing steps that his administration would be taking to make up for this inhumane mishap, including the creation of a center for bioethics at Tuskegee University, a report conducted by the Secretary of Health and Human Services addressing how to better involve minority communities in health related research, better training for medical researchers, the establishment of fellowships for graduate students studying bioethics, and an extension of the National Bioethics Advisory Committee.[45]

While Clinton's apology for the Tuskegee Study was substantive beyond his brief condemnations of the slave trade and slavery and satisfied the guidelines of Lazare's "apology process," he never did make a formal apology for the US government's support of slavery that shaped American life and culture more than any other institution during the nation's formative years. Clinton is not alone in this respect. Just as no American president has ever apologized for the decision to drop the atomic bomb on Hiroshima or Nagasaki (as acts of war to be distinguished from domestic issues), no American president has officially apologized for slavery.

Without nearly as much at stake as US presidents and elected political officials, nongovernmental entities have issued apologies for slavery, and such undertakings have proliferated during the twenty-first century. The first of the new millennium was a public apology from Aetna, Inc., which in 2000 expressed regret for issuing insurance policies to slaveholders for their human property during the 1850s. Aetna would have never apologized had it not been for the findings of lawyer and reparations activist Deadria C. Farmer-Paellmann, who contacted this Fortune 500 corporation and asked it not only to apologize for supporting slavery one 150 years ago but also to pay restitution. "Aetna has long acknowledged that for several years shortly after its founding in 1853 that the company *may have* insured the lives of slaves," an Aetna spokesperson said in March 2000. "We express our deep regret over any participation at all in the deplorable practice." Though reluctant and cautious, this apology was, in Farmer-Paellmann's estimation, "unprecedented."[46]

Following Aetna's admission of guilt, other companies issued similar apologies, such as the *Hartford Courant* newspaper, J. P. Morgan Chase, and the Wachovia Corporation. In the first decade of the new millennium following the lead of Brown University (under the direction of its first black president, Ruth Simmons), a handful of universities, including the University of Alabama, the College of William and Mary, Emory University, and Harvard University,

---

45   William J. Clinton "President William J. Clinton's Remarks," in *Tuskegee's Truths,* ed. Reverby, 574–77.

46   Deadria C. Farmer-Paellmann, "Excerpt from *Black Exodus: The Ex-Slave Pension Movement Reader,*" in *Should America Pay?* ed. Winbush, 22–31.

began researching and acknowledging how their institutions benefitted from slavery. Georgetown University, Princeton University, and the University of Pennsylvania are among the most recent US universities to examine their past links to slavery. In the process, some of these schools expressed regret over their institutions' participation in this institution. These apologies were in some cases contentious. Former University of Alabama law professor Alfred L. Brophy has revealed how many white faculty and students in Tuscaloosa were vehemently opposed to their university's 2004 apology to the descendants of slaves who were the property of faculty members or were enslaved on campus.

Data does not currently exist on the impact that non-governmental apologies to African Americans may have had on politicians. At a minimum, it is not a stretch to conjecture that these dialogues have been recognized by some political spokespersons.

GEORGE W. BUSH'S ATONEMENTS WITH AFRICAN AMERICANS

Whereas Clinton was widely praised for his good favor with black people, Bush was considered by many in the black community to be an opponent to black progress. Many African Americans probably concurred with Kanye West when on September 2, 2005, he famously blurted out on national television: "George Bush doesn't care about black people."[47] Nevertheless, during his presidency, George W. Bush offered a few apologies to African Americans.

In July 2003, one year after he ordered the Department of Justice to reopen the investigation of the 1964 murder of Johnnie Mae Chappell in Jacksonville, Florida, Bush embarked upon a five-day tour of five African countries— Senegal, South Africa, Botswana, Uganda, and Nigeria. While in Senegal, the first stop of his tour, he visited Gorée Island like Clinton did before him. Unsurprisingly, he was accompanied by Colin Powell and Condoleezza Rice. While at Gorée Island, known for its "Door Of No Return," for about eight minutes Bush addressed his Senegalese audience, describing the horrors of the infamous Middle Passage.

He called the slave trade "one of the greatest crimes of history" and made the following comments about the role of the United States in slavery: "There was a time in my country's history when one in every seven human beings was the property of another. In law, they were regarded only as articles of commerce, having no right to travel, or to marry, or to own possessions." He added, "For 250 years, the captives endured an assault on their culture and their dignity." He described the United States as "a republic founded on equality for all" that "became a prison for millions." Bush even acknowledged that slavery impacted the then present status of African Americans and the state of US race relations.

---

47 Shocroc1, "Bush Does Not Care About Black People," posted April 17, 2006, youtube.com. For a detailed discussion of West's remarks, see Michael Eric Dyson, *Come Hell or High Water: Hurricane Katrina and the Color of Disaster,* New York: Basic Civitas, 2005, 16–33.

"The racial bigotry fed by slavery did not end with slavery or with segregation," he declared. "And many of the issues that still trouble America have roots in the bitter experience of other times."[48]

As much as he deplored slavery and acknowledged that we could use the sentiments of those who decried slavery during the nineteenth century to recognize the existence of "this sin," Bush did not apologize for slavery in the manner (albeit lukewarm) that Clinton did for the slave trade while he visited Uganda in 1998. Still, many in the mainstream media praised Bush's speech and, as was the case with Clinton, implied that he had apologized for slavery and sincerely attacked America's participation in the institution. Prolific scholar of rhetoric and communications Martin J. Medhurst even argued that Bush "delivered the most important speech on American slavery since Abraham Lincoln." Medhurst continued, "as an example of rhetorical artistry, the speech is a masterpiece, putting the brutality of slavery into historical, political, and theological perspective."[49]

Bush's speech may have been rhetorically sophisticated (this is most likely to the credit of one of his many speechwriters), but it was not an adequate apology in the minds of many American Americans. As some of his black critics were quick to point out, Bush did not fare well with black voters and, again like Clinton, chose to condemn US slavery while he was not on American soil and not before an African American audience. As pointed out by Medhurst, according to Bush

it is only bad people who are responsible for slavery, not the American system of government . . . it's the people who were to blame, not the system that, after all, is ultimately vindicated in the speech by none other than God Himself.[50]

It is not unwarranted to conclude that Bush was perhaps seeking to win over black Americans with his token vilification of slavery. Bush "missed a historic opportunity" to apologize for slavery and perhaps to even support reparations for slavery in some form or another. Bush's quasi-apology did, however, make its way into legislation. For instance, he was cited in the House of Representatives' 2008 apology for enslavement and Jim Crow segregation.

Several years after his remarks at Gorée Island, in July 2005, "one of Bush's surrogates"—Ken Mehlman, the chairman of the Republican National Committee who managed Bush's 2004 presidential campaign—apologized to members of the NAACP at their annual convention in Milwaukee. He told them that in the past some in his party were "wrong" for ignoring African American

---

48   George W. Bush, "Remarks by the President on Gorée Island," Gorée Island, Senegal, georgewbush-whitehouse.archives.gov, July 8, 2003.
49   Martin J. Medhurst, "George W. Bush at Gorée Island: American Slavery and the Rhetoric of Redemption," *Quarterly Journal of Speech* 96, August 2010, 257–77.
50   Ibid., 270.

voters and for benefitting from "racial polarizations." Bush was criticized for failing to show up at NAACP annual conferences during his presidency, and many in the black community also questioned the sincerity of Mehlman's and the Republican Party's apology.

In 2007, Bush finally decided to speak before the NAACP at its annual convention. The general purpose of Bush's speech was to highlight his commitment to working with this organization to solve some basic problems pertaining to African Americans and education, home ownership, and health. At several points in his thirty-three-minute oration, Bush touched upon how African Americans were mistreated before the passage of the Voting Rights Act and asserted that "the wound is not fully healed." He did not apologize to his predominantly black audience for these misdeeds in America's past. Instead, he acknowledged the obvious: that the nation's founders supported slavery, that "for nearly 200 years," the United States "failed the test of extending the blessings of liberty to African Americans," and that slavery and Jim Crow segregation placed a "stain on America's founding, a stain that we have not yet wiped clean." Reiterating what one of his surrogates told the group two years earlier, he also remarked that it was a "tragedy that the party of Lincoln let go of its historic ties with the African American community."[51]

On several occasions during the end of his second term in office, Bush revisited the subject of black historical victimization. In 2007, Bush offered some brief remarks at the Congressional Gold Medal Ceremony in honor of the Tuskegee Airmen. He began by talking about his general interest in World War II that was sparked by his father's service as a pilot during this war. Bush then compared the experiences of his father's white contemporaries with those of the Tuskegee Airmen who were discriminated against.

"It was different for the men in this room," he said in reference to the African American veterans.

> When America entered World War II, it might have been easy for them to do little for our country. After all, the country didn't do much for them. Even the Nazis asked why African American men would fight for a country that treated them so unfairly.[52]

Bush pointed out that the Tuskegee Airmen embraced the "Double V" campaign and that the act of recognizing their contributions "means that we are doing our small part to ensure that your story will be told and honored for generations to come." He concluded by atoning a bit for how they were not appreciated during their times of great achievement.

---

51 George W. Bush, "President Bush Addresses NAACP Annual Convention," Washington Convention Center, Washington, DC, July 20, 2006.
52 "Tuskegee Airmen Gold Medal Award," US Capitol Rotunda, *C-SPAN*, March 29, 2007.

I would like to offer a gesture to help atone for all the unreturned salutes and unforgivable indignities. And so, on behalf of the office I hold and a country that honors you, I salute you for your service to the United States of America.[53]

In this case, Bush's reconciliation was between himself (representing the nation) and some Tuskegee Airmen. As he did in his repudiation for slavery at Gorée Island four years earlier, Bush did not identify the US government or War Department as being part of a system that mistreated black soldiers like the Tuskegee Airmen. The closest that he came to indicting the US government was saying that "the country"—made up of unidentified individuals—did not treat these black patriots well.

It is worth noting that Bush's remarks were much more apologetic than those delivered by his father at the ceremony for the posthumous pardon Medal of Honor for Corporal Freddie Stowers, who demonstrated valor in a battle against the Germans during the Great War in the Ardennes region in France. In 1991, Stowers became the first African American World War I soldier to be awarded this honor. Bush Sr. mentioned that after he died in 1918, Stowers was recommended to receive this prestigious honor, "but his award was not acted upon." Unlike his son, Bush Sr. did not describe this oversight as constituting a racial injustice.

On October 7, 2008, George W. Bush signed the Emmett Till Unsolved Civil Rights Crime Act as Public Law #110-344 that was introduced by civil rights icon Congressman John Lewis (D-Georgia) and Kenny Hulshof (R-Missouri); it was supported by then Senator Obama and others. The NAACP praised Bush's actions. One journalist suggested that Bush signed the Till Act in his last year in office "to leave something positive" on his "poor civil rights record," and indeed, Bush did not speak out about the significance of this act or the murder of Emmett Till.[54] He never apologized for the miscarriages of justice in the Till case and many more similar cases.

"WITH PROFOUND REGRET"

Bush did not apologize for slavery or for the ensuing oppression of African Americans during the period of Jim Crow segregation while he was on American soil. Yet, during his tenure, more than a few state legislatures and the House of Representatives and Congress did formally apologize for mistreating African Americans in the past.

On June 13, 2005, the US Senate passed Resolution 39, "Lynching Victims Senate Apology." In this resolution, the Senate acknowledged that lynching was a common pastime in American culture that took the lives of more than 4,000

---

53   Ibid.
54   Susan Klopfer, *Who Killed Emmett Till?* Iowa: Author, 2000, 222.

people (mainly African American men) through the first half of the twentieth century and that their predecessors "failed to enact anti-lynching legislation" despite the persistent efforts of many. Offered in the "spirit of true repentance" and "reconciliation," the Senate's formal apology was directed toward the descendants of lynching victims. This event was historic. It was the first time that the US Senate ever apologized to black people for the US government's mistreatment of their ancestors.

The Senate announced its resolution at a ceremonial gathering in the US Capitol that lasted for about forty-five minutes and was covered live by C-SPAN. The apology was quintessentially performative in nature. The program featured brief remarks from several senators and testimonials from descendants of lynching victims. Former Senator Mary Landrieu (D-Louisiana) who sponsored the resolution opened the program by celebrating the efforts of her colleagues from both parties for supporting the resolution. Known by some as being a conservative Democrat, she was outspoken in her backing of this resolution.

She commented that James Allen's path-breaking *Without Sanctuary: Lynching Photography in America* (2000) played an important role in influencing her commitment to getting this resolution passed. She also called lynching "domestic terrorism" several times and proclaimed that the Senate was "culpable" for failing to pass anti-lynching legislation on many occasions. While co-sponsor of the resolution Senator George Allen (R-Virginia) dubbed the event a "solemn historic day" and voiced that Americans needed to "learn from history," Senator John Kerry (D-Massachusetts) was more critical in his remarks. He admitted that he did not know much about lynching until reading *Without Sanctuary*, deemed lynching "torture on American soil" and even a "conspiracy," questioned the integrity of those Senators who had not yet signed the resolution, and even suggested that the lynching of African Americans persisted symbolically in other forms of systematic oppression and inequality.

The testimonials from more than a few African Americans added authenticity to the ceremony. A descendant of Anthony Crawford, an African American man who was lynched in Abbeville, South Carolina, in 1916; Simeon Wright (a cousin of Emmett Till); and the great grandson of Ida B. Wells offered some brief thoughts. Perhaps the most powerful reflections were offered by James Cameron, who survived the famous lynching that took place before a mob of more than 10,000 white onlookers in Marion, Indiana, on August 7, 1930. A ninety-one-year-old Cameron, who opened America's Black Holocaust Museum in 1988, recounted his familiar story as he had done on countless occasions. He died almost exactly a year after this historic moment.

On February 25, 2007, the Virginia General Assembly became the first state legislature to issue some sort of apology for slavery. In Virginia House Joint Resolution No. 728, the Virginia General Assembly described some of the ways that blacks and Native Americans were mistreated in the state. According to the resolution, slavery "ranks as the most horrendous of all depredations of human rights and violations of our founding ideals in our nation's history." Nevertheless, the Virginia General Assembly did not refer to their document as an *apology*.

> Resolved by the House of Delegates, the Senate concurring, That the General Assembly hereby acknowledge *with profound regret* the involuntary servitude of Africans and the exploitation of Native Americans, and call for reconciliation of all Virginians.[55]

Several things stand out about Joint Resolution No. 728. One, acknowledging "with profound regret" is not the same as explicitly and officially apologizing for the past mistreatment of those who were enslaved. Regret implies that one feels sad or disappointed about something that happened. It is not quite the same as admitting guilt with an apology. Two, this quasi-apology addressed the experiences of two distinctly different histories of oppression. Each deserves its own apology. Nevertheless, Virginia's reckoning with slavery seems to have sparked a movement of some sort. Between 2007 and 2017, eight other states— Alabama, Connecticut, Florida, Maryland, New Jersey, North Carolina, Tennessee, and Delaware—have issued apologies and/or expressed "profound regret" for their past support of slavery.

Approximately a year after the Virginia General Assembly grappled with the state's slaveholding past, the US House of Representatives passed a resolution in late July 2008 apologizing for slavery and Jim Crow segregation. The apology was called "unprecedented" by many in the mainstream media. In H. Res. 194, the US House of Representatives, in part taking cues from the legislation of the Commonwealth of Virginia, Bush's comments at Gorée Island in 2004, and Clinton's One America in the 21st Century initiative on race, acknowledged the horrors of slavery and the "rigid system of officially sanctioned racial segregation." Equally important, these politicians conceded that "African-Americans continue to suffer from the complex interplay" between these systems. In their landmark bill, the House of Representatives posited that a "formal apology" was a prerequisite for the United States to be able to "move forward and seek reconciliation, justice, and harmony for all of its citizens." In the end, the House of Representatives declared that slavery was at odds with the country's founding principles and that slavery and Jim Crow segregation were fundamentally inhumane. The apology was straightforward and direct: That the House of Representatives did not outline a concrete plan for redress and instead "apologizes to African Americans on behalf of the people of the United States, for the wrongs

---

55   House Joint Resolution 728 (2007) (emphasis added).

committed against them and their ancestors who suffered under slavery and Jim Crow."[56]

They then indicated that they would be committed to addressing and rectifying the "lingering consequences" of the mistreatment of African Americans during earlier times. How this would actually be achieved was not specified. Approximately five months after Obama assumed office, on June 18, 2009, Congress echoed the House of the Representatives with some modifications. Most important, it did not commit itself to remedying how black Americans were impacted by slavery and Jim Crow segregation, and it added a decisive disclaimer. Congress emphasized that nothing included in this resolution "(A) authorizes or support any claim against the United States; or (B) serves as a settlement of any claim against the United States."[57] This abdication of responsibility was obviously added to thwart the plans of reparationists who had been long pressing the US government to apologize for slavery and act upon this admission of guilt.

In 2016, Delaware—whose General Assembly initially rebuffed ratifying the 13th Amendment—became among the most recent states to "express profound regret" for its role in slavery and its sanctioning of Jim Crow segregation for much of the twentieth century. Though Delaware's apology borrowed a lot of direct language from those of Virginia and the US Senate, Delaware employed some harsher language in describing what life during slavery entailed. For instance, they acknowledged that "women and girls were raped." Like the Senate's apology, they admitted that blacks in Delaware continued to be impacted by the "lasting legacy of slavery." The resolution included five major points, including a direct apology to African Americans and a commitment to supposedly rectify the "lingering consequences of the misdeeds committed against African-Americans under slavery and Jim Crow." Like the resolution from the US Senate, Delaware's apology included a crucial disclaimer: "Be it further resolved that it is the intent of the General Assembly that this joint Resolution shall not be used in, or be the basis of, any type of litigation."[58]

In the near future, more states will most likely join those who have symbolically apologized for slavery and Jim Crow segregation. On the other hand, reparations for slavery and Jim Crow segregation at the state and federal levels will continue to be vehemently opposed and disputed. Those who oppose reparations for slavery tend to invoke the same set of criticisms and attacks that can be found in David Horowitz's 2001 "Ten Reasons Why

---

56   H. Res. 194 (110th): Apologizing for the enslavement and racial segregation of African-Americans (2008).

57   S. Con. Res. 26 (111th): A concurrent resolution apologizing for the enslavement and racial segregation of African Americans (2009).

58   Delaware General Assembly, House Joint Resolution 10, House of Representatives 148th General Assembly (2016), legis.delaware.gov.

Reparations for Slavery Are a Bad Idea and Racist, Too."[59] Among the most popular of anti-reparationists' weak rebuttals are that slavery existed so long ago and no longer impacts African Americans, that slavery used to be a "legal" institution in the United States, that today's white Americans—many of whose ancestors migrated to the United States decades after the passage of the Thirteenth Amendment—had nothing to do with slavery, and that the original victims of the institution are dead.

For many anti-reparationists, what transpired during the antebellum era happened in the past, and there is no need to revisit this shameful past that could, they reason, stand in the way of the progress in race relations that have been made since the often romanticized and oversimplified civil rights movement. Anti-reparationists are often quick to argue that the statute of limitations for claims pertaining to slavery have long expired. It is harder to make this type of argument when dealing with Jim Crow segregation that lasted for several decades after *Brown v. Board of Education* in 1954. The recent past is much harder to ignore than more bygone days. Clinton's apology for the Tuskegee Study that spanned from the Great Depression through the early 1970s at one level reveals this. The success of some black farmers in winning a class action suit against the United States Department of Agriculture for racial discrimination from 1981 until 1996 also demonstrates this. It should, therefore, come as no surprise that numerous crimes committed against African Americans during the more recent past and civil rights movement have been revisited by legal analysts, politicians, and social activists.

REVISITING "ATROCITIES OF THE CIVIL RIGHTS ERA"

In June 2005, prompted by the retrial of Edgar Ray Killen (who approximately forty years earlier was found not guilty of playing a role in the murders of civil rights activists James Chaney, Andrew Goodman, and Michael Schwerner in Philadelphia, Mississippi), journalist Shaila Dewan wrote an interesting article in the "National Report" section of the *New York Times*. At the time, I was still practicing what was for many even then the archaic hobby of collecting hard copies of black history-related newspaper clippings. I still have this article in a file for my section on the civil rights movement for my undergraduate survey course in African American history since Reconstruction.

After first reading this brief yet informative article, I distinctly remember many thoughts racing through my mind. "Why did it take so long for this case, and others, to be handled correctly?" I pondered. During the next academic year, I shared Dewan's findings with my students, emphasizing to them yet another way that the violent legacy of the civil rights movement still rears its head in popular culture and the mainstream media.

---

59   The list appeared as an advertisement in the *Daily Free Press* (Boston) on March 12, 2001.

Legal scholars and historians have certainly researched and written about racially motivated crimes from the civil rights era. But Dewan eloquently and concisely captured the significance of the then upcoming Killen trial. "The trial will be one of the biggest of what some have called the South's 'atonement' trials revisiting the most notorious atrocities of the civil rights era," Dewan wrote. "One after another, new prosecutors have returned to these old crimes, spurred by news media investigations, relatives of the victims, the success of prosecutors and even their own youthful memories."[60] Under the header "A Long Battle for Justice," Dewan provided her readers with a handy chart of cases that were similar to the 1964 murders in Philadelphia, Mississippi.

Between the mid-1990s and 2005, at least half a dozen high-profile "racially provoked crimes" were reinvestigated, including the murders of Medgar Evers, Vernon Dahmer, the "four little girls" in the 16th Street Baptist Church in Birmingham, Alabama, Ben Chester White, and Emmett Till. Among other things, this phenomenon suggests that the passage of time—in these cases between thirty and forty years—plays a major role in providing the distance, separation, and perspective, thus allowing cooler heads to prevail. What was considered acceptable for many during the 1960s was considered wrong decades later.

Though many segregationists and racists who came of age during the 1950s and 1960s were still alive in the decades following the passage of the Voting Rights Act and racial discrimination had certainly not disappeared, by the late twentieth century and early twenty-first century some progress had been made in race relations in the South and throughout the nation. This was accompanied by an interest in reappraising past injustices committed against African Americans. Still, despite the passage of time, these reckonings with a dark period of recent American history were often met with resistance from some whites, who argued that bringing up these past atrocities served no purpose other than creating racial animosities that had allegedly been overcome.

Many of the victims' loved ones, journalists, scholars, and activists relentlessly pursued justice for these martyrs of the civil rights era. This determination to never forget history and to publicize past injustices has, in a few cases, yielded some sense of retributive justice, however limited and symbolic

Some of these reinvestigations have led to the convictions of elderly perpetrators who were finally held accountable for their crimes. Perhaps more than any other single event, historians have considered the lynching of Emmett Till in 1955 to have been one of the primary catalysts of the post–World War II civil rights movement. The reopening of the Emmett Till case by the US Department of Justice in 2004 (in order to determine whether others had been involved in

---

60 Shaila Dewan, "Revisiting '64 Civil Rights Deaths, This Time in a Murder Trial," *New York Times*, June 12, 2005, 26.

Till's murder) was monumental but resulted in no convictions. Till's mother, Mamie Till-Mobley, who incessantly kept her son's memory alive and unsuccessfully attempted to get a hearing from President Eisenhower, died before her son's case was reopened and in a minor sense redressed.

One of the main reasons that the Till case was reopened was because people continued to memorialize his tragic death in the ensuing decades. In addition to Till's mother, who relentlessly sought justice for her son and wrote a powerful memoir in 2003, by the time that the case was reopened, a large body of scholarship and several important documentaries had been produced on the case. Directed by Stanley Nelson, the award-winning *The Murder of Emmett Till* was released in 2003 and aired on PBS's popular *American Experience* series. Building upon the "Awakenings (1954–1956)" episode from the *Eyes on the Prize* documentary that first aired in January 1987, Nelson's documentary provides an excellent general overview of Till's murder and its aftermath.

In 2005, director Keith Beauchamp released his highly anticipated *The Untold Story of Emmett Till* that also revisited the details of Till's murder. Beauchamp first became interested in this case in 1996, and by 2000, began sharing "new" information that he learned about the murder with Mississippi state officials. He claimed to have discovered that as many as fourteen other people may have been involved in some way in the murder of Till. Beauchamp's research and documentary has been credited with influencing the FBI's and the Department of Justice's reopening of the case. After Till's body was exhumed and an autopsy was performed, by February 2007, no credible evidence validated Beauchamp's claim, and the case was officially closed. Although Stanley's and Beauchamp's findings did not result in any further prosecutions, these films, especially Beauchamp's, were catalysts for a historic reinvestigation. As historian Terry Wagner has pointed out, "the evidence connecting art to impact is rarely as well-documented as it was in the reinvestigation of Till's death."[61]

Shortly after Till was murdered, FBI Director J. Edgar Hoover wrote a memo to Attorney General Herbert G. Brownell in which he expressed no sympathy for what happened to Till and concluded that "there was no indication to date of a violation of the Federal Kidnapping Statute or a Federal Civil Rights Statute."[62] The US government never said that Hoover was wrong in his handling of the Till case. It took more than fifty-two years for some type of apologies to be offered for Till's murder. On May 9, 2007, the Emmett Till Memorial Commission of Tallahatchie County, Mississippi, signed a symbolic "Resolution of the Emmett Till Commission." In this brief document that was extended in the spirit of "reconciliation" and "healing the wounds of the past,"

---

61   Terry Wagner, "America's Civil Rights Revolution: Three Documentaries about Emmett Till's Murder in Mississippi," *History Journal of Film, Radio and Television* 30, 2010, 187.

62   J. Edgar Hoover to Herbert G. Brownell, pbs.org, September 6, 1955 .

the commission's twenty-member board of directors acknowledged that the Till case was a "terrible miscarriage of justice." They pledged:

> We state candidly and with deep regret the failure to effectively pursue justice. We wish to say to the family of Emmett Till that we are profoundly sorry for what was done in this community to your loved one. We the citizens of Tallahatchie County acknowledge the horrific nature of this crime. Its legacy has haunted our community.[63]

This remains the most extensive "official" apology for Till's murder.

A year later, the Emmett Till Unsolved Civil Rights Crime Act (hereafter the Till Act) was signed into law by President Bush (after it had passed the House in June 2007 and the Senate in September 2008). It called upon the FBI and "other entities within the Department of Justice" to "expeditiously investigate unsolved civil rights murders" that happened prior to December 31, 1969, and to provide "all the necessary resources" to do so. Like the 1994 conviction of Byron De La Beckwith for murdering NAACP field secretary Medgar Evers in Mississippi in 1963, this act represented a turning point in the struggle for black historical retributive justice. While the Till Act indicated that the investigations should be carried out in a speedy and efficient manner "due to the amount of time that has passed since the murders," there are no apologies in the act and Congress never publicly expressed regret that it waited for more than four decades following the Civil Rights Act to take legal steps to address these past wrongs.

According to legal scholar Barbara A. Schwabauer, the Till Act is "overtly symbolic" and "attempts to close a chapter in American history by effectively turning a blind eye to the complex workings of racism." Just as Clinton and Bush blamed individuals and not the US government for slavery and other past atrocities committed against black people, the architects of the Till Act, Schwabauer argues, had a "limited view of racial justice for the twenty-first century" mainly because they focused on identifying individual perpetrators and on "vilifying an intentional racism" that laid the context for the murders of many civil rights activists.[64] The Till Act also transformed various types of "victims" into heroes of the civil rights movement, even if they were not necessarily civil rights activists. These victims became symbols, as Till did. The fourteen-year-old child who was visiting relatives in Money, Mississippi, from Chicago was not murdered for being an activist. Till was one of the many African American men and women who was murdered because he was black and transgressed so-called southern racial etiquette norms. Similarly, the "four little girls" who were killed in the 16th Street Baptist Church in 1963 were awarded the Congressional Gold Medal

---

63 "Resolution of the Emmett Till Commission," etmctallahatchie.com, May 9, 2007 .
64 Barbara A. Schwabauer, "The Emmett Till Unsolved Civil Rights Crime Act: The Cold Case of Racism in the Criminal Justice System," *Ohio State Law Journal* 71, 2010, 656.

in 2013 by Obama not for their civil rights activism, but because their deaths, in Obama's words, "helped trigger triumph and a more just and equal and fair America."[65]

Schwabauer also posed a provocative question that crossed my mind when first reading Shaila Dewan's 2005 editorial. In the Till Act, Congress noted that the FBI and Department of Justice should act "expeditiously" in investigating cold cases from the civil rights era. "What makes this particular instance of racial injustice so urgent today?" asked Schwabauer.[66] At the surface level, the Till Act was the byproduct of new leads in the case that were publicized as well as by the efforts of politicians and activists. While there are many possible answers to Schwabauer's inquiry, it is clear that the supporters of the Till Act avoided making connections between past and present racial injustice and concretely situated crimes during the civil rights era in a distant past, implying that racism and racial violence no longer take place.

Following the passage of the Till Act, in May 2010 Attorney General Eric Holder identified a list of 122 relevant victims who were killed between 1951 and 1968. In August 2011, he produced another report that included the infamous lynching of Claude Neale in 1934. As pointed out by scholar Michael Newton, the vast majority of these cases were closed because those responsible for the murders had died. Families of the victims were offered non-public "hand-delivered" personal apologies that indicated that the FBI and Department of Justice were closing the cases for this reason. "Please accept our sincere condolences on the loss of your [relationship inserted]," concluded these form letters.[67]

Most historical scholarship and research by nongovernment employed scholars does not often directly shape or influence public policy. In a few instances, however, such publications have helped raise the consciousness of politicians to revisit past atrocities and even issue apologies. Sponsors of the Senate's resolution repeatedly said that the findings and images from *Without Sanctuary* exposed them to the horrific nature of this once common practice. Just as Beauchamp's research helped lead to the reinvestigation of the murder of Emmett Till and later, indirectly, the passage of the Till Act, historian Danielle McGuire's gut-wrenching book *At the Dark End of the Street: Black Women, Rape, and Resistance* played a direct role in the historic 2011 apology resolution that the Alabama House granted to Recy Taylor. The then ninety-one-year-old Taylor was raped by seven white men in Abbeville, Alabama, in 1944, and despite major protests, her assailants were not convicted.

The language in the historic resolution—"Expressing Regret for the State of Alabama's Involvement in the Failure to Prosecute Crimes Committed Against

---

65   Scott Wilson, "'Four Little Girls' Honored with Congressional Gold Medal," *Washington Post*, May 24, 2013.

66   Schwabauer, " The Emmett Till Unsolved Civil Rights Crime Act," 674.

67   Michael Newton, *Unsolved Civil Rights Murder Cases, 1934–1970*, Jefferson, NC: McFarland & Company, 2016, 5.

Recy Taylor"—did not mince words. After briefly recounting what happened to Taylor sixty-seven years ago, the resolution called the state's inaction a "deplorable lack of justice" and "sense of shame for all Alabamians." The state acknowledged its wrongdoing for not prosecuting those who committed the crimes, called its inaction "morally abhorrent and repugnant," and offered its "deepest sympathies and solemn regrets to Taylor and her family." Like the Senate's and various states' apologies for slavery and pardons like the one granted to the "Scottsboro Boys" in 2013, the Alabama House also made it clear that the resolution could not be used "in any manner whatsoever as support" for reparations.[68] Once again, it was alright for political authorities to revisit racial injustice as long as it would not be tangibly compensated. Though she felt vindicated by the resolution, Taylor (the subject of a 2017 documentary) has been living with the trauma of this crime for more than seventy years. As Danielle McGuire remarked at an event in honor of Taylor, the apology may have been "an important step towards healing past wounds and recognizing Taylor's humanity," but it did not correct this injustice.[69]

BETTER LATE THAN NEVER?: POSTHUMOUS PARDONING

Building upon previous efforts dating back to the late 1980s, on August 17, 2016, the anniversary of Marcus Garvey's birth, Garvey's son Julius Garvey and others reignited a movement to get a posthumous pardon for the Universal Negro Improvement Association founder from Obama by holding a press conference at the National Press Club in Washington, DC. Months earlier, a petition for pardoning Garvey was sent to the Department of Justice and the president's office. (Garvey's son and a group of activists argued that J. Edgar Hoover's charges against Garvey for mail fraud that led to his imprisonment in 1925 and eventual deportation in 1927 were trumped up and ill-founded.) The first black president did not show any signs of being interested in exonerating this controversial Pan-African nationalist who, for a brief period of time during the early years of the Harlem Renaissance, was at the helm of the largest black mass movement. In 2011, Obama's pardon attorney told Jamaican lawyer Donovan Parker, who was spearheading this movement, that a pardon for Garvey was not going to happen. It is said that Obama was also asked to pardon Garvey by the Jamaican prime minister during his 2015 visit to Garvey's native land.[70]

---

68   Benjamin Greenberg, "Recy Taylor Gets a Personal Sorry, But No Apology From Alabama," Colorlines.com, March 22, 2011; "Pardons and Paroles Board, Scottsboro Boys Act, posthumous pardons for certain convictions prior to 1932," Alabama Senate Bill 97, April 4, 2013.

69   The Associated Press, "Still No Justice for Civil Rights Era Rape Victims," thegrio.com, October 10, 2010.

70   Julia Porterfield, "Activists Ask Obama for Posthumous Pardon of Black Nationalist Leader Marcus Garvey," Washington Times, August 18, 2016.

The United States Department of Justice has a clear stance on its views toward posthumous pardons. Its "Policy on Posthumous Pardon Applications" suggests that a presidential pardon for Garvey or others convicted of federal crimes is highly unlikely:

It is the general policy of the Department of Justice not to accept for processing applications for posthumous pardons for federal convictions. The policy against processing posthumous pardon petitions is grounded in the belief that the time of the officials involved in the clemency process is better spent on the pardon and commutation requests of living persons. Many posthumous pardon requests would likely be based on a claim of manifest injustice, and given that decades have passed since the commission of the offense and the historical record would have to be scoured objectively and comprehensively to investigate such claims, it is the Department's position that the limited resources available to process applications for Presidential pardon are best dedicated to applications submitted by living persons who can truly benefit from a grant of clemency. The policy also recognizes that applications for posthumous pardons are less likely to involve the issues that generally are explored in routine pardon investigations (such as the recent, or ongoing, rehabilitative efforts of a defendant), and are therefore less likely to benefit from the investigative techniques commonly used in the pardon process.[71]

The recent movement to posthumously pardon Garvey is not unique. There have been other efforts to clear the names of other black historical icons and "ordinary" black citizens that have in some cases resulted in posthumous pardons of some nature.

For instance, in August 2005, the Georgia State Board of Pardons and Paroles issued an interesting kind of posthumous pardon to Lena Baker who—in a speedy trial and by a jury composed of all white males—was found guilty of murdering her abusive white male employer in 1944. A year later, she was executed by electrocution. In her defense, she said that she killed her abuser in an act of self-defense. While her descendants campaigned to clear her name, by the late 1990s, her case received increased attention from scholars. Most important, in 2001 scholar Lela Bond Phillips released a brief biography on Baker, *The Lena Baker Story*.

In their 2006 annual report, the Georgia State Board of Pardons and Paroles briefly mentioned the Baker case, calling the pardon an act of honoring Baker's family. The "official" pardon was given to Baker's great-grandnephew, Roosevelt Curry. They summarized what they determined: "The Parole Board did not find Lena Baker innocent of the crime. The Board concluded that it was a grievous error to deny clemency in 1945 to Ms. Baker, and this case called out for mercy."

---

71   The United States Department of Justice, "Policy on Posthumous Pardon Applications," justice.gov.

The board continued, "Ms. Baker's case was only the third parole to be granted posthumously by the Parole Board in the sixty-two-year history of the agency."[72] Though it began to be covered by the mainstream media weeks before the pardon was granted, this pardon was not public. In a private meeting, the pardon was given directly to Baker's descendants. A few politicians did speak out about the decision. State Representative Tyrone Brooks, for instance, viewed this pardon as a step in the right direction. "I see a reawakening of elected and appointed officials to recognize the injustices of the past," he added, "We have a responsibility to correct those wrongs as much we can."[73]

Among the most famous recent pardons were those granted to members of the so-called "Scottsboro Boys" by the Alabama Board of Pardoners in 2013. This benchmark case that gained national and international attention involved nine African American youth from age 12 to 19 who in 1931 were falsely convicted of raping two white women. It is considered one of the greatest miscarriages of justice in US legal history.[74] The Scottsboro Boys Act allowing this pardon to occur established procedures for considering posthumous pardons "to remedy social injustice associated with racial discrimination." Like the Senate's apology for slavery, the act included an important disclaimer.

> Nothing in this act, or any determination made by the Alabama Board of Pardons and Paroles pursuant to this act, shall give rise to any liability for any act or omission of governmental entity or otherwise give rise to any legal claim, suit, or action, including for reparations to a surviving family member of a person pardoned under this act to a posthumously pardoned person's estate.[75]

This act was signed nearly twenty-five years after Clarence Norris, the last survivor of this ordeal, died. After signing the act, Alabama Governor J. Bentley announced that these men had "finally received justice." In describing the significance of these pardons, Senator Arthur Orr (R-Alabama) commented:

> Today is a reminder that it is never too late to right a wrong. We cannot go back in time and change the course of history, but we can change how we respond to history . . . The passage of time and doing nothing is no excuse. This hearing marks a significant milestone for these young men, their families, and for our great state by officially recognizing and correcting a tremendous wrong.[76]

---

72   Georgia State Board of Pardons and Paroles, *Annual Report 2006*, pap.georgia.gov.
73   Associated Press, "Georgia Pardons Black Woman Who Was Executed in '45," *The Boston Globe*, August 31, 2005.
74   See Dan T. Carter, *Scottsboro: A Tragedy of the American South*, Baton Rouge: Louisiana State University Press, 1969.
75   "Pardons and Paroles Board, Scottsboro Boys Act, posthumous pardons for certain convictions prior to 1932," Alabama Senate Bill 97, April 4, 2013.
76   Alan Blinder, "Alabama Pardons 3 'Scottsboro Boys' After 80 Years," *New York Times*, November 22, 2013, A14.

Other politicians echoed Orr's sentiments. James A. Miller, author of *Remembering Scottsboro: The Tragedy of an Infamous Trial*, offered much more critical and insightful comments, noting that the pardon was indeed "long overdue," but he stressed that he did not consider this action a solution or justice, especially since the victims were already deceased and they had few surviving family members alive at the time of the pardon.[77]

In the end, this pardon that included no restitution was a symbolic act that sought to close a discussion on one of the greatest tragedies in the history of the American legal system. Black history professors will, nevertheless, continue to focus on how these nine young black men were victimized rather than how they were eventually pardoned.

Several more recent posthumous pardons and movements for others are also noteworthy. Approximately a year before Lena Baker was executed, on June 16, 1944, fourteen-year-old George Stinney was executed in Columbia, South Carolina, for the murder of two white girls, ages eight and eleven. After he was executed, Stinney's family continued to profess his innocence and to decry the handling of his trial. Others noticed the craziness of this case. In 1988, novelist David Stout wrote a book based upon the case and several years later director John Erman released a television movie, *Carolina Skeletons*, that may have helped generate interest in this case. In 2013, a group of lawyers filed a motion for a new trial on the grounds that there was a lack of evidence (there was, for instance, no signed confession to the crime), the denial of counsel, and an inadequate defense. Considering the amount of time that had elapsed since Stinney was executed and the case's relative obscurity, this reinvestigation was widely publicized. For instance, in March 2014 the weekly *People* magazine that usually focuses on the lives of the rich and famous published an informative essay on Stinney's case.

After a two-day hearing in late January 2014, the following conclusion was reached in mid-December 2014: "The Court finds fundamental Constitutional violations of due process exists in the 1944 prosecution of George Stinney Jr. and hereby vacates the judgement." In vacating Stinney's conviction, the judge called the case "a truly unfortunate episode in our history." Carmen T. Mullen added, "From time to time, we are called to look back to examine our still-recent history and correct injustices when possible. Our common law provides for extraordinary relief, equitable in nature, when great and fundamental injustice has occurred."[78] As was the case with other similar situations, no retribution was paid to Stinney's family. Mullen's admission that the execution of Stinney was an "injustice" did not amount to a formal apology that had further consequences. Nonetheless, Stinney's surviving siblings could perhaps finally feel some sense of vindication, albeit limited.

---

77   Brian Lyman, "Alabama Grants Posthumous Pardons to Scottsboro Boys," *USA Today*, November 21, 2013.

78   As Presiding Circuit Court Judge Carmen Tevis Mullen ordered *in State of South Carolina v. George Stinney, Jr.*, December 16, 2014.

A posthumous pardon of a different nature than Stinney's that has recently gained some attention pertains to the first black heavyweight champion of the world, Jack Johnson, who was erroneously convicted by an all-white jury of violating the Mann Act in 1913. Passed three years earlier, the Mann Act sought to curb forced prostitution and prevent young women, often immigrants, from being beguiled into participating in "the world's oldest profession" by making it a felony to transport "any woman or girl" across state lines or to or from any foreign country "for the purposes of prostitution or debauchery, or for any other immoral practice."[79] It seems to be common knowledge among historians, certainly within African Americanist circles, that this often manipulated law was used as a tool to knock down this brash black man who dated and married white women, mercilessly defeated white boxers, and defied what black men during the "nadir" period were expected to be by white society. Federal agents from the US Department of Justice were determined to secure evidence demonstrating that Johnson had violated the Mann Act and they were successful in this quest.

Instead of serving his sentence of one year and one day in prison, the defiant pugilist lived abroad in exile. When he returned to the United States in 1920, he served his unjust prison sentence in the US Penitentiary, Leavenworth. Johnson's life story is somewhat well-known today. Not only have many informative biographies and micro-studies on Johnson been published, but in 2005, award-winning filmmaker Ken Burns released his exhaustive documentary *Unforgiveable Blackness: The Rise and Fall of Jack Johnson*. As is often the case with PBS films produced during the digital era, there is an excellent website for this nonhagiographical documentary that includes a wealth of resources, lesson plans, and primary documents. Around the time that Burns's documentary was released, Senator John McCain (R-Arizona) and Republican House Representative Peter T. King (R-New York) began campaigning for a posthumous pardon for Johnson. Burns and others joined this cause as well. In 2009 and 2011, Johnson apologists succeeded in getting the Senate and the House to pass resolutions posthumously pardoning Johnson. Though US presidents have issued posthumous pardons to individuals, they are not common, and Obama, like Bush, did not show any interest in granting Johnson this absolution.

On December 9, 2015, the Senate passed a resolution that opined that Johnson "should receive a posthumous pardon for the racially motivated conviction in 1913." The resolution summarized Johnson's accomplishment and overviewed the racist climate in which he lived, noting that "between 1901 and 1910, 754 African Americans were lynched, some for simply being 'too familiar' with white women." In the document, "Federal authorities" are also held responsible for mustering up charges against Johnson. The first point of the resolution is the most important: "That it remains the sense of Congress that Jack Johnson should

---

79 The Mann Act, 18 U.S.C.A. § 2421 et seq., 1910.

receive a posthumous pardon—(1) to expunge a racially motivated abuse of the prosecutorial authority of the Federal Government from the annals of criminal justice in the United States."[80]

On the day that the resolution was passed, McCain reiterated what the resolution asked for and called upon Obama to act. "Jack Johnson is a boxing legend and pioneer whose reputation was wrongly tarnished by a racially motivated conviction more than a century ago," McCain proclaimed. "[I]t's past time for President Obama to right this injustice, restore the legacy of a great American athlete, and close a shameful chapter in our nation's history."[81] Co-sponsor Senator Harry Reid (D-Nevada) added, "The record of history must finally be corrected to restore Jack Johnson's good name ... Today we showed we will never stop working toward righting our past wrongs. It's time to put this injustice behind us."[82] In June 2016, McCain and Reid issued another call to Obama to pardon Johnson in honor of the 70th anniversary of Johnson's death. McCain reiterated: "[W]e are reminded of the cruel injustices of our nation's past that led to this great athlete's wrongful conviction more than a century ago," McCain proclaimed:

> With just months left in President Obama's term in office, now is the time for him to finally do the right thing and issue a posthumous pardon for Jack Johnson. We must right this historical wrong, restore the legacy of a great American athlete, and close a shameful chapter in our nation's history.[83]

Why did McCain, in particular, feel so strongly about Johnson's case? There are certainly many other posthumous pardons that could be sought for African Americans who suffered more than Johnson did. Perhaps McCain's quest to pardon Johnson is the byproduct of his love of boxing. Perhaps Johnson's athletic prowess earned him an honorary status for McCain and other white politicians. Whatever the case may be, McCain's genuine and enduring commitment to this cause cannot be questioned. Why have American presidents been so reluctant to pardon Johnson? Maybe this has something to do with his controversial nature, something that Burns figures effectively and prominently into *Unforgiveable Blackness*.

---

80   S. Con. Res. 5, 113th Congress: A concurrent resolution expressing the sense of Congress that John Arthur "Jack" Johnson should receive a posthumous pardon for the racially motivated conviction in 1913 that diminished the athletic, cultural, and historic significance of Jack Johnson and unduly tarnished his reputation (2013–2014).

81   "Congress Passes McCain-Reid Resolution Urging Posthumous Pardon for Jack Johnson," December 9, 2015, mccain.senate.gov.

82   "McCain, Reid, King & Meeks Call on President Obama to Issue Posthumous Pardon for Jack Johnson," June 30, 2016, mccain.senate.gov.

83   "Congress Passes McCain-Reid Resolution Urging Posthumous Pardon for Jack Johnson," mccain.senate.gov, December 9, 2015; "McCain, Reid, King & Meeks Call Upon President Obama to Issue Posthumous Pardon for Jack Johnson," mccain.senate.gov, June 30, 2016.

On April 21, 2018, supposedly egged on by actor and boxing fan Sylvester Stallone, Donald Trump randomly tweeted that he was "considering a Full Pardon" for Johnson. Then, on May 24, 2018, the divisive 45th President of the United States, who several weeks earlier claimed that his approval rating among African Americans doubled because of Kanye West's endorsement, signed an Executive Grant of Clemency for the first black heavyweight champion of the world. During a thirteen-minute-long ceremony in the Oval Office, attended by, among others, Stallone, undefeated WBC heavyweight title-holder Deontay Wilder, London-born three-time heavyweight champion Lennox Lewis, and Johnson's maternal great-great niece Linda Bell Haywood, a jovial Trump announced that during a "period of tremendous racial tension" in the United States, Johnson was "treated very rough, very rough." Unsurprisingly, he celebrated himself for righting a wrong (without indicting those who falsely persecuted Johnson) and, in his words, for "taking this very righteous step." Predictably, he also could not resist criticizing Obama and his predecessors for not correcting "a wrong that occurred in our history." While WBC President Mauricio Sulaiman, Lewis, Stallone, and Wilder all pandered to Trump and offered shallow tributes to Johnson, Johnson's descendant Haywood spoke eloquently, stressing that the persecution of her "uncle" (as she referred to Johnson) impacted her family's memories of him. She lamented that she was not alone in once feeling ashamed of Johnson's life and legacy. "By this pardon being signed," she said, "that would help rewrite history, and erase the shame and humiliation that my family felt for my uncle." While Haywood's comments are understandable (she was, no doubt, caught up in the moment and overcome by intense emotions), Trump did not in any way "rewrite history." Further, when viewed within the context of his past and present racial politics, his posthumous pardoning of Johnson is a symbolic gesture at best.[84]

Several years ago, sports columnist and author William C. Rhoden posited, perhaps facetiously, that maybe Obama was putting aside a pardon Johnson for "one of the final acts of his presidency." He understood how and why Obama strategically avoided publicly addressing the historical mistreatment of black people. More important, he also offered a viable explanation for why a pardon for Johnson was significant and contentious in a manner that Trump, McCain, and others did not, and intimately related to a broader black struggle against historical injustice. "The issue says something about our reluctance to look back, to do the work needed to fix the flawed foundation of a nation conceived in democracy but built on the backs of millions of slaves," Rhoden concluded, "It's not only Jack Johnson who needs the pardon. We do."[85]

---

84 "Remarks by President Trump at Pardoning of Jack Arthur 'Jack' Johnson," Oval Office, Washington, DC, May 24, 2018. For a hilarious commentary on Trump's pardon, see Michael Harriot, "Jack Johnson Posthumously Tells Donald Trump to Kiss His Ass," May 24, 2018, theroot.com.

85 William C. Rhoden, "A Century Later, Jack Johnson Awaits a Nation's Absolution," *New York Times*, December 4, 2015, B14.

Afterword

Displaying the Black Past

Five months after it officially opened its doors to the general public in late September 2016, I was finally able to visit the National Museum of African American History and Culture (NMAAHC) on the National Mall at 14th Street and Constitution Avenue, NW in Washington, DC. I make it to the nation's capital several times each year and had originally planned to visit this state-of-the-art facility sometime by Thanksgiving at the latest. I soon discovered that this would not be possible. Friends, colleagues, and those with inside connections warned me that my chances of entering this popular tourist destination before the spring of 2017 were slim. In late 2016, when I checked the availability of time entry passes online, there were none available until late in the spring of 2017. "How can this be?" I thought to myself, "Is African American history really *this* popular?" After visiting the museum, I understood the hype. A headline from the *Washington Post* in early October 2016—"More Visitors Want to Go to the New African American Museum than the Building Can Handle"— rang true indeed.

During its opening weekend, more than 30,000 people visited the museum. On average, about 7,000 guests and tourists of all ages and backgrounds, especially African Americans, drop in on the museum daily. As I write, more than one million people from all over the nation and world have visited the NMAAHC since it opened its doors. Through the summer of 2017, of the nineteen Smithsonian museums, only the National Air and Space Museum, the National Museum of Natural History, and the National Museum of American History have been more popular.

Late during Black History Month in 2017, I was in Washington, DC and, with LaShawn Harris who also specializes in African American history, we decided that we would venture to 14th Street and Constitution Avenue, NW to see whether we would be able to convince those manning the entrance to let us in. After all, as one who has devoted most of his life to studying and writing about black history, I felt some sense of entitlement (yes, I realize how self-centered this sounds) to be able to get into this monumental place. Shortly before noon, my affable companion gingerly approached one of the museum employees in a red vest while I anxiously awaited off to the side. To my surprise and joy, she returned with two passes.

Starting at Level Four (because the wraparound line to enter the David M. Rubenstein History Galleries in the Concourse was intimidating), I spent four hours attempting to digest an endless onslaught of historical information, artifacts, panels, multimedia presentations, and memorabilia. After leaving the museum stimulated and exhausted, I realized that four hours was not nearly enough time for me to adequately take in everything that this space has to offer. (I have heard that the average stay at the museum is about six hours.)

Several days later, I returned to the museum at 10:00 a.m. (when the museum opens daily), hoping once again to get in as a ticketless "walk-up" visitor. Alone this time, I approached a staff member outside of the south porch main entrance who looked like she would be sympathetic to my predicament and asked if I could obtain a "walk-up" pass. The polite museum employee told me that it was a very busy day and that I could wait in a section on the Madison Drive side of the building until about 1:00 p.m. for the opportunity to acquire a same-day pass. A bit deflated, I decided to go to the north side entrance to see if I could somehow once again gain entrance.

To my great delight, an African American high school teacher from Prince George's County, Maryland, was posted at this entrance announcing that she had some extra tickets. Trying to be as calm as possible and respectful to other ticketless bystanders, I bolted over to this generous educator and got my "Golden Ticket." During this visit, I remained at the museum for about five hours. What made this visit particularly memorable was overhearing the conversations of and observing the countless—for the most part African American—elementary, middle school, and high school students. I was happily surprised when I overheard one black female teenager chastising her classmate for rushing her through the exhibits. When taking in images of lynching, I overheard another teenaged black female exalt, "That's messed up!" and while standing in line at the Emmett Till Memorial, another African American high school student nervously whispered to her friend, "I don't want to see this."

Following this second visit, I concluded that I needed to visit the museum at least one more time in order to write an informed assessment of it. So on March 1, 2017, at about noon, I arrived at the museum and while standing in a long line, once again without an entry pass, a gracious black woman directly in front of me offered several extra tickets to those behind her. I took advantage of this opportunity. During this visit, I surveyed all of the galleries for about three hours. I concluded by treating myself to a pricey meal at the museum's surprisingly excellent cafeteria, the Sweet Home Café. While devouring shrimp and grits, I looked up and saw a large photo of the determined Greensboro Four posted at the Woolworth's lunch counter and other images of African Americans cooking and breaking bread together. Even in this space, I was surrounded by the black past.

Thanks to the generosity of a member of the museum's Scholarly Advisory Committee who I recently reestablished contact with, in early July 2017 I visited the museum again, mainly to see if any changes had been made during the three months since my last visit. No major alterations had been made. I did, however, notice that more materials and resources had been added to the Explore More! educational space, especially to the Robert Frederick Smith Explore Your Family History Center.

I have visited numerous African American historical sites and museums and the NMAAHC is, hands down, the most comprehensive, cutting-edge, ultramodern, and awe-inspiring museum focusing on the black American experience. I agree with children's author Tonya Bolden who proclaimed: "It's an experience like no other."[1] I was profoundly moved by what I witnessed, experienced, and, in some cases, learned and discovered about a past that I believe that I am tremendously familiar with.

Typically speaking, the primary function of museums is to amass, display, protect, and exhibit historical materials and artifacts to the public for educational and entertainment purposes. Because the vast majority of African Americans were denied their most basic human and civil rights during nearly 80 percent of the total black presence in this country, the curators of black museums face a significant challenge: to offer a snapshot of the African American experience that tactfully balances the prevailing themes of victimization/oppression and perseverance/resistance.

In the late twentieth and twenty-first centuries, this issue has preoccupied those involved in working with displaying black history. "African American history does contain certain difficult, controversial, and sensitive topics—as does all American history," president of Engaging, LLC, Max A. van Balgooy observes.

> As historical museums and historical sites, we have a great responsibility to share all of the lessons of history, whether it moves through successes and failures, tragedy and delight, laughter and sadness. Favoring one without the other can mislead our listeners, giving them only an incomplete understanding of our past and present.[2]

Echoing Balgooy, NMAAHC founding director historian Lonnie G. Bunch III described what he believed an underlying goal of the Smithsonian Institution's nineteenth museum ought to be. "I think the museum needs to be a place that finds the right tension between moments of pain and stories of resiliency and uplift." He continues:

> There should be moments where visitors should cry as they ponder the pains of the past, but they will also find much of the joy and hope that have been a cornerstone of the African-American experience.[3]

1   Tonya Bolden, *How to Build a Museum*, New York: Viking, 2016, 54.
2   Max A. van Balgooy, "Introduction," in *African American History and Culture at Museums and Historical Sites*, ed. Max A. van Balgooy, xiv, New York: Roman and Littlefield, 2015.
3   Lonnie G. Bunch III, "Making a Way Out of No Way," *Smithsonian* 47, September 2016, 28.

Keeping such observations in mind, in the remainder of this "Afterword," I briefly reflect upon how the NMAAHC presents African American history to the general public and can potentially shape its visitors' views of the black past. Despite its undeniable impressiveness and incredible scope, the museum can be criticized for its shortcomings. Because of its overwhelmingly massive collection, I am not going to pretend that my account is by any means comprehensive.

Among the first major and thoughtful reviews of NMAAHC was Pulitzer Prize-winning co-chief art critic of the *New York Times* Holland Carter's balanced appraisal from September 2016, "The Smithsonian's African American Museum Is Here At Last. And It Uplifts and Upsets." By and large, the US mainstream media and popular press has heaped praise on the museum. Several of the books on the museum sold in the gift shop are informative, namely the museum's *Official Guide* and Mabel O. Wilson's *Begin with the Past: Building the National Museum of African American History and Culture.* But they are also understandably celebratory.

As one not formally trained in public history, museum studies, or museology, I believe that African Americanist historians should be aware of the role that museums can play in helping to influence how people view black history. After all, it could be argued that museums influence the general public's views of history more than the books that many historians write. I concur with historian John Fleming who two decades ago argued that African American museums served to "transmit cultural values" and can "help by giving us a sense of history that allows us to call upon our experiences to interpret the past and to use that knowledge to shape and influence the future."[4]

"IT'S AN EXPERIENCE LIKE NO OTHER":

The National Museum of African American History and Culture
With more than 100,000 square feet of exhibition space, the NMAAHC has about twenty Exhibition Stories that are housed in six major levels. Located underground, Levels C3 ("Slavery and Freedom, 1400–1877"), C2 ("Defending Freedom, Defining Freedom: The Era of Segregation, 1876–1968"), and C1 ("A Changing America: 1968 and Beyond") constitute the David M. Rubenstein History Galleries spanning from approximately 1400 until the present. Level C, the Concourse, includes the Sweet Home Café, the Oprah Winfrey Theatre, a serene Contemplative Court, a History Orientation Gallery, a "Century in the Making," and an area reserved for future special exhibitions.

On the ground level, where one enters the museum, is the spacious and beautifully designed Heritage Hall that has an information desk, an Orientation Theatre, and a museum gift shop that includes all sorts of black history

---

4   John E. Fleming, "African-American Museums, History, and the American Ideal," *The Journal of American History* 81, December 1994, 1026.

memorabilia and a limited collection of books. It would be interesting to know the politics behind how the decisions were made about the books to feature and the frequency of changes to the selections. Level Two, Explore More!, has a family center, a library and archives section, classroom space, and a Center for African American Media Arts. For me, the most intriguing component on this level is the "Follow the Greenbook" interactive exhibit. From a monitor nicely fit into the dashboard and front window of an older replica car, visitors are schooled about the challenges that African Americans faced when they embarked on road trips to the South. Level Three, Community Galleries, showcases four sections dealing with blacks in America's wars, African Americans in sports, the significance of "place" in black life and culture, and various expressions of resistance. Level Four, Culture Galleries, focuses on various black "cultural expressions," including musical traditions and contributions, visual arts (mainly paintings), and blacks' contributions to Hollywood film, drama, television, and comedy.

Though those with minimal knowledge of African American history may be overwhelmed by the wealth of information packed into the countless panels and first-rate interactive exhibitions and revealed by the more than 36,000 artifacts on display and even somewhat confused by the layout of the museum (especially if one gets sidetracked or makes a wrong turn in the History Galleries), anyone who visits the museum will learn something new about African American history.

The History Galleries present the black experience from the era of European Exploration and the early years of the transatlantic slave trade through the Obama presidency in a conventional manner. By this, I mean that the information is presented in a way that mirrors the presentation in major black history textbooks, like *From Slavery to Freedom: A History of African Americans* or *The African American Odyssey*. The elegantly illustrated commemorative textbook that was produced for the museum, *Dream a World Anew: The African American Experience and the Shaping of America* (whose title echoes that of Robin D. G. Kelley and Earl Lewis's anthology *To Make Our World Anew*), also follows a normative approach to African American history, featuring essays from older generations of scholars and historians. Peniel E. Joseph is the only contributor who hails from the hip-hop generation.

When taking the large, glass-encased elevator from the Concourse, down to the History Galleries, a dozen flashpoints appear painted on the brick wall in the following order: Today, 2008, 1984, 1968, 1954, 1948, 1865, 1863, 1808, 1776, 1565, and 1400. Other dates, of course, could have been selected and those without knowledge in African American history would probably not know why some of these dates were selected. Most would probably have no problem identifying 2008 as the year when Obama became America's first black president. During my visits, different museum staff members offered brief, and in some cases imprecise, descriptions of what transpired during these years.

While the transatlantic slave trade, the rise of sugar, the Middle Passage, and enslaved Africans' west African roots are described in "Slavery and Freedom," there could have been more about the various African kingdoms and states from which Africans were imported into North America. Many Afrocentric theorists—like, for instance, the late Asa G. Hilliard who in 1992 authored an article unambiguously entitled "The Meaning of KMT (Ancient Egyptian) History for Contemporary African American Experience"—would certainly be disappointed with the lack of any attention paid to ancient African civilizations and Cheikh Anta Diop's theory of African cultural unity that has inspired many. Overall, the discussions of the transatlantic slave trade, slavery during the colonial and antebellum eras, emancipation, and the Civil War are thorough, and visitors are presented with useful information regarding the number of enslaved Africans imported into and living in North America and the United States at different points during the seventeenth, eighteenth, and nineteenth centuries.

The collection of maps highlighting slavery's expansion from the era of the "New Nation" through the Civil War are particularly illuminating. Actual ads for runaway slaves as well as many brief descriptions that appear on one wall are jarring. The statues that are in Level C3 representing the era of slavery are quite predictable—Benjamin Banneker, Thomas Jefferson, Phillis Wheatley, Elizabeth Freeman, Clara Brown, Robert Smalls, and Toussaint L'Ouverture. Though a small Bible that "likely" belonged to Nat Turner is on display, nobody who led an armed slave revolt or conspiracy in the United States such as Jemmy, Turner, Denmark Vesey, Gabriel Prosser, or John Brown are memorialized with a statue.

Though illuminating, the section on the transatlantic slave trade and slavery did not stress the horrors of these institutions. In portraying the slave trade, there are edifying visuals and audios: a large digital map of the Atlantic Ocean, a section on Olaudah Equiano's famous experience, a wall with the names of the slavers and the numbers of Africans they transported, and an eerie dark and narrow corridor that contains iron ballasts from the São José that sank near the Cape of Good Hope in 1794. Captive Africans are called "commodities" and the Middle Passage is described as being "the traumatic journey from western Africa to the Caribbean and the Americas" and as "a mixture of captivity and commerce" by which "enslaved Africans were dispersed throughout the Atlantic World and forced to leave their homeland and loved ones behind." In one panel, "Ship Full of Sorrow," enslaved Africans are depicted as resisting: "Rather than endure the horrors of enslavement, many jumped into the shark-infested waters." While certainly educational, the NMAAHC's depiction of the Middle Passage is mild when compared with the way the Charles H. Wright Museum of African American History in Detroit treats this horrific phenomenon. This museum's once controversial replica slaver is a transformative experience, especially for young visitors.

While visitors see runaway slave ads, slave auction announcements, a pair of shackles and a whip, a blown-up image of a black man being burned at the stake after the 1741 "New York Conspiracy," and the famous photo of Private Gordon's "scarred back," the museum curators do not stress the violence associated with slavery, an institution that was brutal and even genocidal in nature. After all, approximately 50 percent of all enslaved children died before the age of five, and despite what "culture and community" slavery scholars may have argued during the 1970s and 1980s, oppression impacted enslaved African Americans profoundly. The section on the American Revolution is excellent, highlighting the various roles played by blacks as well as the changing demographics in enslaved and free populations during the revolutionary era. Still, the prevailing myth of Crispus Attucks that historian Mitch Kachun meticulously deconstructs in *First Martyr of Liberty: Crispus Attucks in American Memory* (2017) is unsurprisingly celebrated.

Following "Slavery and Freedom: 1400–1877," the next exhibition focuses on the vast era of segregation spanning from the controversial election of 1876, signaling the end of Reconstruction, through the assassination of Martin Luther King Jr. in 1968. While the periodization of this level is understandable, the vital "nadir" period is not emphasized. There is a fairly comprehensive section dedicated to Jim Crow segregation that has a component on black leadership during this crucial era. Echoing archaic yet enduring trends in African American historiography as well as the sentiments of the vast majority of black public intellectuals, the museum perpetuates the Booker T. Washington–W. E. B. Du Bois dichotomy, siding with Du Bois, the routinely anointed epitome of the protest tradition of black thought.

There are dozens of brief video presentations throughout the museum. In "The Debate," a five-minute video directed by Stanley Nelson and written by Marcia Smith, the strategies of Washington, Ida B. Wells, and Du Bois are compared. The interpretation is facile and conventional. "In the wake of Reconstruction, as African Americans continued their struggle for equality," narrator Corene Lavhan opens the video, "they debated how best to move forward." Ignoring the great diversity of black thought during the Progressive Era, Lavhan declares: "Three prominent voices emerged" (these being Ida B. Wells, W. E. B. Du Bois, and Booker T. Washington). Setting aside what they had in common, it is stressed that "each advocated a different strategy." Characterized solely upon popular excerpts from his famous 1895 Atlanta Exposition oration, Washington is dubbed an accommodationist who simply advised African Americans to work hard, avoid confrontations with white America, and exercise patience.

Wells and Du Bois, on the other hand, are portrayed as being activists and agents of protest. "Du Bois believed that critical thinking and protests were necessary in the face of discrimination," whereas "Wells was even more critical of the South's violence." After citing Washington as advising that blacks begin at "the bottom of life"/ "not at the top," the narrator notes: "But activist Du Bois encouraged African Americans to seek civil rights and, if possible, attend college." This dismissal of Washington is replicated in the museum's textbook, *Dream a World Anew*. Ignoring Washington's complexity, historian Spencer R. Crew dubs the founder of Tuskegee Institute "the prominent black educator who encouraged African Americans to accept second-class, segregated status as they pulled themselves up economically."[5]

In addition to depicting black life during the era of Jim Crow segregation through the first half of the twentieth century, Level 2 includes extensive information on the modern civil rights movement. Among the most popular sections in this exhibit area are the segregated railroad passenger car from the Southern Railroad Company, the amazing interactive lunch counters, and the Emmett Till Memorial.

Unsurprisingly, "A Changing America: 1968 and Beyond" is the least expansive of the exhibitions in the History Galleries. Though the representation of the multilayered and often romanticized Black Power era is elaborate and highlights the diversity of the period's activists, the exhibit breezes through the "Beyond." The 1970s, 1980s, and 1990s are all described in very generic terms. The 1970s is depicted as a decade that gave rise to black "political firsts," African American "cultural rebirth," Affirmative Action, and an expanding black middle-class (despite the fact that "others stayed trapped within cycles of poverty"). The 1980s are dubbed "years of paradox" marked most by gains by professional blacks, Reaganomics, drugs, incarceration, and hip-hop; to depict the 1990s, there is a two-minute video and references to The Anita Hill–Clarence Thomas case, the Million Man March, and the Million Woman March.

In this sense (that is, a limited portrayal of the African American experience after the Black Power era), the museum's curators followed the trend in the African American historical profession of underappreciating contemporary black history. Based upon this exhibit, one would be led to think that the most important things that happened in the post-Black Power era were the ascendency of Oprah Winfrey and the presidency of Barack Obama. By predictably ending the History Galleries with a tribute to Obama, the NMAAHC perpetuates the popular myth that the first black president was a bona fide black leader and that his presidency profoundly altered the course of African American history.

BLACK HEROES ARE GREAT, BUT WHERE IS "THE FATHER OF BLACK HISTORY"?

The Charles H. Wright Museum of African American History in Detroit, Michigan, used to hold the distinction of housing the "world's largest

---

5 Spencer R. Crew, "From Reconstruction to the Civil Rights Movement," in *Dream a World Anew*, ed. Kinshasha Holman Conwill, 99, Washington, DC: Smithsonian Books, 2016.

permanent exhibit" on black history. Of course, now this claim-to-fame belongs to the NMAAHC. Detroit's once premier black history museum is dwarfed by the newest Smithsonian museum. The NMAAHC includes so much that it would be unreasonable to argue that more panels, videos, interactive exhibits, artifacts, or sections should be included. At the same time, it is clear that deliberate decisions were made about who and what to include and showcase and who and what to mention in passing and essentially leave out. Creating a space for "all Americans" with entertainment value was certainly considered when these decisions were made.

While I do not think that certain athletes, musicians, entertainers, war heroes, and "black firsts" who did not necessarily shape the black experience profoundly or work on behalf of the struggle for African Americans' civil and human rights should have received as much or more attention than some black leaders, activists, and freedom fighters, I understand why such decisions were made. "Sports: Leveling the Playing Field" and "Musical Crossroads" seem to be especially popular with the vast majority of visitors, especially African American youth. For example, scores of visitors line up to take photos of the statues of Peter Norman, Tommie Smith, and John Carlos on the podium at the 1968 Olympics in Mexico City.

The relatively elaborate display in honor for Ben Carson is intriguing, especially given his conservative and controversial racial politics. One could also say the same about the tribute to Michael Jordan. There is a statue of him and an area called The Michael Jordan Hall. The Oprah Winfrey Theatre on the Concourse level and "The Oprah Effect" located in "A Changing America: 1968 and Beyond" makes more sense given her influence on US popular culture and black female identity, not to mention the fact that the multimillionaire donated $21 million to the museum.

There are more than a few surprising omissions of famous African American historical icons and at least one that I find baffling. While scholar-activists like Du Bois and James Baldwin are featured in several places, the contributions of Carter G. Woodson, "The Father of Black History," are virtually ignored. It is now common knowledge that Woodson did more than any other individual to institutionalize and popularize the study and commemoration of African American history during the first half of the twentieth century. Yet, based upon my inspection of the NMAAHC, his work is represented only in passing.

In a section featuring African Americans' educational achievements, there is a first edition copy of Woodson's 1928 *Negro Makers of History*. Resembling an explanatory footnote, the description is as follows: "Known as the Father of Black History, Carter G. Woodson (1875–1950) dedicated his career to eradicating myths and misconceptions about the achievements of African Americans. Woodson established Negro History Week and founded the [Association for the Study of Negro Life and History], an outlet for black scholars to publish original research." In another display, playwright Willis Richardson's *Plays and Pageants from the Life of the Negro* (1930) is exhibited (Woodson helped write it), and a reproduction of the cover of the first volume of *The Journal of Negro History* is displayed with six other African American magazine and journal covers in a section entitled "Printing for Progress."

I was not able to locate one single photo of Woodson in the NMAAHC. (I confess that I might have missed it given the countless number of images in the massive space.)

The minimal attention to Woodson is even more peculiar when one notices that many of his contemporaries—Jack Johnson, Madam C. J. Walker, Maggie Lena Walker, Ida Cox, Garrett Morgan, Bert Williams, George Walker, Oscar Micheaux, Marshall "Major" Taylor, and Samuel Coleridge-Taylor, just to name a handful—received more attention than he did. The lack of detailed attention afforded to Woodson is also striking because, in his words, Lonnie Bunch III strove to "root the history told inside the Museum in the context of Washington, DC" in part because of the large and influential black population in the nation's capital.[6]

Woodson lived in his "office-home" at 1538 9th Street, NW, in the historic Shaw neighborhood from 1922 until 1950. Perhaps because his home is an NPS historic site, the museum curators did not think that it was necessary to have a special exhibit for Woodson. This explanation, however, is not really convincing because an excellent exhibition is devoted to Mary McLeod Bethune and the National Council of Negro Women (NCNW). In a large room, the office of the NCNW has been essentially reconstructed. Visitors can even sit at a replica of the group's meeting table. Bunch stressed that the museum would not have been possible without "scholarly insights." Yet Woodson is also underappreciated in the museum's commemorative textbook, *Dream a World Anew: The African American Experience and the Shaping of America*. In his essay "Making a Way Out of No Way," historian Alfred A. Moss discusses early black learned and scholarly organizations and mentions Woodson and the ASNLH in passing, dating the organization's founding in 1916 (and not 1915, the actual date). Not only is there no photo of Woodson in *Dream a World Anew*, but there is more information on Woodson's contemporaries like jockey Isaac Burns Murphy.

REVISITING "THE PAINFUL ASPECTS OF HISTORY"

On the eve of the NMAAHC's historic grand opening, while reflecting upon the challenges that he and his colleagues encountered when determining exactly "what the museum should be," Lonnie G. Bunch III recounted:

---

6   Mabel O. Wilson, *Begin with the Past: Building the National Museum of African American History and Culture*, Washington, DC: Smithsonian Books, 2016, 134.

There were those who felt it was impossible, in a federally funded museum, to explore candidly some of the painful aspects of history, such as slavery and discrimination. Others felt strongly that the museum had the responsibility to shape the mindset of future generations, and should do so without discussing moments that might depict African-Americans simply as victims . . . Conversely, some believed that this institution should be a holocaust museum that depicted "what they did to us."[7]

For Bunch, "moments of pain" and "stories of resiliency and uplift" needed to coexist. In her detailed architectural overview of the museum, scholar Mabel O. Wilson insists that the NMAAHC "ultimately shows how Americans—museum experts, politicians, architects, philanthropists, and citizens—worked together to launch a new vision of how museums can address the difficult history of race and racism."[8] I agree with museum reviewer Holland Cotter's observation that Bunch's focus "rings hollow to many at a time when violence is harming African Americans." Yet, he might exaggerate with his assertion that Bunch and his curators "have made centuries-old history of that violence clear in the opening display of some 3,500 objects, selected from the 40,000 in the museum's collection."[9]

The NMAAHC is by no means a black holocaust museum in the sense that James Cameron's America's Black Holocaust Museum (ABHM) in Milwaukee, Wisconsin is. The ABHM is unambiguous in publicizing its focus. "The four hundred-year history of captured Africans and their descendants has many similarities with the Holocaust experiences of European Jews—and other victims of mass atrocities," note the ABHM curators.[10] For obvious political reasons, in describing the atrocities faced, endured, and confronted by African Americans, the NMAAHC echoes Obama's judicious sentiments at the 2012 groundbreaking ceremony. It is balanced and strategic. For the most part, the Community and Cultural Galleries highlight how African Americans were able to survive, break down barriers, and impact American culture. At the same time, in the Community Galleries in "The Power of Place," there is an excellent section on the 1921 Tulsa Race Riot that describes the event as being a "massacre" during which "white mobs rampaged through the thriving black community of Greenwood, looting, burning homes, churches, and businesses and murdering scores of African Americans." There is also an exhibit on Angola, the Louisiana State Penitentiary and former slave plantation, that draws concrete connections between the past and the present incarnation and criminalization of African Americans.

---

7   Bunch, "Making a Way Out of No Way," 28.
8   Wilson, *Begin with the Past*, 10.
9   Holland Cotter, "The Smithsonian's African American Museum Is Here At Last. And It Uplifts and Upsets," *New York Times*, September 22, 2106, F2.
10   See abhmuseum.org/what-is-the-black-holocaust.

Though the Middle Passage and slavery could have been presented in a more graphic manner, throughout the History Galleries there are numerous displays, images, and panels that underscore anti-black violence that was commonplace through the era of the conventional civil rights movement. In "Defending Freedom, Defining Freedom: The Era of Segregation, 1877–1968," there are two large reminders of anti-black violence—a guard tower from the Angola prison and a chapel-like room dedicated to Emmett Till that includes the actual casket that the Chicago native was buried in. Inside the casket is a life-size print of Till's mangled and distorted face as it appeared on the day of the funeral. Media coverage, testimonies, photographs, and *Eyes on the Prize*-like footage in the Emmett Till Memorial effectively transport the viewer back in time. In a panel entitled "A Climate of Fear," the violence that blacks faced daily during the era of Jim Crow segregation is discussed and numerous graphic images of lynchings are presented. In presenting such troubling photographs, the curators of the NMAAHC decided to do what those of the ABHM did not: warn visitors about the disturbing images with signs outlined boldly in red. Moreover, if visitors become overwhelmed with emotion, the museum has a Contemplative Court (a space for reflection) as well as even an on-site grief counselor. It would be interesting to know how often people request this resource; how the museum's experts were trained for these roles; and how they comfort, help, and advise their patrons.

In addition to the murder of Emmett Till, the many acts of violence commit-ted against African Americans and their allies that the museum most effectively addresses include the following: "violent reprisals" to slave revolts and conspira-cies; the Fort Pillow Massacre; the convict lease system; The Frazier Baker case; the Red Summer of 1919 and other previous and later race riots; the lynching of Matthew Williams (a souvenir piece of the lynch rope used to hang him is on display), the murder of John C. Perkins in 1946; the Recy Taylor case; "The Rape of Gertrude Perkins" in 1949 by two white police officers; the bombing of the 16th Street Baptist Church (visitors will see bits of glass from the church's windows); the murders of Schwerner, Chaney, and Goodman and many other civil rights activists; and the Attica Uprising.

THE NEW MILLENNIUM "BLACK MUSEUM MOVEMENT" IN PERSPECTIVE

The new museum in Washington, DC, has a long history dating back to the founding of the National Memorial Association, Inc., in 1916. In more contemporary terms, the NMAAHC represents the pinnacle of what could be called the new millennium "black museum movement." That is, during the last several decades, there has been a revival of a "black museum movement" that dates back most concretely to the early 1960s until the founding of the African American Museums Association (now the Association of African American Museums) in 1978 when more than a few major and pioneering

African American museums were founded. Called "neighborhood" museums by scholar Andrea A. Burns, these institutions centered black life and sought to serve as correctives to mainstream US museums that marginalized the black experience and strove to educate and validate members of black communities through outreach.[11] Among them were the DuSable Museum of African American History in Chicago, the International African American Museum in Detroit, the Anacostia Community Museum in Washington, DC, the African American Museum of Art and History in Minneapolis, and the African American Museum of Philadelphia. By the 1980s, there were more than one hundred museums dedicated to African American history and culture throughout the nation. During the culture wars and debates about multiculturalism during the 1980s and 1990s, several black museums were relocated, expanded, funded by major corporations, and (in some cases) mainstreamed.

By the dawning of the new millennium, the Association of African American Museums reported that there were slightly more than two hundred African American museums of various types scattered throughout the United States. Based upon their operating budgets, the leading African American museums today include the Charles H. Wright Museum of African American History, the National Civil Rights Museum in Memphis, the National Underground Railroad Freedom Center in Cincinnati, the Center for Civil and Human Rights in Atlanta, the Studio Museum in Harlem, and, of course, the NMAAHC.[12] The most recently opened African American history museums include the Legacy Museum in Montgomery, Alabama and the Mississippi Civil Rights Museum.

While the NMAAHC "is the only *national* museum devoted exclusively to the documentation of African American life, history, and culture," it is certainly not the only wide-ranging, expansive, and chronologically conscious African American history museum. Before the founding of the NMAAHC, the largest museum devoted to the African American experience was the Charles H. Wright Museum of African American History that was reopened in Detroit, Michigan in 1997 at 315 East Warren near the Michigan Science Center and the Detroit Institute of Arts in the heart of the Detroit Historic District. When it opened, the museum was hailed as "the world's largest" museum devoted to African American history and culture that boasted more than 30,000 artifacts, a collection of important archives, an amazing permanent exhibit, and the awe-inspiring Ford Freedom Rotunda.

By the dawning of the new millennium, however, the museum was "facing serious financial challenges" and discussions of its possible closing began

---

11   See Andrea A. Burns, *From Storefront to Monument: Tracing the Public History of the Black Museum Movement*, Amherst: University of Massachusetts Press, 2013.

12   LaNesha DeBardelaben, "The Future of African American Museums and the Role of the Scholar Administrator Within Them," unpublished paper, December 31, 2015.

surfacing. Some in the black community were also questioning the museum's effectiveness, as it was epitomized by one reporter for the *Michigan Citizen* who charged that the museum was an "eyesore" and "failed to effectively market itself to the community it is supposed to represent." In 2001, the museum had a "disastrous fiscal year."[13] During the 2000s, the museum has had to cut its staff and engage in sustained membership drives, fundraising campaigns, and outreach efforts. When the city of Detroit filed for Chapter 9 bankruptcy in the summer of 2013, discussions pertaining to the Charles H. Wright Museum of African American History shifted quite drastically once again. It was no longer hailed for its remarkable attributes. Attention was directed to how the museum would survive the unprecedented hard times for the Motor City. Once again, after Detroit filed for bankruptcy, rumors surfaced that the museum was on the verge of potentially closing its doors, and media coverage on the museum has highlighted the challenges that it has faced. The future of Detroit's black history museum is unclear. Perhaps given the much discussed and debated gentrification taking place in the city, there may be increased investment in this awesome black cultural institution.

Though its popularity will most likely wane in the coming years, the evolution and future of the NMAAHC will not mirror that of the Charles H. Wright Museum of African American History, for obvious reasons. After all, the NMAAHC is a federally and privately funded Smithsonian Institution museum. As such, it is not controversial. It is not a black holocaust museum. Instead, it commits more to fulfilling its "four pillars" that center on portraying African American history in a manner that is palpable not to *all* Americans, as it claimed, but instead to various cross-sections of the US public. This magnificent Smithsonian museum is certainly an educational tool. But it also provides its visitors with much entertainment. As indicated on the museum's website, "it provides an opportunity for those who are interested in African American culture to explore and revel in this history through interactive exhibitions." At bottom, it demonstrates how for centuries African Americans succeeded in "making a way out of no way." The NMAAHC has already profoundly shaped how millions of Americans understand the African American historical experience, and it will undoubtedly continue to do so. Representations of black history such as those presented in the NMAAHC are refreshing in an era during which the black past is being strategically used in so many different manners by a range of people in the United States.

As this book has demonstrated, during the late twentieth century and the

---

13   "Crisis at Charles H. Wright Museum; Black Business Leaders to Donate $1 Million to Save Museum," *The Michigan Chronicle*, April 6, 2004, A1; "Museum Needs Our Support," *The Michigan Chronicle*, April 13, 2004, A6; Glenn W. Morgan Jr., "Charles H. Wright Museum of African American History: The Black Community's White Elephant," *The Michigan Citizen*, May 16, 2004, A6; "Saving Our History; CEO Discusses State and Efforts to Sustain Museum, First of Two-Part Series," *The Michigan Chronicle*, April 13, 2004, A1.

new millennium, African American history has been interpreted and enlisted by diverse groups of people in American society for a variety of reasons. These representations as manifested in US popular culture and politics have at times been restorative, creative, and practical. These portrayals must, however, more often than not be scrutinized and contextualized. What they end up meaning ultimately depends on one's approach to and knowledge of African American history and culture.

Index